FAITH ACROSS TRADITIONS

ESSAYS FROM TEN YEARS OF
DIALOGUE AT CONCILIAR POST

EDITED BY
JACOB J. PRAHLOW

Faith Across Traditions: Essays from Ten Years of Dialogue at Conciliar Post
© 2024 by Jacob Prahlow

Published by Arise Press, 639 Gravois Bluffs Blvd, Ste I, Saint Louis, MO 63026. Printed by AKD Publishing.

All rights reserved. No part of this book may be reproduced, stored in a retrieval system, or transmitted in any form or by any means—electronic, mechanical, photocopy, recording, or otherwise—without written permission of the published, except for brief quotations in printed reviews.

Scripture quotations marked (ESV) are taken from the ESV® Bible (The Holy Bible, English Standard Version®), © 2001 by Crossway, a publishing ministry of Good News Publishers. Used by permission. All rights reserved. The ESV text may not be quoted in any publication made available to the public by a Creative Commons license. The ESV may not be translated in whole or in part into any other language. **www.esv.org**

Scripture quotations marked (NIV) are taken from the Holy Bible, New International Version®, NIV®. Copyright © 1973, 1978, 1984, 2011 by Biblica, Inc.™ Used by permission of Zondervan. All rights reserved worldwide. The "NIV" and "New International Version" are trademarks registered in the United States Patent and Trademark Office by Biblica, Inc.™ **www.zondervan.com**

Scripture quotations marked (NRSV) are taken from the New Revised Standard Version Bible, copyright © 1989 National Council of the Churches of Christ in the United States of America. Used by permission. All rights reserved worldwide. **www.nrsvbibles.org**

Scripture quotations marked (NKJV) are taken from the New King James Version®. Copyright © 1982 by Thomas Nelson. Used by permission. All rights reserved. **www.thomasnelson.com**

Scripture quotations marked (NET) are from the NET Bible® copyright ©1996, 2019 by Biblical Studies Press, L.L.C. Quoted by permission. All rights reserved. **www.netbible.com**

All rights reserved by publishing authors and used with permission.

ISBN 979-8-9892650-1-5
Printed in the United States of America

Table of Contents

Introduction — 11

Conversions and Denominations — 15
Why Would a Protestant Convert to Eastern Orthodoxy, *Cabe* — 17
Why I Didn't Convert to Orthodoxy, *Humphrey* — 25
Why I'm Not Reformed (But Admire Them Anyway), *Ehrett* — 35
Lex Orandi, Lex Credendi, *Kim* — 41
The Non-Denominational Reformation, *Prahlow* — 45
Is Protestantism a Heresy, *Cabe* — 51
The Logic of Closed Communion, *Ehrett* — 61
Do You Have to Be Anti-Western to Be Eastern Orthodox, *Cabe* — 65

Adventus, Byrkett — 73

The Church Calendar — 75
On the Advent of Christ, *Prahlow* — 77
Christmas Is About the Cross, *Aldhizer* — 81
Christmas Is About the Incarnation, *Cabe* — 87
Remembering Christmas, *Maynard* — 97
God Is With Us, *Byrkett* — 101
The Fast Before the Feast, *Kishi* — 105
Holy Week, *Hyland* — 109
What Day Did Jesus Die, *Prahlow* — 111

Through the Rain, Grubb — 119

Ethics and the Christian Life — 121
The Sermon on the Mount and Christian Ethics, *Prahlow* — 123
Let Justice Roll Down, *Justice* — 127
What Re-Enchantment Really Means, *Ehrett* — 131
John Wesley and Small Groups, *Dickey* — 137
Recovering Koinonia, *Walker* — 141
Toward a Spirituality of Christian Work, *Aldhizer* — 145
A Christian Defense of Video Games, *Casberg* — 149
Confessions of a Single Mom, *Barrett* — 153
The Insufficiency of Spontaneous Prayer, *Landsman* — 157

A Sonnet on the Occasion of Super Tuesday, Casberg — 161

Faith in the Public Square — 163
Could Liberals & Conservatives Follow the Same Christ, *Tillman* — 165
An Open Letter to Christian Bakers in Indiana, *Johnson* — 173
Dear White Christians, It's Time for Us to Listen, *Quick* — 175
Social Justice Without Resurrection Is Dead, *Aldhizer* — 181
Gnostic Anthropology and Identity Politics, *Ehrett* — 185
CRT and Its Dissidents, *Walker* — 187

God Remembers, Lambert — 193

Scripture and Interpretation — 195
The New Testament in Order, *Prahlow* — 197
Books Removed From the NT, *Bryan* — 207
Visiting D.C.'s Museum of the Bible, *Ehrett* — 215
Augustine on Biblical Interpretation, *Dickey* — 219
In Praise of the English Bible, *Rebholtz* — 225
Maccabees in the New Testament, *Bryan* — 229
Sola Scriptura's Relevance for the Modern Church, *Hall* — 239

Longings, Schendel — 243

Tradition and Traditions — 245
The Desert Fathers Play *Pokémon Go*, *Casberg* — 247
Tradition Is the Answer to Questions We've Forgotten, *White* — 251
Acts of Baptism, *Prahlow* — 257
Mary, Mother of God, Mother of the Church, *Hyland* — 261
Things I'd Rather Do on Sunday Morning, *Casberg* — 267
What John Calvin Taught Me, *Schellhase* — 271
Why Is Christian Liturgy So Repetitive, *Quick* — 275
Three Things That Need to Change About Church, *White* — 279
What's the Point of the Sermon, *Kim* — 285
How Should We Choose the Church We Attend, *Aldhizer* — 293

Empty Hands, Byrkett — 295

Sin and Salvation — 297
The Natural Desire to See God, *Winter* — 299
The Pandemic and the Wrath of God, *Fletcher* — 309
It Is Not a Sin to Wear a Facemask, *Townsend* — 315
On Original Sin and Racism, *Cline* — 321
The Atonement of Irenaeus, *Bryan* — 331
Dare We Hope for the Salvation of All, *Winter* — 337
The Problem of Predestination, *Aldhizer* — 343

Is Christian Existentialism Unbiblical, *Tillman*	349
A Poem to My Anxiety, Salem	355
Sorrow and Grief	**357**
You Are Not Okay, *White*	359
Thoughts, Prayers, and Platitudes, *Quick*	363
The Longest Lent, *Byrkett*	367
The Lost Art of Evangelical Weeping, *Cline*	371
Why God Allows Spiritual Dryness in the Christian Life, *Hall*	379
Dealing with Pain and Suffering, *McMeans*	385
The Art of Grieving, *Byrkett*	389
Contributor Biographies	**393**
Acknowledgements	**401**

Introduction
Jacob J. Prahlow

Ten years ago, we launched *Conciliar Post* in a very different world.

There was no Covid. Vine was the trendy short-form video platform. Taylor Swift had not yet ventured into pop music. Joe Biden was serving as Vice President. Donald Trump wasn't even a politician. *Obergefell* was a year away. Bill Gates topped the world billionaires list. *Roe V. Wade* was the law of the land. X was still called Twitter (alright, that is *still* true in 2024). Substack did not even exist yet, so people blogged. We were eager to launch our website into that world.

In many ways, it was a different world.

But in some ways, 2014 looked a lot like 2024.

People argued on the internet. The political process seemed unfixable. NFL officiating was broken. Trust in institutions crumbled. Conversations about faith, race, sex, politics, culture, and relationships were contentious and frustrating. To paraphrase the words of Stephen Covey, most people did not listen with the intent to understand other perspectives, but with the intent to reply and be proven right.

Into that context, we launched *Conciliar Post* as a website to promote dialogue that informed, encouraged, and challenged Christians from across traditions. In a world of fundamentalisms that possess all the answers and postmodernism that decries true answers, we aimed to seriously, thoughtfully, critically, and faithfully reflect upon life, faith, and our world.

It was a noble pursuit. Yet despite the sometimes-crushing weight of our world, this remains a worthy work.

Our world still needs *accessible* dialogue. Paywalls and subscriptions are the name of the game today. And while we affirm content creators' rights to monetize and make money from their work, we remain committed to a different approach at *Conciliar Post*.

Our world also desperately needs *charitable* dialogue, perhaps now more than ever. Our technology and social media-saturated echo chambers are still a problem. The politicization and rhetoricalization of faith remain corrosive. There is much we can learn from one another, both about how to have complex conversations and how to do so in a spirit of love and understanding for our interlocutors.

And our world still needs *robust Christian* dialogue. Even as the Church moves into its third millennium and the distinctives of denominational Christianity shift, theological particulars remain, and the Church continues to possess her prophetic voice for a world in need of rescue by the coming King.

With *Faith Across Traditions*, we are excited to continue looking forward even as we celebrate our tenth anniversary by looking back. The essays in this volume represent the best of the best when it comes to *Conciliar Post*: accessible, charitable, robust Christian dialogue on a variety of topics from an outstanding group of writers, thinkers, and human beings who seek to love God and love one another.

This volume represents a collective invitation from the *Conciliar Post* team: an invitation to remember and reflect on how you have changed over the past ten years amid the ongoing changes in our world. And also an invitation to continue this dialogue in the future. Our watching world needs Christians speaking in accessible, charitable, and distinctly Christian ways. Will you join us?

*****

The essays in this volume were selected based on engagement, popularity, and continued resonance. For a variety of reasons, some excellent and popular articles were unable to be included, and we encourage you to find them online. Furthermore, we invite you to take up and read the included essays selectively. Find something that interests you and dig in. You will find that many selections reference other parts of the conversation at *Conciliar Post*. Consider exploring those other articles.

Become part of the conversation by weighing in online at www.conciliarpost.com

Conversions and Denominations

"Why are you the *kind* of Christian that you are?" represents one of the most common questions asked at *Conciliar Post*. The essays in this first section address this question head-on, reflecting on why authors have converted (or not) and the implications of those decisions for faith and life.

Essays

Why Would a Protestant Convert to Eastern Orthodoxy, *Cabe*

Why I Didn't Convert to Orthodoxy, *Humphrey*

Why I'm Not Reformed (But Admire Them Anyway), *Ehrett*

Lex Orandi, Lex Credendi, Kim

The Non-Denominational Reformation, *Prahlow*

Is Protestantism a Heresy, *Cabe*

The Logic of Closed Communion, *Ehrett*

Do You Have to Be Anti-Western to Be Eastern Orthodox, *Cabe*

Faith Across Traditions

Why Would a Protestant Convert to Eastern Orthodoxy?
Benjamin Cabe

Why would a Protestant Christian convert to Eastern Orthodox Christianity? Such a question cannot be answered through the use of dogmatic assertions or theoretical musings. For such a question presupposes a particular person's journey of faith. And such a journey can only be spoken of from experience.[1] Similarly, Christianity at its core is an encounter with Christ—a relationship—not a formal set of dogmas. It is not my aim to embark on the process of comparative religion. The journey I wish to take you on is my own: how a nominal Protestant Christian, and his family, found the fulness of Christ in the Eastern Orthodox Church.

My Christian Background

I grew up as an active participant in a non-denominational Protestant church in rural Michigan. At this same church I met a woman who would, in 2009, become my wife. My father, a music pastor and missionary, along with my mother, led their five children, of whom I am the fourth, to faith in Christ. Through the promptings of my older sister I asked Jesus into my heart at the age of six. Seeing no major reason, at the time, to be baptized right away, I waited until I was ten. At fifteen, while in Africa, God audibly spoke to me: an experience that rocked my world.

Around this time I began reading every book on theology and philosophy that I could get my hands on—beginning, of course, with C.S. Lewis. By seventeen I had delved into Plato and Aristotle and eventually wound up following the timeline of history and reading a variety of philosophers and theologians. At that point in time, my World Religion's Professor began offering free Koine Greek lessons before class; this kick-started my interest in biblical Greek, though I am still an amateur. I can see, though only in part, that God has used

---

[1] When this experience is communicated, however, the listener (or reader in this case) can participate in that person's journey.

all of these interests as instruments to pave the way towards union with Him through Eastern Orthodoxy.

At eighteen, as my reading list would have proclaimed, I was really *into* Christianity. But the reading list is pretty much where it stopped. Christianity was in my head but not my heart, and I did not even realize that this was a problem.

Between 2007 and 2009 I went through several phases. I was a professing Christian, a skeptic, agnostic, neoplatonic dualist, a priori enthusiast, a "who gives a f***ist" . . . Between what I was reading and what I was undergoing during that period of time my entire life was thrown completely out of balance.

And then I got married.

We lived together as newlyweds 2000 miles away from where we grew up . . . and we did alright. We were attending a Baptist church and it was really good for us. We got involved and I began attempting to "lead" as I perceived a godly husband should—though I didn't really know what this should look like. When we moved back to our hometown a year later we fell back into a stupor—floating along nominally and attending the church we grew up in.

Until we found out we were pregnant.

The Beautiful Crisis
"Honey, that says positive." She was holding out the pregnancy test. We were both in disbelief. It was summer 2011; we were in our second year of marriage. Finding out you're going to be a dad will straighten you out really fast. I was working as a barista in a small coffee shop. My wife, a nurse, was working in home health care. The plan up to that point had been to continue the road toward my PhD in philosophy—I really liked metaphysics. But not anymore. That was the first thing that had to go, I knew it. I needed a real job, not a PhD in a field where I might not even find a job—and would most likely go crazy trying to explain sunlight to people looking at shadows. The second thing we realized was we needed to get serious about life—what were we doing? And most importantly we needed to get serious about God.

The next several months consisted of job and soul searching. For the first time as a couple, we began to wake up, sing hymns, and read scripture together. We also began praying in the evenings before bed. At that point, we were only attending church to see our old friends. That wasn't a good reason. So we went church "shopping" and found a new, solid, Bible believing church. And it was good for us.

Around this time our son was born.

The Road from Protestantism to the Eastern Orthodox Church

When we first switched from the church we grew up in to a different—though still non-denominational—protestant church, we were really convicted by the preaching. I remember it vividly. We were laying in bed on a Sunday evening and a dread feeling of conviction came upon me. It felt like a rotting in my soul . . . like if I didn't say something, I would slowly decompose in my own filth. I opened my mouth hesitantly and began to confess all kinds of things to my wife. And she did the same. The Spirit of God was clearly present. We wept; over our sins but also out of joy because, having confessed, we were free. But as we continued to attend the same church over the next few months we quickly realized that we needed something different. We needed more. There had to be more than appropriating, and then distributing, "get-out-of-hell-free cards". There had to be more than "God looking down on us from above." The question that was singeing the edges of my mind was this: How can I keep Christ in front of me every moment of every day? What I was really asking was, how do we abide in Christ?

Until that point, if you would have walked into our apartment off the street, you wouldn't have seen any indication that we believed . . . anything. Except maybe the Bible on the nightstand . . . maybe. But there was no physical evidence that we were Christians. Growing up, we weren't explicitly taught that the physical was *bad* but the mindset we were grafted into took on a form of dualism. "The body and the material universe is *bad*. Earth isn't our home.[1] The spiritual is good." And so, in our formative years we naturally misunderstood, and poked fun at,—*Lord, have mercy*—any kind of Christianity that incorporated the physical world. (In retrospect, I can see how it was so easy for me, upon reading Plato, to accept the theory of forms and a dualistic view of the world.)

---

[1] The Orthodox affirm that human beings were made for earth and so the earth *is* our home; it will be restored at the end of all things.

But not any more.

I had two thoughts. The first was to get a picture of Christ to hang in my living room as a visible representation of His presence. I didn't want one of those soft, happy-go-lucky pictures of a hipster-model-looking shepherd, I wanted something real. The style I had in mind turned out to be that of iconography—this is before I even knew what an icon was. The second thought was to get a cross to put around my neck. These two thoughts thrust me into a third: *Christianity has been around for a really long time surely someone has already thought of this.* And so I began searching to find out what early Christians did to abide in Christ.

This catapulted me into a study of the history of Christianity—something I'd never ventured to read into before. I was shocked. Why hadn't I read the history of my own faith before now? For being somewhat well read, I was caught with my pants down when it came to Christian history and the Church Fathers. Up to that point, I had always naively thought that after the apostles died the church fell into serious disarray until Luther. What I found, however, was astounding, encouraging, and eye-opening. There were schisms and heresies circulating in the early church for sure, but the Church was never overcome by the gates of hades.[1]

Why hasn't anyone told me about the history of Christianity? I asked myself. *Why hasn't anyone told me about the Church Fathers?* What amazed me even more was how little I really knew about my own faith. And so I read. And kept reading. And then I read some more. It wasn't dry facts about dead bishops that captivated me. On the contrary, as I began reading the lives of the saints and how they lived, worshiped, and prayed, I felt the presence of the very saints, about whom I was reading, pulling me closer to Christ.

It became readily apparent, from the historical point of view, that there were only two options: the Roman Catholic Church and the Eastern Orthodox Church. So I began learning as much as I could about the two Churches. What captivated me about the Eastern Church was the balance between the rational and the experiential. Around this time, my wife, son, and I were invited to dinner with an Orthodox priest and his wife. I'd seen Fr. Gregory a few times before. My parents were really good friends with him—my father met him on

---

[1] Matthew 16:18

a missions trip about a year prior to my interest in Church history—and we all went to dinner together. I wasn't planning on saying anything, but about three-quarters of the way through the meal my mom turned to Fr. Gregory and said, "I think Ben has a question for you about the Orthodox Church." I am eternally grateful that she said this because it sparked a conversation with Fr. Gregory that would continue, through email and regular meetings, for over a year.

Fr. Gregory responded to my questions and suggested books about the Orthodox faith. Our email correspondence spans over a hundred printed pages—in the future I hope to publish these emails on Conciliar Post under the title "Conversations with an Orthodox Priest." The Orthodox Faith was vibrant and had a lot to offer. The fact that it has withstood the test of time really spoke to me. The Orthodox Church still worships and encourages parishioners to live, with minor adjustments of course, as it did 2000 years ago.

And this is where it began to get real.

As I looked at how a Christian should live in order to keep Christ the focus of their life, I realized I needed to begin practicing what I read instead of merely ruminating on it. So I began waking up to say morning prayers and in the evening Mallory and I would stand together for evening prayers. Fr. Gregory had given me a prayer rope—black wool with 100 knots—and told me about the Jesus Prayer: *Lord, Jesus Christ, Son of God have mercy on me, a sinner*. And I began practicing it as well. This affected a major change in me. We began attending the Orthodox Church where Fr. Gregory was priest—which at that point was an hour away—as we continued to read about Orthodoxy.

As I continued to participate in daily prayers throughout the week and in the Divine Liturgy on Sundays—though at that point not being able to go forward for to participate in the Eucharist—the doctrines I once mocked became clearer and clearer. It wasn't as much a rational explication of the doctrines that convinced me of their truth but rather an experience of them. (Though I didn't neglect the rational by any means—a healthy balance of both is necessary.) It was the fact that I was changing, by God's grace, through the practice of daily prayers, participation in the Liturgy, reverencing the icons, and fasting. There was something *very real* happening to me. I later found out that I was—and by God's grace still am—being healed.

The Orthodox Church views Christianity and the gospel, not as a courtroom but, as a hospital. I would like to talk about this view more in a later article but for now it will suffice to say that through participation in the life of the Church and reading, I underwent a significant change in how I viewed the world. Suddenly, everything began to be an opportunity to give thanks to God. The presence of Christ pervaded everything. The world took on a different meaning; I *began*—I say began and I am still beginning—for the first time in my life, to love other people. I wasn't as angry all the time. My wife and I began to resolve conflict much faster. Overall, it was incredibly encouraging to see that what the Church was offering to me was *working*.

Our Conversion
We were participating in the Church as much as we could. But that wasn't enough. It was necessary, in my mind, that we convert so that we could participate fully in the life of the Church. I expressed this desire to Mallory and she too felt like it was the right thing to do—although she didn't feel the imperative as much as I.

From what I've read, and from people I've spoken to, it is typically much more difficult for women to convert from protestantism to Orthodoxy than men. When asked, Mallory responded, "Well at first I just thought this was another phase. But when he began praying and participating in the Church and he stopped swearing and punching holes in the wall, I thought there may be something to this Orthodox thing." She also mentioned that it was encouraging to see that worship wasn't based on stylistic preference (strange fire, maybe?). When we enter the Church and participate in the liturgy we are *stepping out of time and into the kingdom* where the king is being worshiped 24/7. We step into this worship, together with the saints and the angels who are *always* worshipping, as often as we can. The Liturgical calendar has been set up to help us participate in this manner, in the kingdom. By participating in the Liturgical cycle the Church takes us on a journey. This journey is a rhythmic pattern of daily prayers, the iconic significance of sleeping (death) rising from sleep (resurrection), weekly fasting, the Eucharist on Sunday (the 8th day), and extended periods of fasting throughout the year—as a preparation for the feasts (Nativity, Pascha, etc.).

A Few Other Things that Struck Us About Orthodoxy
Even though we didn't know it before our journey to Orthodoxy, we both had a very impoverished Christianity—and an impoverished

view of the world. Unbeknownst to myself, I was a deist (God created and then walked away from the world). I regarded God to be "the man upstairs" and humans to be "downstairs." Fr. Stephen Freeman talks about this misunderstanding of Christianity in his book *Everywhere Present* where he calls it a "two-story universe." One result of this way of thinking—even if it's not cognizant—is banishing God from the world (in a very physical sense). When we do this what is left are "four walls and a sermon." The reality is, however, that the whole world is held together by God, and God *works through* the created world to affect our salvation. Any decent theology about the incarnation will recognize this—although the natural implications of this aren't always accepted.

Orthodox worship was formed (after the resurrection of Christ) based on these implications: on the fact that we are physical and spiritual beings. It is the soul and the body that compose the human, not one or the other but both together. This being so, it's important that we use both in worship. In the Eastern Church we use candles, icons, and incense. We bow, prostrate, and kiss. We baptize our children and allow them to take the Eucharist—because rational understanding is not necessary for salvation but participation *in Christ* is. All of these things are based on the reality that Christianity is an experiential reality and, as human beings, the gospel is not merely an ethereal, rational truth. All of these things bound up together affected a major paradigm shift in our Western mind. All of these things were contributing factors in our conversion.

On Sunday, September 15, 2013, two years after we began searching, we were brought into full communion with the Orthodox Church. The story has many other facets to it as well—at the beginning of those two years unbeknownst to us Fr. Gregory, feeling called by God to our area, sent a letter to His Bishop requesting to start a mission (Orthodox term for a church plant) in Southwest Michigan. Two years later, alongside us being brought into the Church, on September 15, 2013 we held our first Divine Liturgy, which was served by Fr. Gregory, at the Orthodox Mission in Southwestern Michigan currently known as Holy Resurrection.

In summation there are a few things I'd like to say. This account of our conversion from protestantism to Eastern Orthodox Christianity is just one of many. As others have said, I feel like the journey is just now beginning. I do not want to give you the impression that we are perfect little Christians now that we have converted. Far from it. In fact, things actually got much harder after our conversion. But healing is possible; and it is Christ, the healer, whom we seek.

I would like to highlight again that I am not trying to set forward a systematic defense of the dogmas of the Orthodox Church. This being the case I would also like to affirm that doctrine is very important and, having also looked at things rationally, Orthodoxy not only *works* it also holds up under scrutiny. I affirm and accept the Orthodox faith and doctrine in its entirety—and where doctrines of other traditions vary, I believe it is an aberration from the truth revealed through the Church. For there are beliefs I now hold that, when I was a protestant, I once mocked—and at this I am ashamed. So what convinced me otherwise? It was participation in the life of the Church and *experience* of these things—tied tandem, of course, with a healthy and balanced intellectual search as well. For Christianity is something you must experience and participate in, not something you can speak about from a distance.

In closing I ask that you pray to God for me, His servant, that he may have mercy on me and my family and remember us in His kingdom. In the name of the Father and the Son and the Holy Spirit to whom be all glory, honor, and worship, now and ever and unto ages of ages. Amen.

Why I Didn't Convert to Eastern Orthodoxy
TJ Humphrey

The eye cannot say to the hand, "I don't need you!" And the head cannot say to the feet, "I don't need you!"[1]

A few years ago my wife and I went to a Greek festival hosted by a Greek Orthodox Church in downtown St. Louis. As we were walking around the building trying to decide which food looked most appetizing to us, we stumbled across a bookstore right inside the doors of the church. The avid reader in me picked up a book by an author I had never heard of before and I began thumbing my way through it. It was so refreshingly succinct, beautifully articulated, and...well...different from what I had become so accustomed to in Western Christianity. I found the author saying things that I always felt like I wanted to say but had been too reluctant to do so out of fear of being ostracized. But, here was this author making bold claims about the communal nature of salvation, the self-punishment of hell, the importance of the Church Fathers, the necessity of prayer for salvation, etc. I had grown incredibly weary of aspects of Christianity that were solely based off of individualistic intellectual assent. I also sensed a tremendous depth to what the author was saying. It was clear that he really knew what he was talking about as he spoke of prayer. He also seemed to reflect a tradition, a history, that was so much bigger than himself at the same time. So, needless to say, the book spoke to me. The author, of course, was Kallistos Ware and the book was a simple little book titled, "How Are We Saved?"

That day marked the beginning of a very intense spiritual journey for me. I desired to learn more about the Orthodox faith and the Patristic way. So, I began where most Protestants begin, especially those who have been parked in the Reformed camp for a while. I began with the intellectual side of things. I wanted to better understand the church's theological teachings. I began attending Vespers services at a couple of the local parishes nearby and I sought out conversation partners in local Orthodox parishioners and priests alike. Even though the whole experience was a bit like trying to drink from a firehose, I felt

---

[1] 1 Corinthians 12:15

spiritually dehydrated enough to take it on. My prayer life was in shambles and I was genuinely burnt out from the ministry I was a part of. Orthodoxy was an awful lot to seek—to understand—but I felt there was something therapeutic in wrestling through it all. I quickly found that Orthodoxy is much more comprehensive than the versions of Western Christianity that I had been a part of. There wasn't merely a deep theological perspective, but a way in which one was to live it out through asceticism. What really drew me in from there was the notion that there was no question for the Orthodox as to what the life of individual prayer and corporate worship is supposed to look like. I had grown weary of constantly seeking to innovate worship services around my own personality whenever I was leading the liturgy on Sunday mornings in my church. I was also extremely bothered by how much prayer, especially silent prayer, was underemphasized, neglected and deprioritized within the Reformed tradition. Orthodoxy presented a way in which God's people are to gather for worship and it taught a way in which people should embody prayer. I found something remedial in these things.

I also began to dabble more and more in Eastern Orthodox writings. I read all of John Zizioulas's books and most of Dumitu Staniloae's as well. "St. Silouan the Athonite,"[1] by Elder Sophrony became my favorite book (still is) and I read all that I could of Elder Sophrony and his disciple, Archimadrite Zacharias. Later on, someone introduced me to John Behr and I soaked his teachings in like a sponge. After reading the works of all of these modern figures, I began to read the Church Fathers that they cited so frequently. I committed large amounts of time to studying Irenaeus, John Chrysostom, Gregory Palamas and Ignatius of Antioch. Both Zizioulas and Staniloae, however, really triggered a love in me for the Cappadocian Fathers and Maximus the Confessor, and I read them all fairly extensively.

I was hooked and was definitely in a puppy love sort of phase with all things Orthodox. It wasn't too long after that when I began to notice a disturbing trend, however. My wife, in her perceptive wisdom, picked up on it right from the start. She never shared in the love which was slowly kindled in my heart for the Orthodox faith. I was initially confused as to why she wasn't as enthused about this newfound version of the faith as I was. But, as I began seeing the things she was

---

[1] Zizioulas, John. *Being As Communion*. Crestwood: St. Vladimir's Seminary Press, 1985. 26.

pushing back against, I began to gradually come out of my puppy love infatuation and see exactly what she was talking about.

Here is where the Orthodox lost me (or, us): I wasn't looking for a new faith. To paraphrase Kallistos Ware, I was looking for a "fuller version" of the faith that I already had. This attitude, however, was not enough for many of the real life Eastern Orthodox relationships that I had developed. I was expected to renounce and reject the entirety of my Christian past. All things Protestant were to become an anathema to me. My Orthodox acquaintances were baffled that I didn't hate all things Western and Protestant as much as they did. I simply couldn't disqualify all of the grace that I had experienced as a Protestant. I couldn't bite the hand that had fed me for so long.

Those of us who are searching are not all the 1990's version of Frank Schaeffer. We are not all utterly scarred from and enthusiastically pissed off about our spiritual upbringings. The anti-Western tirade that is launched by so many Orthodox converts, which is often applauded and supported by Orthodox leaders, truly bothered me. I couldn't convert and become another anti-Western poster child for the Orthodox, and that is where I saw my journey quickly heading. I couldn't tell my devout Christian friends (Protestant and Catholic alike) that they were "heretics" and "schismatics"—many of them had never even heard of the Eastern Orthodox Church before. I could never say the types of things to them that were being said to me as I was inquiring about Orthodoxy. Orthodox people, laity and priests alike, were delighted to meet with me whenever I had questions because they always enjoyed opportunities for "evangelism." I didn't understand how I, someone who had been following Christ for several years, needed to be "evangelized." I couldn't, in turn, treat my non-Orthodox friends as if they were non-Christian and "evangelize" them into Orthodoxy. I couldn't treat them as if they weren't a part of the authentic Church of Christ.

Many Orthodox would accuse me of being too worldly, assuming that I am only seeking to embrace modern Western sentiments towards political correctness and inclusiveness. This is not the case whatsoever. I wouldn't resist telling my non-Orthodox Christian friends that they were heretical and not truly a part of the Church because I am simply seeking to abstain from hurting their feelings. I would resist telling them such an atrocious thing because it would be utterly untrue. I found Christ in Protestantism or, better, Christ found me through Protestantism. I never would deny such a thing nor expect others around me to do so.

After sharing my frustrations with a priest and later on with a monk, they both told me to do that which brings my heart peace. After taking their guidance to heart and spending several months in fasting and prayer, I did exactly what they told me. I quit gravitating towards Orthodoxy because the journey was not bringing me any peace whatsoever. I realized that, at the center of it all, I could not pursue Christ-like humility and Orthodoxy at the same time. I couldn't pronounce other Christians as being estranged from God's Kingdom while believing that I was in. I couldn't believe that the vast majority of the Christians that I know, most of whom know absolutely nothing about the Orthodox Church, had never found the true Way of Christ and union with Him. I could never believe that my Western Christian friends were heretical.

In the end, it wasn't the theology or the worship which soured me. What soured me was an elitist attitude that several Orthodox embody and what these particular people expected of me. I recall Frank Schaeffer saying in a few of his lectures that "salvation is a mystery" to the Orthodox. Many of the Orthodox that I have known agree with this notion...as long as you are becoming Orthodox. If not, then salvation is no longer so mysterious...because you aren't acquiring it. As I mentioned before, Kallistos Ware is known for saying that Orthodoxy is a "fuller version of the faith." Again, many of the Orthodox people that I know would agree as long as you are on your way to becoming Orthodox. If this is not the case, the lesser version of the faith is actually no faith at all. As Metropolitan John Zizioulas notes, "As the late Fr Georges Florovsky likes to repeat, the authentic catholicity of the Church must include both the West and the East."[1] Many of the Orthodox that I have known would, again, agree with such a statement as long as the "West" mentioned here is Orthodoxy in the West, not the actual Western Church itself.

At this point I want to iterate a very important caveat. I am not seeking to critique all Orthodox Christians here. This is not a reaction to the whole of Orthodoxy, but to my very limited interaction with it. Many people who have interacted with Orthodoxy or even converted in this community have stories that are vastly different from my own and I fully acknowledge that. I am not looking to mount a critique

---

[1] Ibid.

against the Eastern Orthodox Church but against an attitude within parts of the Eastern Orthodox community that I have had direct personal contact with. I also know that Orthodox readers will react in a few different ways. Some will truly believe that I am a heretic and am doing nothing more than spouting off a bunch of delusional rubbish. Others will understand where I am coming from (even if they disagree with me on several points) because they have seen similar trends within the Orthodox fold and they lament such tendencies. They will say, "This is unfortunate because this is not the way Orthodoxy is meant to be." Let me be clear, again, I am not seeking to launch a full-on attack of the Eastern Orthodox Church. I am simply seeking to share my own story because I think it is good for Eastern Orthodox readers out there to hear it, whether they agree with me or not. I also write this for my Western Christian friends who have been shamed by our Eastern brothers and sisters for finding Christ in the Western Church, and for choosing to continue to pursue him there. I know people who have been hurt very deeply by the dismissive and spitefully elitist attitudes of loved ones who have converted to Orthodoxy.

With all that I have said so far, you can probably imagine that some of the recent happenings within the Orthodox world have been fairly unsettling for me. I have been reading about all of the controversy leading up to the recent Council in Crete and the subsequent aftershock which followed it. The reaction towards Crete within the Orthodox world, especially in terms of section 6 of the text "Relations of the Orthodox Church with the Rest of the Christian World," really bothers me. Here is what I am talking about. This was written by a Metropolitan before the Council ever convened:

> "The Orthodox Church of Christ never lost the 'unity of faith and the communion of the Holy Spirit' and does not accept the theory of the restoration of the unity of those "who believe in Christ," because it believes that the unity of those who believe in Christ already exists in the unity of all of Her baptized children, between themselves and with Christ, in Her correct faith, where no heretics or schismatics are present, for which reason She prays for their return to Orthodoxy in repentance."

My heart sunk even further as I read about the reaction from Mt. Athos as well (remember, my favorite book is "St. Silouan the

Athonite"). The monks there believe that the Patriarch of Constantinople to be facilitating the "pan-heresy of ecumenism."

It is a weird and utterly off-putting notion for me; that in order to pursue unity with the Orthodox my "schismatic" and "heretical" self has to convert, especially whenever I personally never left the membership of any Orthodox parish to begin with. Furthermore, whenever I recognize the grace of Christ within your tradition while you denounce God's grace within my own, it doesn't give me the impression that I am the one being schismatic.

I can't help but reflect upon the writings of St. Ignatius of Antioch as I read through and hear about much of the Orthodox world's negative reaction to some of the conclusions of the Council in Crete. I sense that a lot of this negative outburst finds its origin in the writings of St. Ignatius (how could it not?). Others quote him directly to support their claims. While I get that St. Ignatius writes that the churches should "do nothing without the bishop"[7] and be on their guard against the heretics who break themselves off, I can't help but think that the context is quite a bit different in today's world than the one in which Ignatius was living.

For one, the early Church was quite united already under the teachings of the Apostles and the establishment of the elders. This is vastly different from today's world. There was no such thing as denominations back then. So, one had to be proactively and intentionally divisive if they wanted to sever off from the Church and go their own way.

In addition to this, the divisions that existed back then between the bishops and the heretics were quite a bit more severe than the divisions which exist between the Orthodox bishops and the Western Church today. Listen to how St. Ignatius describes the heretics of his day:

> "For they speak of Christ, not that they may preach Christ, but that they may reject Christ; and they speak of the law, not that they may establish the law, but that they may proclaim things contrary to it. For they alienate Christ from the Father, and the law from Christ. They also calumniate His being born of the Virgin; they are ashamed of His cross; they deny His passion; and they do not believe His resurrection. They introduce God as a Being unknown; they suppose Christ to be

unbegotten; and as to the Spirit, they do not admit that He exists. Some of them say that the Son is a mere man, and that the Father, Son, and Holy Spirit are but the same person, and that the creation is the work of God, not by Christ, but by some other strange power."

I personally do not know of any Western Christians, Catholic or Protestant, who would adhere themselves to any point of this heretical tradition as described by St. Ignatius. Given that this is the case, perhaps the word "heretic" needs to be reconsidered just a bit. I sincerely hope that my Orthodox friends can see that the wedge which divides us Western Christians from their bishops is much less severe than the divisive issues that St. Ignatius is speaking of.

Lastly, there is a double standard in the perspective of those who desire to withhold unity from us Western Christians. I don't understand how those who don't adhere to the Orthodox bishop are somehow heretical whenever those who don't observe the one Eucharist that St. Ignatius speaks of are not.

> "Take ye heed, then, to have but one Eucharist. For there is one flesh of our Lord Jesus Christ, and one cup to show forth the unity of His blood; one altar; as there is one bishop, along with the presbytery and deacons, my fellow-servants: that so, whatsoever ye do, ye may do it according to the will of God."

Metropolitan John Zizioulas elaborates further:

> "As the combination of the existing fragmentary liturgical evidence of the first centuries allows us to know, the 'whole Church' dwelling in a certain city would 'come together' mainly on a Sunday to 'break bread.' This synaxis would be the only one in that particular place in the sense that it would include the 'whole Church.'"[1]

Is there one Eastern Orthodox eucharist within a region under the headship of one Eastern Orthodox bishop, or do we often find multiple eucharists under multiple bishops in a region? Do not the various jurisdictions (OCA, ROCOR, Antiochian, Greek, Romanian, Serbian, etc.) have their own churches within close proximity to one another that celebrate their own eucharistic services under the

---

[1] Ibid., 150.

oversight of their own bishops? Within my own city (St. Louis) I know that all of the various parishes do not come together for the Eucharistic Liturgy, but rather do their own thing on Sundays. Is this not contrary to what St. Ignatius is instructing us in? Does this embody the oneness that he speaks of whenever Orthodox churches are divided along lines of ethnicity?

Delving further in terms of the office of Bishop:

> "The office of bishop in the early Church is essentially that of the president of the Eucharistic assembly. All the liturgical and canonical elements in the ordination of a bishop presuppose the primitive situation whereby there was in each city Church—one bishop (all bishops' names in the early Church, beginning with the times of Ignatius of Antioch, bear connection with a particular city), who was surrounded by the college of presbyters (he was in fact one of the presbyters himself) and was called "presbyter" for a long time (cf. Irenaeus). What the emergence of the parish did was to destroy this structure, a destruction which affected not only the episcopal office but also that of the presbyter. For it meant that from then on the eucharist did not require the presence of presbyters as a college—an essential aspect of the original significance of the presbyterium—in order to exist as local Church. An individual presbyter was thus enough to create and lead a eucharistic gathering—a parish. Could that gathering be called 'Church'?"[1]

Zizioulas goes on to argue here and elsewhere (he touches on the subject in all of his books that I have read) that whenever the ancient Church shifted from having two different types of services (Dom Gregory Dix refers these services as the Synaxis Service and the Eucharistic Service; J.J. Von Allmon refers to them as The Service of the Word and the Service of the Eucharist), much was compromised liturgically and ecclesiologically that has affected the entirety of Christendom. Thus, to reiterate and rephrase the question with which Zizioulas ends that last quote: Can any of us really call our gatherings "Church" whenever they stand in stark contrast to how things were done in the ancient Church?

---

[1] Ibid., 250.

Zizioulas also elaborates on the liturgical shifts that have affected Orthodoxy throughout the ages in his book, "The Eucharistic Communion and the World."[1] While he acknowledges that "the form of the Liturgy and all the services is preserved with almost complete faithfulness and exactitude," he also urges his readers to think through the changes from Byzantine times "which had an indirect and destructive influence on the iconic symbolism of the Liturgy." He then goes on to note four changes:

a) The skevophylakion disappeared from the churches, altering the symbolism behind the Little and Great Entrances.

b) The distinctions between the episcopal and presbyterial liturgies dissolved.

c) Because of the adoption of individualistic and rationalistic attitudes, he says: "We Orthodox have come to the point of not knowing what to do with our Liturgy and our Tradition. Those who kiss the icons or the priest's hand do it out of habit, without knowing why, and under the mocking gaze of those who know better." By this he means that there are some who have been so swayed by the Enlightenment within Orthodoxy that much of the symbolism in Orthodox worship has become, "pious naivete," "nonsense," "superstition," and "magic" to those who "know better."

d) Piety has taken over much of the Orthodox world, thus stripping much of the grandeur of the eschatological symbolism in the Liturgy down to simpler forms. He gives the examples of how people prefer country chapels over the cathedrals, prayers read rather than prayers chanted, modest vestments rather than elaborately decorated ones.

I am not trying to make an elaborate argument against Eastern Orthodox theology or ecclesiology. For one, Western Christianity falls quite short of St. Ignatius' teaching here as well. Secondly, Metropolitan Zizioulas is already critiquing his own tradition from within it; I don't wish to add anything (nor am I qualified to do so), but just to point out what he has already said.

I simply want to ask those Orthodox who would deem me a heretic and not worthy of being reunited with: "Why do I (and other Western

---

[1] Zizioulas, John. *The Eucharistic Communion and the World*. London: T & T Clark, 2011. 95.

Christians) need to follow St. Ignatius's writings whenever it comes to the teaching on the bishops, but you do not need to follow his teaching and the teaching of other Church Fathers whenever it comes to observing the one Eucharist under the one bishop? How are Western Christians heretics and deviants of Tradition when the Orthodox Church has also not been entirely faithful in terms of maintaining the original mode of worship of the ancient Church, as noted by its own prominent theologians?"

As I come to a close, I suppose I also want to address the notion that is emphasized by many Orthodox today, that the Divine Liturgy has been handed down in an unaltered way throughout the ages. I often hear the claim that the Apostle Paul or any of the other Apostles would readily recognize the modern Orthodox liturgy. I completely agree that there is much in the Eastern liturgies that ancient Christians would readily recognize. The same could also be said of the traditional Western Rites as well. I do think that the Orthodox need to be challenged in their perspective on this a bit, though. As we see in Zizoulas' notes above, things have not remained completely unchanged by time. We Westerners are not the only ones who have wavered from the ancient ways, nor are we the only ones who have innovated the traditions we've received:

One Orthodox worship service on Sunday mornings is not the two services of the ancient Church. Something was changed by merging them together.

Letting the catechumens remain in the service is not the same as dismissing them.

Multiple Bishops in one city does not equate with the one Bishop in ancient Christendom, and multiple Eucharists in one city is not the same as having one Eucharist under one Bishop in one city.

Removing the ancient processionals for the sake of convenience or time is not the same as keeping them.

Altering the motions of the Entrances is not the same as leaving them unaltered.

Why I'm Not Reformed (But Admire Them Anyway)
John Ehrett

I have a complicated relationship with Reformed theology.

Growing up, I first encountered Calvinist ideas in early high school. I was floored by the thought that anyone might really embrace a kind of theological "hard determinism," in which anything could ultimately be causally attributed to God. It took only a little dot-connecting to see the implications: without free will, the Fall itself was an "act of God"... which, it seemed, would inevitably make God the Author of evil. That's a simplistic critique, and a familiar one, but I've never been altogether convinced that it's off base.

So, I reasoned to myself, *I'm not a Calvinist.* But as the years passed and my social circle expanded, I found myself increasingly puzzled by the patterns I observed. Almost without exception, the staunchest Calvinists I knew were singularly committed to their faith, and felt strongly about seriously engaging its intellectual implications. (I'd learn later that I wasn't the only one noticing this trend; my teen years happened to coincide with the heyday of the "Young, Restless, and Reformed" movement, a kind of Calvinist renaissance spearheaded by magnetic evangelical leaders). Though I might've disagreed—strongly—with any theology that predicated eternal damnation upon "hidden decrees" of God, I couldn't question these folks' sincere love of God and Scripture. To be fully honest, I sometimes wondered what I was missing.

The high-water mark of my interest in the "doctrines of grace" came during my freshman year of college. I'd started attending a church within the Sovereign Grace Movement, a small denomination that fused elements of the Reformed and charismatic traditions (needless to say, this was quite the departure from my Lutheran upbringing). For the first few months, my biggest complaint was that the sermons were really long; where my objections to Calvinism were concerned, I'd reached a sort of détente. After all, why fixate on such obviously divisive minutiae when there was a whole world to engage?

But then, all the old feelings came back. And I can still remember the sermon that did it—the last message I ever sat through at that church. The pastor described everyone in the world as running headlong toward damnation: a single unified mass of sinners, moving faster and faster as they surged toward an infinite abyss. And some of these runners, the pastor explained, were miraculously plucked from the horde by God and spirited away into eternal bliss. Everyone else simply went on to their destruction.

Something primal in me revolted. How could a God of such naked caprice—a God who was omnipotent, but plainly not all-benevolent—ever rightfully command human love and worship? (I'd later hear this problem phrased as "the major difference between God and Satan is that God only wants *most* people to go to hell). Again, I realize that caricature isn't fair to the thoughtfully Reformed, but the principle of the thing was potent enough to turn me off Calvinism almost for good.

There's a current in some high-level theological scholarship that echoes this critique. In *A Secular Age*, Charles Taylor lays the blame for contemporary irreligiosity at the feet of Calvin's heirs. In Taylor's telling, the medieval ebb and flow of sin and salvation—of Carnival and Confession—gave way to a puritanical ethic of dread as Calvinist theological ideas took root. That Puritanism, which imposed impossible demands of holiness on the faithful, would later pave the way for a despondent modern nihilism. For its part, Anthony Kronman's *Confessions of a Born-Again Pagan* delivers a muted version of Taylor's critique, suggesting that any metaphysics of God that prioritizes his "will" (that is, God's sovereignty) will necessarily lay the emotional groundwork for anti-theism. And not to be outdone, the inimitable David Bentley Hart brutally takes the Reformed tradition to task in his recent volume *The Hidden and the Manifest*:
The God of absolute will who was born in the late Middle Ages had by the late sixteenth century so successfully usurped the place of the true God that few theologians could recognize him for the imposter that he was. And the piety he inspired was, in some measure, a kind of blasphemous piety: a servile and fatalistic adoration of boundless power masquerading as a love of righteousness. . . . If this is God, then Feuerbach and Nietzsche were both perfectly correct to see his exaltation as an impoverishment and abasement of the human at the hands of a celestial despot.

I certainly don't have the historical or theological mojo to go head-to-head with a Taylor or a Hart on the merits of their arguments: it's quite possible their "genealogies of nihilism" recount a bitterly true story. Yet at the same time, I can't help but think there's a certain unfairness underlying these caustic jabs at Reformed thought. Confirmation bias is a devil of a thing, after all.

There's a lot in the Reformed tradition that I know I'll never agree with. I can't see myself ever coming around on the issue of "limited atonement," or the notion that God's revealed will is utterly different from his hidden will, or that God's "love" means something radically different from how we understand the term. But notwithstanding these and other objections, over the last year or so I've become increasingly aware of the ways in which Reformed theology manifests a unique and important beauty. Cynical just-so stories about how Calvinism spawned nihilism must inevitably neglect that beauty, and in so doing they tell an incomplete tale.

Though there have definitely been times in my life when I'd never have admitted it, I've learned an enormous amount from the Reformed heritage over the years. People like me—who find that their soteriological sensibilities run in a decidedly non-Calvinist direction—are often, perhaps, too unwilling to admit this sort of thing. Four specific issues stand out: the Reformed tradition's robust sense of "holy dread"; the tradition's commitment to rigorously engaging the Bible on its own terms; the tradition's resistance to faddishness and corresponding embrace of its own rigor; and the tradition's longstanding willingness to seriously engage the cultural forms of a given age.

Holy Dread

If the popularity of "The Shack" means anything at all, it's a testament to how an essentially therapeutic view of the divine has embedded itself in modern culture. (And there are radical differences, for what it's worth, between this god and the restorative Deity envisioned in the Orthodox tradition: the former demands nothing at all, while the latter demands nothing less than our radical ontological transformation.) The deistic figurehead of late Western theism is sovereign over bumper stickers and Precious Moments figurines.

Whether or not one embraces the associated metaphysics, it's undeniable that the Calvinist God reduces this pretender's throne to rubble. In an age of theological apathy, the Reformed faith unabashedly deploys the language of sin and redemption, fire and light, hell and heaven. This stands in stark contrast to the fog of sentimentality that surrounds much public "God-talk." The idea that there really are ways we *ought* or *ought not* live, irrespective of our preferences or rationalizations, is a positively scandalous sentiment. When so much of culture has forgotten its sense of sacred awe, Calvinism forces the world to confront that ultimacy anew: the terrible beauty of a genuinely holy God.

To declare that God is sovereign is necessarily to declare that God does not exist for one's own pleasure. There will always—*must always*—be questions the human mind can never answer about the foundations of reality. Learning to live with that inevitable uncertainty is the root of any true intellectual humility, and for better or worse, the Reformed have modeled that humility for centuries.

The Vitality of Scripture
This is a thorny topic for those who, like me, are occasionally uncomfortable with the ways in which the Reformation-era concept of sola scriptura has mutated over time (e.g., the notion of a "self-authenticating" biblical canon that can exist apart from the Church). But consider this: the theological alternative to a rigorously Reformed approach to the Bible is very rarely a deep dive into patristic history and context. Agree or disagree with the parameters of study ("no historical-critical method allowed!"), it's undeniable that some of the most thoughtful engagement with biblical texts has come from thoroughly Reformed writers. By contrast, evangelical authors who abandon entrenched concepts of "inerrancy" typically end up invoking far mushier sources of spiritual guidance (just page through anything by Rob Bell or Rachel Held Evans—the readings of the Bible that emerge often bear a suspicious resemblance to the current Huffington Post opinion pages).

It's one thing to argue that Protestant paradigms for approaching the Bible are often much more historically contingent than many are willing to admit. "Post-evangelical" writers like Bell and Held Evans get that right. But it's quite another to substitute, as they and others often do, a thin theological gruel that uses the "right language" while stripping culturally disfavored biblical texts of any claim to moral force. Before post-Protestants tear down the dogmatic fences of their forerunners, they at least ought to know why those fences were put up.

The Life of the Mind

Reformed theology—even in its more contemporary varieties—has vigorously resisted the dumbing-down effects of modern culture. (Any tradition willing to unironically invoke the wisdom of the Puritans can't be accused of selling out for social prestige.) Reformed thought has long been characterized by intricate, interlocking systems of analysis—the framework of "covenant theology" particularly stands out—with implications for multiple areas of life. Those systems are intellectually demanding: they compel adherents to seriously think through the authority structures they accept and their reasons for doing so, while simultaneously raising the specter of epistemic uncertainty (can a mind clouded by sin ever truly come to grasp truth? If so, how?). That's a far cry from the fideism of pop Christianity (whether or not one agrees with the underlying assumptions), and in an Internet-glutted age obsessed with clickbaity slogans, it's a breath of fresh air. Reformed thought expects seriousness and intellectual engagement from Christians of every age and station, and many have risen to that challenge.

Cultural Engagement

The Reformed tradition—at least in its twentieth-century expressions—has been far less hostile to meaningful engagement with secular culture than many other strains of Protestantism. This is no doubt attributable in part to the influence of Abraham Kuyper, famous for his expansive understanding of God's sovereignty in the world, and Francis Schaeffer, pioneer of the "worldview studies" commonly seen today.

Here a brief digression is in order. In the past, I've criticized the tendency of some "worldview studies" proponents to reduce belief systems down to sets of (sometimes unrepresentative) propositions. A version of this argument also made the rounds in classical-education circles last spring. But again, context matters: it's one thing to say that certain framings of religious belief systems don't "work" at the level of graduate study, but quite another to suggest that the teaching approach doesn't work *at all*. The alternative to "worldview studies" is almost never going to be a serious explanation of rival theologies and philosophies through the lens of history; the alternative will instead be a knee-jerk aversion or an undercooked syncretism.

Worldview studies, done right, require careful engagement with intellectual traditions and their cultural artifacts. That interaction isn't squared with any flight into "Christian kitsch" or subcultural sequestration. Taking other beliefs seriously requires some degree of sincere understanding—even an imperfect one—and by popularizing the concept of "worldview," Reformed thought has helped to make that possible.

None of this is intended to paper over the significant theological differences that keep me from being Reformed. This side of eternity, there may be no way to definitively resolve the questions at issue. But that said, in an American religious marketplace that tends to desaturate the power of real religious convictions, the Reformed tradition retains an undeniable vitality.

And that, I think, is well worth admiring.

Lex Orandi, Lex Credendi
Chad Kim

Luther and Lutherans have the market cornered on justification, *sola fide*. Calvin and Reformed thinkers spend all their time trying to elaborate on the notion of election (I wish I had a nice Latin word for it, but I digress). Baptists, well I guess it would be *sola Scriptura*, at the very least something about the individual conscience of the believer and reading Scripture. These are all traditions that I have been shaped by in my theological journey. Seven years ago, almost to the month, I was confirmed in the Episcopal Church. I have never been able to get a grasp on what precisely is the *subiectum theologicae* for Episcopalians. What is the focus of theological conversation and speculation?

I'm new to Conciliar Post. And, without knowing anything about me, it might be hard to understand the spirit or background with which I come to this difficulty of understanding what makes Anglican theology... well, Anglican.

So, by way of introduction, both to the question at hand, and because I'm a new author on this blog, I will provide you a quick sketch. My parents raised me as a Southern Baptist, my dad's family having ties to Jerry Falwell and Independent Fundamentalist Baptists. In sixth grade, my parents sent me to a Reformed school based on the Westminster Confession because apparently Baptists are not into specialized secondary education. I studied philosophy at Oklahoma Baptist University, received an M. Div. from Princeton Seminary and and currently study at St. Louis University for my doctorate. Oh yeah, and I was confirmed in the Episcopal Church while studying at Princeton. Why did I tell you all that? Well, I have been shaped and "tradition-ed" by such a diverse set of theological, political and social commitments, that I am not sure either, where I belong or where I want to stay.

I recognize that I over-simplified the above theological traditions, who clearly had more to say than what I reduced them to, but–when in a pinch or when a non-theological trained person asks me what makes each distinct–I can resort to those simple ideas. Yet when it comes to Anglicans, I'm stumped. When I tried being Presbyterian in high school, I was taken in by the sheer logical force and air tight reasoning of the arguments given to me by my Reformed teachers. When I quit going to church in college, I hated the God I had come to believe in because I thought I had everything figured out in my air tight Reformed system (man was I wrong). I think the reason I became Episcopalian was because I loved hymn music and a more conservative liturgy. Despite the fact that I loved philosophy, theology, and thinking, I came to the Episcopalian church for other, less rational reasons. This has always bothered me because I *love* a good logical, rational debate. The Episcopal church gave me the freedom to argue or consider pretty much whatever I wanted. As long as coffee was being served after the service, Episcopalians don't get their feathers ruffled by much. At first this was liberating. Then, I started to wonder what actually people were committed to.

To this point in my life, the best summary of Episcopal theology I know is the dictum *lex orandi, lex credendi*. Literally, this means "law of praying, law of believing", or, in a more idiomatic translation, "as one prays so one believes." This emerges from the Anglican commitment to the *Book of Common Prayer* as the standard form for prayer, worship, and piety for Anglicans. Reformed people have the *Institutes*. Lutherans have *Luther's Catechism*. Baptists have the Bible (and the Sinner's Prayer). It always seemed odd that in an Episcopal church you are more likely to find a hymnal and the *Book of Common Prayer* than a Bible in the pews. But, if the primary concern of theology for Anglicans is derived from how the pray, of course they would only have the *Book of Common Prayer*!

Some of my more knowledgeable readers might recognize that usually the *via media* is the traditional shorthand way of summarizing Anglican theology. While that certainly is a portion of it, I personally find the *lex orandi, lex credendi*, to be somewhat more binding, as well as a better interpretation of what is going on in calling Anglican theology *via media*. The reason Anglicans are looked upon as the *via media*—as I understand it—is basically due to the middle ground position taken in the *1559 Book of Common Prayer* on the question of what is happening at Eucharist. Basically, the route taken in this iteration was that you could read into the liturgy a more Reformed view of the Eucharist, as an "outward sign of an invisible grace." This did not require the parishioner to hold to a view of transubstantiation, as in the Catholic Church. I don't bring this up to go through various views of communion, but simply to illustrate the meaning of *via media*.

But, if this is all it means to be Anglican, we have essentially committed ourselves to the logical fallacy of the false middle. Whereas, if you look at *lex orandi, lex credendi*, as at the core of the Anglican identity, there isn't a theological battle to be had over the nature of the Eucharist, except to say, "We believe what we pray, in the liturgy." Two sides can disagree on the particulars, but we all share one bread. This ability to stand for something, while also standing for unity is a beautiful thing. Sometimes the drive for unity can lead to a position that is essentially the least common denominator and the only goal is to make everyone happy. At its best, the Anglican can continue to pray with a unified voice, even though those gathered at the table understand its meaning in different ways. Maybe more to the point, Anglicans are committed to a *spiritual identity* rather than a *purely systematic theological identity*. A student of mine asked me why I went to the Episcopal church, and the best answer I could provide was, "When I wake up on Sunday morning, the place I feel most at home is at St. Michael's." I didn't always like the preaching. I disagreed with people on a number of theological issues. But, we shared one prayer, one creed, one baptism and one bread.

This identity that I have lived in for about seven years now, I have continued to explore and struggle with, but it has also shaped me more than I realized. As a youth director at a church, I had to do a funeral for a student who committed suicide. I was asked by well-meaning youth and friends what I believed about where this student would go after their death. I told them, quite frankly it wasn't up to me, but as the prayer book says, "God's property is always to have mercy." Now, of course, this is a quote from the book of James, but I had it memorized as the prayer we say before communion in the older Rite One liturgy. We acknowledge before we approach the altar that the only reason anyone is able to receive grace and the healing gifts of the sacrament is due to God's unfailing mercy. We can't know for certain what is the future of this child who was created in the image of God, but we affirm what we know in through prayer and the liturgy that our God is a God of mercy, *always*.

When my grandfather ("Papaw" as I call him) was in the hospital with a heart attack, my sister and brother asked me how we should pray. We were raised Southern Baptist where the most authentic way to pray was extemporaneously. Needless to say, I didn't know what words to say when we had just heard this awful news and were sitting together at my parents counter. When I went to pray, in my head were the words from compline in the *Book of Common Prayer*:

> *"Keep watch, dear Lord, with those who work, or watch or weep this night, and give your angels charge over those who sleep. Tend the sick, Lord Christ; give rest to the weary, bless the dying, soothe the suffering, pity the afflicted, shield the joyous; and all for your love's sake. Amen."*

Even still, I know I could not have come up with words more beautiful or true. To me prayers of this kind provide great comfort, because I don't have to have the perfect word on the tip of my tongue. I can pray with the great crowd of witnesses, how Anglicans and Christians have been praying for centuries. It is not about me, but how a community prays together, as one.

The Non-Denominational Reformation
Jacob J. Prahlow

Every 500 years or so in the history of the Christian church, a significant restructuring seems to take place.

Around the year 500, a church council at Chalcedon published what most of Christendom calls the clearest explanation of orthodox Christology: Christ is one person with two natures. However, large swaths of Christians—the Oriental Orthodox (such as the Coptic, Syrian, and Ethiopian churches) and the Church of the East—found the Chalcedon Definition lacking. And so the first major division in Christianity occurred.

About 500 years later, a hot-headed Bishop of Rome (or at least his hot-headed legates) and an angry Bishop of Constantinople mutually excommunicated each other, leading to nearly 1000 years of division between the western Roman Catholic and Eastern Orthodox churches.[1]

Some 500 years after that, a tempermental Augustinian monk in Germany posted some theses for academic disputation that started a firestorm of theological controversy, reformation, and church divisions—resulting in the proliferation of thousands of Protestant denominations.[2]

Historically Speaking

Now, the historian in me is obligated to note that using a clean, round number (500 years) to delineate these dates is somewhat artificial. There's nothing inherently special about the passage of 500 years that leads Christians to say to one another, "I don't like how you do church

---

[1] Ostensibly over the *filioque* controversy (about from whom the Holy Spirit proceeds, the (original) Father or the (western addition) Father and Son.
[2] It's commonly said that there are some 33,000 Christian denominations in the world. There are some problems with the methodology and taxonomy of this number; Gordon-Conwell estimates some 47,000 denominations, while others advocate for a more general "about 200 major denominations plus thousands of independent and non-denominational churches" approach.

anymore." But humans enjoy describing the past in easy-to-remember terms that serve as useful baselines for historical knowledge, whether or not they encompass the totality of historical truth (476, 1492, or July 4th, anyone?). Even so, given Christianity's track record so far, you might expect another monumental moment to occur any year now, since it's been about 500 years since the last major shakeup in Christendom.

The argument I wish to make in this article, is that we've already begun to see the next great restructuring of Christianity: *the rise of non-denominational Christianity.*

The Rise and Spread of Non-Denominationalism
The ongoing increase in non-denominational churches worldwide follows the basic pattern of Christianity's previous shakeups. A series of significant theological and organizational battles occurs, typically in one relatively isolated geographical region, followed by a relatively rapid spread of the movement into other areas. As the change spreads, the movement undergoes a period of reorganization and coming to terms with the new structure (institutionalization).

Following the denominational wars in the United States (and elsewhere) during the 20th century, non-denominational churches began to emerge.[1] Thus far, historians have not yet determined who the initial non-denominational reformer was, though factors such as a post-World War II emphasis on personal freedom, growing disillusionment with denominational infighting, the rise of trans-denominational movements (such as the Civil Rights Movement, Billy Graham's Crusades, and the rise of parachurch ministries), and the tremendous success of the megachurch movement are likely influences.

Today, non-denominational churches are seemingly everywhere, and they're increasing in number. From 1976 until 2014, the number of non-denominational churches increased by over 400% in the United

---

[1] While we can trace a form of non-denominationalism back to seventeenth century Scotland, the movement did not begin in earnest until 20th century North America. In terms of historical parallel, I would liken this to the Protestant Reformation: we could (and some do) speak about historical predecessors to Luther (namely, Wycliffe and Hus), though Luther bears the standard as the progenitor of the Protestant Reformation.

States.[1] Several years ago, the Hartford Institute estimated that some 12 million American Christians called themselves non-denominational.[2] Although accurate numbers are difficult to find, it's possible that some 100 million Christians around the world identify as non-denominational today.[3]

Case Study: St. Louis, MO
Saint Louis, the city in which I live, provides a fascinating case study of this growth. Traditionally split between Roman Catholics and Lutherans, Saint Louis has become home to many non-denominational churches, several of which are very large and influential.[4] But equally fascinating are the number of churches that are *not* non-denominational but *act as if they are*. In St. Louis, several large and growing churches throughout the city have denominational ties that a) are not obvious unless you ask, b) do not appear on any signage, and c) are routinely deemphasized even in those churches. Churches like The Journey, The Crossing, The Gathering, and The Rock are non-denominational in form and function, even though they retain denominational connections.

Saint Louis is by no means an exception when it comes to these trends. The Hartford Institute lists six non-denominational churches among the ten largest churches in the United States, and most of the churches appearing near the top of this list do not obviously affiliate with a denomination, even if ties are still present.[5] The growth of non-denominational churches in the US (and around the world) in the past fifty years has been rapid and shows no signs of slowing, even influencing churches with long-standing denominational ties.

---

[1] Ed Stetzer, "The Rapid Rise of Nondenominational Christianity," *Christianity Today*, 12 June 2015.
[2] Scott Thumma, "A Report on the 2010 National Profile of U.S. Nondenominational and Independent Churches," *Hartford Institute For Religion Research*.
[3] The Status of Global Christianity, 2017.
[4] Grace Church, Faith Church, Saint Louis Family Church, and Word of Life Church are four of the largest that are recorded on most registries of megachurches (1,000+/weekend).
[5] The Hartford Institute for Religion Research, "Database of Megachurches in the U.S."

Moving Toward Institution

Another sign of the non-denominational reformation is the emerging institutionalization of this movement through multisite churches and church networks.

Multisite churches are Christian gatherings where a single church organization holds services at two or more geographical locations. Church networks, while a little less clearly defined at this point, are more extensive groupings of churches, often with a common approach, geography, or mission. In essence, networks tend to function as resource sharing centers that attempt to sidestep the nuanced battles over theology and praxis that has come to define many denominations.

I postulate that the emergence of multisites and networks—both of which are still in their relatively early stages—represents the next step in the non-denominational reformation, the move towards institutionalization. These churches are coming to realize their need to better organize and define themselves, and the multisite and network movements are the most common forms of that institutionalization. Just as French, Swiss, and German churches had to wrestle with questions of succession and ongoing ministry after the the initial reforms of Luther, Calvin, and Zwingli, so also non-denominational churches (as a movement) are beginning to wrestle with how their shakeup can last more than a generation or two.

Considering Some Problems

To be clear: my contention about the non-denominational reformation is a theory about the currents of Christianity, a theory with much to work out and many more questions to answer—both theologically and methodologically. On these topics, a number of questions remain that need to be addressed in order to better understand the state of the global Christian church with respect to the non-denominational reformation.

Is non-denominational an accurate term to use? By-and-large, non-denominational churches have emerged out of particular circumstances and situations rather than as a wholesale response to a particular council, person, or church. In contrast to non-Chalcedonian churches, mainline Protestants, and (to a different degree) the Catholic and Orthodox churches, non-denominational churches don't have a clearly defining trait. As currently used, the term "non-denominational" lacks a defining origin or characteristic other than simply "not belonging to one of the many organizational structures of denominational Christianity." As a result, the terminology around churches that are non-denominational can vary considerably ("independent" is also sometimes used) and can be fuzzy.

How do we count and categorize non-denominational churches? We desperately need better ways to count and categorize non-denominational churches. For years, church statisticians have relied on central denominational offices to provide information on the number of churches, congregants, baptisms, and so forth that have been used as the counting numbers for tracking church growth and decline. Existing studies by Gordon-Conwell, the Hartford Institute, Pew Forum, and (even) Wikipedia tend to lump these churches into a broad "other" category. This makes it nearly impossible to fully account for the number of non-denominational churches in existence in the United States, let alone in geographies with less infrastructure or fewer surveys from Pew or Gallup running about.

Is non-denominationalism simply a regional (i.e., North American) movement? Within Christendom, it is sometimes difficult to discern between a regional movement and the start of something much larger. There have been numerous more-or-less regional movements within Christianity which were influential for a time and then faded (for example, Gnosticism, pietism, and quietism). So it could be that non-denominational Christianity is a largely regional phenomenon that's been exported to particular places around the world. Of course, most of the significant events that have shaped global Christianity began as regional issues. In 451, Chalcedonian Christological debates may have seemed like an eastern problem; in 1054 it was clearly a Rome v. Constantinople issue; and in 1517, many people thought the debate would remain confined to German universities. While non-denominationalism began (at least in its present form) and is most popular in North America, it is by no means a specifically North American form of Christianity. You can find non-denominational churches (and non-denominational churches that have taken the steps of going multisite or using networks) worldwide.[1]

---

[1] See Warren Bird's database of Global Megachurches.

What about movement churches? The general difficulties of tracking non-denominational churches are compounded when it comes to "movement" churches, those congregations which haven't official shed denominational ties but still functionally operate as non-denominational bodies that are more closely aligned to a network than a denomination.[1] Above I noted several local congregations in St. Louis that are functionally non-denominational but retain their denominational ties; one of these churches is even in the process of officially becoming non-denominational. Keeping track of that sort of information would be incredibly helpful when looking at the non-denominational reformation, although no standards yet exist to help with that process.

Conclusion

The spread of non-denominational churches shows no signs of stopping (or slowing down) even as North American culture moves away from treating Christian identity as normative. I've suggested that this movement may represent the next great shift in Christendom, following in the paradigm shifts of Chalcedon, the Great Schism, and the Protestant Reformation. To better understand this trend, however, some key questions need to be answered about how we understand non-denominationalism and monitor its development. May Christ's Church on earth continue to take root in our world, even as we look for these answers.

---

[1] This isn't a problem new to non-denominational churches either; statisticians have long struggled to accurately assess how many churches belong to the Pentecostal and Charismatic movements which, historically, have transcended denominational lines.

Is Protestantism a Heresy?
Benjamin Cabe

Is Protestantism a heresy? This question has recently been asked of me by a number of sincere Protestants. Well-meaning as they are, their questions have put me in a dangerous position. On the one hand, I could answer as I have addressed similar, though less pointed, questions by hearkening to my ignorance and the mercy of our gracious God. On the other, such an answer may lead those I love, among whom I count you as one, to believe that Protestantism is an equal alternative to Orthodoxy. And so, I am faced with a dilemma.

Saint Raphael of Brooklyn faced a similar dilemma in 1911 when he wrote concerning the American branch of Anglican and Eastern Orthodox Churches' union. The tenderness of the first letter, he grievously relates, proved to be "harmful and confusing." So, after carefully studying *The Book of Common Prayer* used in Anglican Churches, he wrote a second and third letter with "great reluctance." It is with such reluctance that I write. For, regardless of how I answer—or if I choose to remain silent—I risk either alienating or accidentally misleading those with whom I long to be united. Thus, fearing the loss of brethren on either side—but mostly the loss of brethren who might come into the Fold—it is incumbent upon me to respond. Love compels me.[1]

Many would like me to say that all Trinitarian Christianities are created equal; that it does not matter where you belong; that there is a kind of *mere Christianity* that can unite us, though invisibly, as the Church (*ekklesia*). But a unity in *mere Christianity*, such as we seemed to have achieved here on Conciliar Post, is a kind of meeting hall, as C. S. Lewis describe it, not the unity of the Church. The unity of the Church is based in the mystery of the Holy Trinity, it is a unity explicitly effected through the Eucharist (1 Corinthians 10:16-17), a mystery that calls us to union with one another, and to Christ in the same manner Christ is one with the Father (John 17:20-26). This kind of union is not based on a stripped down list of *essentials*, as Paul

---

[1] "The unity of the Church follows of necessity from the unity of God." (Alexei Khomiakov, *The Church is One*. 10).

notes, but in the total unity of mind and judgment (1 Corinthians 1:10). This is of the utmost importance: the Church is the Body of Christ and Christ is not divided, so how can His Church be? With these considerations, it seems that an invisible church based on the unity of a few distinct dogmas that all Trinitarian Christians believe, cannot be what the writers of Holy Scripture had in mind.[1]

It is natural that a Protestant understanding of the church, and church unity, would consist in a "least common denominator" model since such a model is the only unity any Protestant church achieves. Due to this phenomenon, there will always be a variety of opposing views within the walls of any given Protestant church. Many Protestants may wonder why Orthodox and Roman Catholics will not accept such a model of unity where we can "agree to disagree" on things they consider to be "non-essential." The biggest problem with this way of thinking is that, for the church of history, those other things *are* essential. Further, we are forced to ask if, even today, a least common denominator model is viable within the Protestant world. Historically, Protestants have never been united in any substantial sense.

George Aldhizer, who identifies as a Reformed Christian, wrote in a recent article,
> once one begins to do historical research on the Reformation, one finds that Protestants never intended to be fundamentally united with one another. There was no comfortableness with a generic "evangelicalism," or a unity on the *five solas*, or a simple appeal to an "invisible church." Countries, governments, and lands were separated based on distinct practices of the Lord's Supper (among other things), there was simply no *Gospel Coalition* or *Christianity Today* or mutual love of Billy Graham with which to create a common ground authoritative center. Maybe if we were more historically aware of the origins of our traditions, Protestants wouldn't be

---

[1] It should be noted that within the walls of the Orthodox Church, you will find a distinction between *essentials* (dogma) and *theological opinion* (theologoumenon). This "list" developed as the early Christians fought against the heretical teachings of the time. In this sense, we can say that Christian dogma developed in articulation in order to refute false teachings. This is why we have the creeds. It should also be noted that these *essentials* are agreed upon in every branch of Orthodoxy—unlike in Protestantism where the lists of essentials all differ from one another.

so comfortable with each other's supposedly "minor" or "non-essential" beliefs.

It seems clear that neither ecumenism nor the Church (*ekklesia*) can be based on a kind of abstract *essentialism*. The Church is *one* body because of *the* One Body into which we were baptized and of which we partake (1 Corinthians 12:13; 1 Corinthians 10:16-17). That is, the Church is a concrete reality that exists in the world, though She is not of the world, where She physically receives as members those who are baptized into Her Fold. This Church cannot be divided into various sects, nor can she be overcome (corrupted) by the secularism of the world (cf. Matthew 16:17-19). Historically, and even today, to safeguard this unity, the Church has placed outside of Her Fold those who, even after being confronted by a council of the Church, willfully propound false teachings (cf. Matthew 18:15-20). Such was the case with Arius and countless others who propounded false teachings. Arius refused to accept the admonishment of the Church at the council of Nicaea and so he was excommunicated, or excommunicated himself in a sense by willfully placing himself outside of the Church.[1] This means, above all, that he was deprived of the Church's sacraments: the Eucharist, *par excellence*.

But Arius, among others, continued to practice their mutated form of Christianity, deceiving many. This raises a peculiar question: are the sacraments offered "outside" of the Church valid? Is Baptism administered within an heretical sect "valid"? St. Cyprian deals with this in one of his letters (letter 72). He says no (Matthew 18:18). With such an answer echoed in various others throughout history, this is an issue we must take seriously. But with a radical disinterest in the church of history and a total rejection of the sacraments by a portion of Evangelicalism today (a re-hashing in part of the ancient gnostic heresy), how do we speak about this issue?

---

[1] Many in the Evangelical community may doubt that "excommunication" does anything to affect one's "status" of being in the Church. This is natural for a community that has neither a solid understanding of Apostolic Succession nor a substantial ecclesiology. It seems that Western Christianity has abandoned ecclesiology in all its forms—neither understanding it, nor taking it seriously. However, with what is said in scripture and proclaimed by Christians universally (until the Reformation) about apostolic succession / the laying on of hands / the unity of the Church / the ability to bind and lose things on earth that will be bound and loosed in heaven, we should take this seriously (Matthew 18:18).

I suppose the question comes down to, as Joseph Green points out in a recent article, what is the standard of measure? Protestants would like us to believe that Scripture alone can tell us what we need to know, individually, without relying on anyone else's interpretation. It is this method, however, that led to the tens of thousands of Protestant denominations in existence today. Still, to be logically consistent with S*ola scriptura*, as Joseph points out, it would seem that sermons should only consist of scripture reading without any attempt at explanation on the part of the pastor. Instead, we are left with tens of thousands opposing interpretations of scripture in the Protestant world. So, with everyone disagreeing on what scripture actually means, how do you know what it means?

Instead of answering the original question, I want to pose another. How do you know you are *in* the church of the Apostles? How do you know you believe what the Apostles believed? How do you know what you believe about God is true? Such questions are frightening when you begin to think about them. Do I believe what I believe because of when and where I was born in history? How do I know it's the Holy Spirit and not just *me?* After all, the heart is deceitful above all things (Jeremiah 17:9). Such questions plagued me prior to our conversion to Orthodoxy.

A writer in the fifth century offers some wise advice: you can know what you believe is true if it can be found in antiquity and if it is view held universally regardless of time period or place.[1] If there is some contention on these two points, he writes that we must look for a consensus among people who *lived* the faith, not just philosophized. These three rules, Antiquity, Universality, and Consensus, can be helpful for us in our journey today. So, did the majority of Christians throughout time agree upon dogmas that reflect a kind of Protestantism or Orthodoxy (and Catholicism)? Any reader of Church history will be able to answer readily.

"What kind of Christian would you have you been in 4th century Egypt or 8th century Gaul, or 12th century Greece?" asks Fr. Josiah Trenham in his latest book, *Rock and Sand.* "Certainly not a Protestant since there were no protestants. There were only Orthodox and heretics." But we are not in the 4th, 8th, or 12th centuries. Post 16th century Christendom looks far different. In our time, the term

---

[1] St. Vincent of Lerins.

"Christian" has been broadened to include those who reject the Church and Her Tradition—an action that, every other time in Church history would have carried with it the title "heretic."

Early in the second century, a disciple of the Apostle John named Ignatius tells us that where the bishop is, there is the Church (*Smyrnaeans*, 8). And that there is *one* Eucharist and *one* Altar (*Philadelphians*, 4), and anyone outside of this Altar (the Church) is deprived of the Bread of God (*Ephesians*, 5). Further still, Ignatius proclaims that, "If any man follows him that makes a schism in the Church, he shall not inherit the kingdom of God" (*Philadelphians*, 3). A little later in the second century, Irenaeus names the twelve Bishops of Rome, up to that point in history, who were received by the laying on of hands, the first of whom by the Apostles themselves, and tells us that "by this succession, the ecclesiastical tradition from the apostles, and the preaching of the truth, have come down to us. And this is most abundant proof that there is one and the same vivifying faith, which has been preserved in the Church from the apostles until now, and handed down in truth."[1] He goes on to say that we can tell what is the truth by seeing if what is propounded existed before the one who propounded it.[2] That is, if it is grounded in the life of the Church all throughout history. After all, it is the Church that scripture proclaims to be the pillar and ground of truth (1 Timothy 3:15).

Irenaeus continues by exhorting us to, "learn the truth from those who possess that succession of the Church which is from the apostles, and among whom exists that which is sound and blameless in conduct, as well as that which is unadulterated and incorrupt in speech." These men who possess this Apostolic Succession are "they [that] expound the Scriptures to us without danger, neither blaspheming God, nor dishonoring the patriarchs, nor despising the prophets."[3] Again, we must "read the Scriptures in company with those who are presbyters in the Church, among whom is the apostolic doctrine, as I have pointed out."[4]

So how do you know what you believe about God is true? How do you know you are in the Church of the apostles? According to the witness

---

[1] *Against Heresies*, 3.3.3.
[2] Ibid., 3.4.3.
[3] Ibid., 4.26.5.
[4] Ibid., 4.32.1.

of scripture and history, we must *receive* the faith and not turn aside from it; and we receive it from the unbroken succession of the Apostles *in* the Church. Scripture constantly talks about holding on to that which we *received*. Paul exhorts us, over and over again, to hold on to the traditions delivered to us (1 Corinthians 11:2) whether by *word* or epistle (2 Thessalonians 2:15). Again he tells us to avoid those who hold teachings contrary to what we "learned" (Romans 16:17) and that he who teaches a gospel contrary to what we *received* is accursed (Galatians 1:8-9). Paul tells Timothy not to "neglect the gift in him" by the "laying on of hands" (1 Timothy 4:14). In the same epistle, Paul cautions Timothy not to "hastily lay hands" on anyone (1 Timothy 5:22). Further, Paul explains that he will be a "good minister" if he "instructs the brethren in all these things" (1 Timothy 4:6) and that in the latter days many will depart from this teaching, the faith (1 Timothy 4). Being *in the Church* and learning *from the Church* is the standard according to scripture and antiquity—a standard that is reaffirmed over and over again throughout history.

True knowledge is [that which consists in] the doctrine of the apostles, and the ancient constitution of the Church throughout all the world, and the distinctive manifestation of the body of Christ according to the successions of the bishops, by which they have handed down that Church which exists in every place, and has come even unto us, being guarded and preserved without any forging of Scriptures, by a very complete system of doctrine, and neither receiving addition nor [suffering] curtailment [in the truths which she believes]; and [it consists in] reading [the word of God] without falsification, and a lawful and diligent exposition in harmony with the Scriptures, both without danger and without blasphemy; and [above all, it consists in] the pre-eminent gift of love, which is more precious than knowledge, more glorious than prophecy, and which excels all the other gifts [of God]."[1]

We are told, further, by Irenaeus who was writing against "all the heresies" at the time, that, "[it is also incumbent] to hold in suspicion others who depart from the primitive succession, and assemble themselves together in any place whatsoever, [looking upon them either as heretics of perverse minds, or as schismatics puffed up and self-pleasing, or again as hypocrites, acting thus for the sake of lucre and vainglory. For all these have fallen from the truth. And the heretics, indeed who bring strange fire to the altar of God — namely,

---

[1] Ibid., 4.33.8.

strange doctrines, — shall be burned up by the fire from heaven, as were Nadab and Abiud.[1] From such people we [who hold the doctrine of the apostles] should "keep aloof."[2]

So is Protestantism a heresy? Forgive me, but I will not answer this question. I CANNOT answer the question. Alexei Khomiakov, writing in the 19th century, relates that the (Orthodox) Church can only judge Herself.[3] It seems clear, however, that Protestantism is not, and cannot, be considered grounded in history—something that both the Orthodox and the Roman Catholics can claim. With respect to this, and the sayings above, this is a serious reality. But does this mean that there is an absence of God's grace in Protestantism? I do not think so. After all, "All Truth is God's Truth" as Augustine tells us. Certainly there are some, however, that are closer to the Truth than others. And truth is not an abstract concept, but a *person*. A person that desires to bring each of us into *His life,* into *full communion* with Him. Naturally, then, Truth cannot be fully expressed in rhetoric or dogma, but in *worship*. And *how one worships*, is incalculably important. This is why the essence of Orthodox worship has never changed— because Orthodox dogma is inextricably connected to Orthodox worship. As Saint Raphael of Brooklyn writes,

> The Holy Orthodox Church has never perceptibly changed from Apostolic times, and, therefore, no one can go astray in finding out what She teaches. Like Her Lord and Master, though at times surrounded with human malaria—which He in His mercy pardons—She is *the same yesterday, and today, and forever* (Heb. 13:8) the mother and safe deposit of the truth as it is in Jesus (cf. Eph. 4:21).

This is exactly why the Orthodox "do church" the way we do. This is why we have the Apostolic Tradition, a Liturgical Calendar, why we fast during certain periods of the year, why we have confession and the Sacraments of the Church. It is all Christocentric: we are aimed at becoming "partakers of the Divine Nature" (2 Peter 1:3-4) by the purging of our sinful passions and the uniting with Christ, the Truth. And we will be content with nothing less than *full communion* with Christ—and this requires ascetic effort. The *fasting rules*, among other things in the Orthodox Church, are not ends in themselves, but

---

[1] Ibid., 4.26.2.
[2] Ibid., 4.26.4.
[3] Alexei Stepanovich Khomiakov, *The Church is One.*

a means to *reject our self* that we may gain a True Self in Christ.[1] It is true that, on the outside, the structure of the Orthodox Church seems excessive and rule-based. But on the inside, when you are living it (or in my case *trying to live it)*, it looks much different. What once looked like rigid boundaries—rules—dissolves, and all that remains is *love;* ascetic effort and self-sacrifice, as Christ tells us, is the apex of love (John 15:13). To "lay down your life" can mean physical martyrdom or martyrdom through asceticism—the denying of one's will or desires. And so, by way of our daily martyrdom through ascesis we learn to give our whole being to God, as well as prepare for the possibility of our physical martyrdom.

I write all of this without any intention to offend or quarrel. Although I know some may take offense at it, I offer this last thought: as an ex-Protestant, I found that I had reached the limits of what Protestantism could give me. I hit a brick wall. Protestantism was *not enough*. I was compelled, after much study, to join the Orthodox Church. This move was not based on a *preference*. I was, in a sense, forced out of Protestantism. I was deeply disturbed to find that the church I was attending as a Protestant was neither grounded in history nor a part of the succession from the apostles. Though Protestantism may claim the Trinitarian and Christological dogmas handed down to us from the great defenders of the faith, they claim something that is not theirs, for they reject everything else that every one of these defenders held in common faith. Orthodox Christians today, clergy and laity alike, are to be defenders of the faith—a faith that was handed down to us from the Apostles—not in arrogance, but in truth and love.[2]

With this in mind, I must say that not every form of Christianity even if they are Trinitarian is equal in its ability to transform the person into the likeness of God—a perfection we are commanded to achieve (Matthew 5:48). It is telling that Evangelicalism neither accepts, nor produces, Saints. And this is the litmus test of a church: its ability to produce Saints. This raised a troublesome question for me, as a Protestant. If not all Trinitarian Christian "denominations" are created equal, and some are closer to the truth than others. Since Jesus Christ is *The Truth*, then does that mean that my Western Protestant form of Christianity is holding me back from full

---

[1] cf. Matthew 16:25.
[2] cf. Ephesians 4:11-16.

communion with Christ? Though there are many virtues in Protestantism, Protestantism is *not enough*. For love demands *all*.

Where does this leave me as the founder of Conciliar Post? I also struggle with this question. Undoubtedly my desire is to "dialogue" with those of other "traditions" but how is it possible to talk about something that must be practiced to be understood? For Orthodox Christians, theology is worship—and through worship we learn our theology. There can be no parsing of the human person; the human mind cannot be divorced from practice. In Orthodox theology, a popular adaptation of a saying from Evagrius of Ponticus says, "the Theologian is the one who prays." For us, this is where we draw the line. We mustn't merely intellectualize—we must read the lives of the saints, see what they did, what they said to do, and do it ourselves. The road is neither easy nor comfortable. But this is the real test—a true self-sacrifice.

Of course, it is possible to be within the Orthodox Church and be worse off in the long run. Because we will be judged harsher (cf. James 3:1). For this, I must admit that I know many sincere Protestants who are better off than I. And for this, and for speaking, I must ask your forgiveness. I pray you will take some time to reflect on whether your Christian tradition is grounded in antiquity, universality, and consensus, and these questions:

Is your church, and everything it believes grounded in history? Has it added something or taken something away? Does your Christian tradition believe that worship-style is a preference? Is what you believe found in history, grounded in universality, and confirmed by consensus?

In order for the Orthodox Church to look into any charge of heresy, the person in question must first be a part of Her fold. I did not answer the question because most Protestants were never a part of the Orthodox Church in the first place. For this reason, I attempted only to lay out the reasons why I think it is important to be a part of the Church.

Faith Across Traditions

The Logic of Closed Communion
John Ehrett

A few weeks ago, I found myself having a fruitful discussion about Christian unity with a nondenominational friend. His concerns echoed many of those voiced by Peter Leithart in *The End of Protestantism*—fragmentation over comparatively insignificant differences, the mandate of Jesus that his followers be one, and so forth. And I tend to think that many of those observations have force: in a cultural moment where questions of orthodoxy seem less and less bound up with longstanding denominational divides, getting too hung up on the finer points of dogma can feel pretty pedantic.

In response, I referred him to Gene Veith and Trevor Sutton's recent book *Authentic Christianity*, which approaches that question from a distinctly Lutheran perspective. My friend subsequently remarked that confessional Lutheranism was largely off the table for him—no pun intended—due to its practice of "closed communion" (or, as it's sometimes labeled via an annoyingly cutesy neologism, "close communion"). To his mind, this is an archetypal case of unnecessary line-drawing between orthodox Christians.

Essentially, "closed communion" is the practice "whereby only those individuals who are members of [a denomination] or of a church body with which the [denomination] is in altar and pulpit fellowship are ordinarily communed." In other words, Baptists and Presbyterians typically can't receive Communion at a Lutheran church. And this isn't a specifically Lutheran idea—Catholics and Orthodox Christians have the same restriction on the sacrament. But is it warranted?

I freely admit that my views tend to run in an ecumenical direction, and I tend to think the litmus test for "altar fellowship" should be somewhat less rigorous than it is today. But as I've wrestled with this issue over the years, I've come to see that the position I held earlier in my life—that closed communion was a ridiculous and unnecessary impediment to Christian unity—was probably wrong. So, what follows is my best attempt to articulate, in accessible terms, why some version of closed communion does indeed make sense.

In the broadest sense, some restriction on Communion participation is deeply rooted in historical tradition: it has *virtually always* been the practice of the Church to restrict Communion to those identified as Christian believers. The traditional liturgical division of the worship service into the "Service of the Word" and the "Service of the Sacrament" reflects this: in the earliest days of the Church, those who had not been baptized could attend the "Service of the Word" at which the Scriptures were proclaimed, but were not even permitted to *witness* the Eucharist. To adopt a totally open approach to Communion—that is, one in which participants' *religious* affiliation is irrelevant—is to deviate sharply from the historical understanding that the Eucharist is a distinctly *Christian* celebration.

And that particular kind of deviation is explicitly warned against in Scripture: as the Apostle Paul writes in 1 Corinthians 11:27–29: "Whoever eats the bread or drinks the cup of the Lord in an unworthy manner will be guilty of sinning against the body and blood of the Lord. Everyone ought to examine themselves before they eat of the bread and drink from the cup. For those who eat and drink without discerning the body of Christ eat and drink judgment on themselves." Paul's statement could hardly be clearer: the one who fails to recognize Christ's presence "under" the physical forms of the sacrament does so at a distinct risk to themselves. Just as Moses was warned to remove his sandals before entering the presence of God (Ex. 3:5) and Uzzah was struck down for mishandling the Ark of the Covenant where God's presence resided (1 Chron. 13:9–10), encountering God through Communion is not an action taken lightly.

To my mind, these factors compel the conclusion that some form of "closed communion" is not only desirable, but also mandatory—for the sake of those who might otherwise receive the Eucharist to their detriment. But I doubt this is an especially controversial observation (except maybe among denominations that don't take Paul's teaching here as normative—and that's a whole different ballgame). Far more controversial, I think, is the practice of denying Communion to other Christians who affirm the Nicene Creed.

Here, I think, the rationale may properly shift from a strictly theological one to a quasi-sociological one. To my mind, closed communion epitomizes the principle that the faith ought to be practiced within the context of a discrete local congregation. On Sunday morning, the invitation to worship is extended to all; the invitation to the altar, however, is extended only to those who have made themselves accountable to a discernible institutional order beyond themselves. It is, in a sense, an invitation to seek membership.

This "principle of subsidiarity" also entails that an individual living in unrepentant sin—of which the local congregation is presumably aware—may be denied the sacrament until their behavior changes. Because those within a common denomination will, ideally, enforce the discipline imposed of a member congregation, the offender cannot simply go to another parish: if they wish to receive Communion again, they must reckon with their past conduct.

In a cultural environment where younger Christians are increasingly inclined to seek unity between denominations, I find that this way of thinking about closed communion makes more practical sense than the justification often deployed—that "full unity in doctrine" is absolutely necessary for altar fellowship to occur.

There are at least two good reasons for this. First, the definition of "full unity in doctrine" is not at all clear. One might reasonably expect that subscription to the Lutheran Confessions (because they are faithful expositions of Scripture) constitutes a sufficient unity of doctrine for fellowship to occur, but historically this has not been seen as such. Demanding "full unity," absent an obvious norming standard, risks kicking off an endless regress of ever-finer doctrinal hairsplitting. And second, framing the issue strictly as one of doctrinal purity *among orthodox Christians*—such that a member of the Anglican Church in North America must be denied Communion at an LCMS Lutheran congregation *solely* because of minor theological differences—seems to me to be not only unnecessarily pedantic, but readily misunderstood as the denomination implying that other Christians are not truly believers.

At bottom, the goal of church order—that is, the preservation of meaningful internal discipline—strikes me as a quite compelling justification for practicing closed communion. The practice is a way of ensuring that even in an era of splintered denominations, the universal Church may establish and defend standards for its members. It is decidedly *not* a declaration that the members of one tradition are intrinsically "holier" than those of another. And it ought not be understood as such.

Faith Across Traditions

Do You Have to Be Anti-Western to Be Eastern Orthodox?
Benjamin Cabe

TJ Humphrey's latest article, *Why I Didn't Convert to Eastern Orthodoxy*, is making the rounds on the internet as voices on social media and elsewhere join in to echo his main critique. The enthusiasm with which this article was received is indicative of a failure on our part as Eastern Orthodox Christians in general and a failure of Eastern Orthodox Christian converts in particular. What this calls for is not a defense of Holy Orthodoxy but an apology: Dear TJ, (and all others), please forgive me, an Eastern Orthodox convert who is not free from guilt.

TJ's article touches on a number of topics but the main theme which took hold—in the article and in the mind of the commenters—is the elitist and triumphalist attitude adopted by many Eastern Orthodox Christians. TJ comments that,

> It wasn't the theology or the worship which soured me. What soured me was an elitist attitude that several Orthodox embody and what these particular people expected of me . . . I was expected to renounce and reject the entirety of my Christian past. All things Protestant were to become an anathema to me. My Orthodox acquaintances were baffled that I didn't hate all things Western and Protestant as much as they did. I simply couldn't disqualify all of the grace that I had experienced as a Protestant. I couldn't bite the hand that had fed me for so long.[1]

It's true. A hatred towards Western Christianity can be found within certain adherents to Eastern Orthodoxy. And it has been exacerbated in recent times by the influx of tech-savvy Orthodox converts and the rise of "internet Orthodoxy." I am not writing here to defend anti-westernism or arrogant triumphalism in Orthodox Christians but

---

[1] Humphrey, TJ. *Why I Didn't Convert to Eastern Orthodoxy*. N.p.: Conciliar Post, 2016. Web. 18 Aug. 2016. <https://conciliarpost.com/journeys-of-faith/to-my-eastern-orthodox-friends-am-i-really-a-heretic/>.

rather apologize to those hurt and frustrated by it. In addition, I would like to address this question begged by TJ's article: does Eastern Orthodoxy proper, Her spiritual practices and Her liturgical life, require a hatred for all things Western and arrogant triumphalism in all things Orthodox?

TJ writes in his article that he is "not seeking to critique all Orthodox Christians" and that his article "is not a reaction to the whole of Orthodoxy" but to his "very limited interaction with it."[1] While his critique is a direct reaction against "an attitude within parts of the Eastern Orthodox community" with which he "had direct personal contact,"[2] the article's thesis seems to assume that in order to be an Eastern Orthodox Christian you must latch onto an anti-western mentality and speak with an elitist tone. This brings me back to the question above: do you have to be anti-Western and adopt the "anti-Western tirade that is launched by so many Orthodox converts"[3] in order to be Eastern Orthodox? The answer to these questions is an unequivocal no. This is a crucial distinction that is missing in TJ's article—though I do not think its exclusion was purposeful or his fault. Let me explain.

I was stunned and saddened to find that TJ's first experience with Orthodox Christians who do NOT embody triumphalism and anti-western mentalities was actually with Orthodox commenters in discussion of his own article (which is worth checking out, by the way). The fact is that most of TJ's real-life experiences with Eastern Orthodoxy involved interactions with Orthodox Christians who launched countless polemics against Western Christianity. Had TJ continued in those circles it is quite possible that he would have been influenced by their anti-westernism. But he refused to be involved in it—and for this he should be applauded, and we Orthodox Christians should learn from his example.

Why This Elitist Attitude?
It is a fact that the Eastern Orthodox Church has a rich spiritual tradition and heritage. But, one might ask, if Orthodox Christians drink from so deep a well, why are many filled with such an unChrist-like attitude? This is a good question—and to answer it I will put forth an opinion that may or may not be sound. Many Orthodox Christians,

---

[1] Ibid.
[2] Ibid.
[3] Ibid.

converts especially, are filled with an intellectual zeal for the Orthodox faith. This is often called "convert zeal" because of its frequency in new converts and Ortho-interested-almost-converts. People filled with convert zeal seek to "evangelize" the whole world—especially those in their former tradition—into Orthodoxy. A lot of the time it comes across as arrogant and elitist—especially when the people sought by the convert are resisting what he "knows to be the path to union with God." But if he is following the path to union with God, and is drinking from the deep well, why is he so arrogant? Doesn't this discredit him and the effectiveness of the Eastern Orthodox Christian path? No, it does not. It means only that he is a sinner who is still at the beginning of his journey.

Elder Sophrony (who wrote one of the books TJ devoured: *Saint Silouan the Athonite*) was always reticent to make generalizations about the Christian life. But he did define, quite broadly, three stages that everyone goes through on their spiritual journey. First, we experience the "coming to ourselves," like the prodigal son, and the grace and enabling of God to begin the journey. Second, the grace of God retreats and we experience a spiritual desert. Finally, the grace of God returns to those who "proved themselves" in the desert—whose faith was tested and found firm in their "first love."[1] According to Elder Sophrony, the first stage can last anywhere from a few days to seven years and the second stage is where we spend most of our lives as Christians (persevere!). Some die in the desert before reaching the third and final stage—which is when, after much struggle and perseverance, when we are "begotten as sons."

I maintain that most Eastern Orthodox converts, or enthusiasts, who begin to display anti-western tendencies and arrogant triumphalism do so when they get the first taste of God's grace—perhaps something they never experienced in their former tradition. And this experience, of course, rocks their world. During this period of time, prayer and fasting come easily. The Jesus Prayer is always on their tongue and repeated in their heart. They may be constantly aware of death and copiously shed tears of repentance. All of this reaffirms their decision to convert to Orthodoxy. This is where the Orthodox inquirer, filled with convert zeal, comes in. He has found this "new, ancient path" and is experiencing grace upon grace. And so, when someone crosses

---

[1] This is a summary of what Elder Zacharias says in his book, *Remember Thy First Love*, about Elder Sophrony's three stages of the spiritual life.

his path that does not believe it or will not yield to Orthodoxy, he takes great offense and lashes back.

One might wonder, again, how an Orthodox Christian experiencing such grace would (or could!) speak to his brother in arrogance and anger. It is because the grace that he is experiencing was received as a foretaste to sustain him in the desert. But he has not yet striven for, and taken by force, the Kingdom of heaven (Matthew 11:12)—he has been given special grace that he might "remember his first love" when things get tough. In short, he has not yet been perfected.

Unfortunately, graces experienced in the first stage can be misappropriated to confirm a hatred for the "ineffectuality" of his former tradition. This is not always the case, but when someone in the first stage takes this position, it expels the grace of God, leaving the man with little love and a quickly-fading spiritual fervor and zeal (though the "bang people over the head with Orthodoxy" kind of zeal may remain). When the grace of God is withdrawn the man may wonder what is happening and begin to doubt—especially if he is unaware of these three stages of the spiritual life—and, all too often, either fall away from the Christian faith entirely or drift into robotic mode, continuing down the line of anti-Westernism. But Eastern Orthodoxy proper does not, and will never, lead to anti-Westernism. And this is why, I believe, Eastern Orthodox Christianity—or Christianity in general—cannot be written off.

TJ experienced the underbelly of Eastern Orthodoxy—the dirty laundry, as one commentator put it—and it pushed him away. The fact is that there will always be an underbelly, wherever you end up. Another commenter noted that elitism is not found only within Orthodox circles—it can just as much be found with Protestantism. And as one who used to believe all Roman Catholics were bound for hell (*Lord forgive me*), I can personally attest to this fact. Just like the Westboro Baptist Church does not represent Protestantism as a whole, the triumphalism and arrogance of many young converts should not be seen as representative as Orthodoxy as a whole. And neither should it be seen as a prerequisite for being an Orthodox Christian, because it certainly is not! Sure, there will always be tares among the wheat. There will always be Christians who don't *love* like we are instructed to; there will always be Christians who act downright unChristian—a fact that has produced countless atheists. But does that mean that we should reject Christianity?

Definitions
Up to this point we have thrown around words like "anti-western," "triumphalist," and "elitist," without any substantial definition. What do we mean by these terms and what do we not mean—specifically within the context of this article? Anti-westernism in Eastern Orthodoxy seems to find seed in the demonizing of Augustine of Hippo, who is often used as an all-around whipping boy, so to speak. The flaws in Blessed Augustine's theology, and their development and impact on Western Christianity, are then traced through the fabric of Christian history and conflated for use in dramatic, hyperbolic sentences. It is an attractive oversimplification of a complicated issue—especially so to Eastern Orthodox converts who are "scarred from and enthusiastically pissed off about"[1] their spiritual upbringing. "Triumphalist" and "elitist" are terms that carry with them the idea that the only meaningful relationship, or interaction, with God is through the Eastern Orthodox Church—and all other communities are fruitless and all-around worthless. But these three terms are sometimes used flippantly by Evangelicals frustrated by the exclusivity of Eastern Orthodoxy and are not always rightfully applied to the Eastern Orthodox Church (I am not talking about TJ here). So a little explanation is needed.

Orthodox Beliefs about Herself as the Church
There are a number of Eastern Orthodox beliefs and practices that may step on Evangelical toes. For one, the Eastern Orthodox Church practices what is called closed communion—we do not allow anyone who is not Orthodox to partake of the Holy Mysteries, the body and blood of Christ. In addition to Christians of other traditions, the Orthodox Church may withhold communion from certain Orthodox Christians for a number of reasons. Participation in the Holy Mysteries require both unity in mind, spirit, and dogma as well as an active participation in the life of the Church (fasting, almsgiving, confession, etc). Another thing that generally elicits disdain from Western Christians is the belief that the Eastern Orthodox Christian Church contains the fulness of Christian dogma and practice. Where other Christian traditions disagree with Orthodox dogma, those traditions err. An Orthodox Christian will likely believe that there are some non-Orthodox Christian communities that are close to the Truth (in belief and practice) and perhaps some Christian communities that are far from it, all the while maintaining that the

---

[1] Humphrey, TJ. *Why I Didn't Convert to Eastern Orthodoxy*. N.p.: Conciliar Post, 2016. Web. 18 Aug. 2016.

Holy Spirit has safeguarded the dogma and spiritual practices of the Eastern Orthodox Church which is in the fulness of Truth. This is certainly far from the American ideal: "I'm okay, you're okay." There are certain things (many things) on which the Eastern Orthodox Church will not budge. And this bothers a lot of people. But (and this is a big but) none of these beliefs and practices require the Orthodox Christian to hold the West in contempt. These beliefs, in themselves, are not anti-western, triumphalist, or elitist—and neither is the Eastern Orthodox Church—even though those titles may be falsely attributed to Eastern Orthodoxy because of our firm belief that these differences (between Eastern Orthodoxy and any other tradition) are significant. As long as there is "dialogue across Christian Traditions" there will always be things we disagree on. So when we do disagree with a Christian of any tradition (or non-Christian!) it should be charitably (Conciliar Post was built on this principal). This is key. But the main point is that you do not have to be anti-western in order to be pro-eastern. You do not have to shun your friends who aren't Orthodox when you become Orthodox (please don't!).

A Suggestion to My Orthodox Brethren
Earlier we talked about Saint Augustine and how he is sometimes disregarded and disdained by Eastern Orthodox Christians. Some Orthodox Christians would even go so far as to call him a heretic. But the obvious flaw in this way of thinking is that the Eastern Orthodox Church formally recognizes Augustine as a Saint. In fact, Fr. Seraphim Rose, an extremely conservative Orthodox priest, wrote an entire book, entitled *The Place of Blessed Augustine in the Orthodox Church,* in order to defend the Orthodox Church's recognition of Augustine as a Saint against the anti-western ethos prevalent at that time. While we do not agree with everything Saint Augustine had to say, we do admire him for his piety and as a model for repentance. And this is how, I suggest, we view our Western brothers and sisters. In many cases these men and women walk circles around us in their spiritual life (they do around me at least—I am thinking here of my Protestant parents and siblings and Roman Catholic friends). After all, every Sunday, right before partaking of the Holy Eucharist, we affirm that we are the "chief of sinners." But no one can truly confess themselves to be the chief of sinners if he is focused on the failures of his brother.

This is where the rubber meets the road. Orthodox often herald Orthodoxy's spiritual path as a way to healing and a true transformation (it is!) and we hold up the saints as our examples. But our lives, as Orthodox Christians living today, should be a witness to this transformation. We should be glowing with the light of Christ. We should be Christ to everyone we meet. And in this area we have failed TJ and many others.

I have failed you.

Forgive me.

Adventus
Johanna Byrkett

Time dawned and chaos was made order,
man came alive within a garden's border,
within the garden's border man died
when he disobeyed God and bowed to pride.

Darkness and chaos twined the world 'round,
but with the curse a promise was found,
up would grow a tender young shoot;
A King would rise from Jesse's root.

A King would rise like light in the dark,
One unbranded by sin's cruel mark,
to free his people from the grave,
from sin's tyranny, which made them slaves.

The Light of the world, mighty to save,
was born bloody and frail in a dark cave;
He grew up, a tender shoot as foretold,
the prophet cried: "The Lamb of God, behold!"

The Dayspring from on high came down
to open darkened eyes, to wear a thorn-crown;
He died bloody and broken on a cross,
Unbranded by sin, but smeared by its dross.

Day dawned anew when the Light rose,
sin's consequence paid—Death in its throes
was undone within a garden's border;
man, made alive, chaos, made order.

Faith Across Traditions

The Church Calendar

Among the many things that unite different branches of Christianity, the Church Calendar impacts nearly every Christian. Time changes us, and shapes our experience of faith in deeply formative ways. In this section, readers will find essays addressing various parts of the calendar, from Advent to Easter and the year in between.

Essays

On the Advent of Christ, *Prahlow*

Christmas Is About the Cross, *Aldhizer*

Christmas Is About the Incarnation, *Cabe*

Remembering Christmas, *Maynard*

God Is With Us, *Byrkett*

The Fast Before the Feast, *Kishi*

Holy Week, *Hyland*

What Day Did Jesus Die, *Prahlow*

Faith Across Traditions

On the Advent of Christ
Jacob J. Prahlow

God has ventured all in Jesus Christ to save us...."
–Oswald Chambers

Tomorrow Christians around the world will celebrate the birth of Jesus Christ, Messiah of Israel, King of Kings, Lord of Lords, Savior of Creation, Son of God, *Logos* Incarnate, God-become-man. This advent—arrival—and incarnation of the Christ has rightly fostered much contemplation from Christians over the centuries. Ranging from nativity accounts to creeds, and from hymns to Charlie Brown Christmas performances, Christians throughout the ages have celebrated the all-glorious God's birth in a lowly Judean stable. Building from these statements on the centrality of Jesus' birth in Bethlehem, today I offer three suggestions for Christians this Christmas.

Embrace formative traditions. Most importantly, the tradition—the *credo* which has been handed down by generations of Christians—that God has come to earth to save His people from their sins should stand in the forefront of our hearts and minds this Christmas season. As greeting cards and radio stations correctly (if somewhat incessantly) remind us, "Jesus is the reason for the season."

But "tradition" takes on another meaning during this season as well, as in the *things* which we do as part and parcel of Christmas. Making (and eating!) Christmas cookies, fighting the crowds whilst shopping, Christmas caroling, serving at a food pantry, sending an Operation Christmas Child shoebox, attending Advent services, listening to Christmas music on the radio, decking the halls with oodles of lights: these are but some of the traditions which fill our lives in the days and weeks leading up to Christmas.

The best Christmas traditions are those by which we experience God alongside others. For my family, this usually means attending the Christmas Eve service at Valparaiso University's Chapel of the Resurrection, where we worship, fellowship, and commune with some 1,500 other Christians who are celebrating our Savior's birth.

However you celebrate Christmas, traditions—especially the Great Tradition of Christ's birth—remain foundational for how we understand Christ's coming into the world and celebrate that momentous event.

Think hard (about what matters). In a world full of competing narratives, the Christmas season can be particularly troubling. When every other news story reports murder, war, or senseless violence, it's hard to meaningfully talk about "peace on earth." Even within a broadly defined "Christendom" there are controversies which try our minds during the holy-day season. Should we be upset about Starbuck's latest December-themed cups? Ought one be concerned about the "latest" research which demonstrates that Jesus wasn't God, wasn't born of a virgin, and/or didn't exist at all? And what about that "war on Christmas" that we regularly hear about?

Thinking rightly is difficult enough under regular circumstances, but under the additional stresses and busyness of the Christmas season, things can become downright unbearable. Yet this is when Christians must do their best to love God with their minds, to discern which claims are devoid of substance (no one really cares about the color of a disposable coffee cup), which are confused (no meaningful historical evidence suggests anything about Jesus other than what the Christian Church has confessed about his birth, life, death, and resurrection for the past 2,000 years), and which are worth caring about and addressing (Christmas is about God's love, not the commercialization of the toy market or Best Buy holiday deals).

Of course, thinking rightly and loving God with our minds during the Christmas season can be made easier when we recognize and reflect upon the truthful traditions of Christmas. Wolfhart Pannenberg once noted that, "People are prone to look for something new, and all too often the new lacks the profound, substantial meaning enshrined in traditional forms." This does not mean that we should reject out-of-hand every new Christmas tradition, carol, or Hallmark movie. It does mean that we should subject those new experiences and events to thoughtful scrutiny as we think hard about what matters this Christmas. (Sorry Hallmark Channel)

Set intentional time aside for Christ. Today's final suggestion calls us to both be intentional with our time and to set some of that time apart for Jesus. If your life is anything like mine, the past several weeks have been utterly hectic: work, Christmas parties, shopping, work, something in your house broke, more work, more shopping, people came to visit you, final projects, more shopping (because you forgot one item at the store!), traveling, and more. Amid this busyness, it's hard to pause. To take time. To stop. To look outside ourselves. To give thanks. To worship God.

This past Sunday I was reminded of my need to slow down and set aside intentional time for Christ while preparing to sing in our church's Christmas choir. It was an especially busy morning, as I got up early to finish packing for our trip home for Christmas, then headed off to church earlier than normal to practice for service one more time. My morning was one big series of checklists, on which was the item "Sing in Choir." In the middle of practicing, however, our choir director reminded us that we weren't just reciting some words that we had been learning for the past several weeks. No, we were supposed to be glorifying God. Pointing others toward God. Leading people to worship the Great, Glorious God of the Universe who loved us so much that He sent His Son to earth for us.

Singing "Glory to God" could not be a mere item on my checklist. It had to be time which I intentionally dedicated to God, time where my "self" was set aside for the sake of one greater than me. I submit that we all need to foster *selfless* moments this Christmas, even brief moments of time where we orient ourselves toward Christ in honor, thanksgiving, worship, and service to Him. Those moments could come at any point this Christmas: in the middle of a worship service, while your kids open presents, before anyone else wakes up on Christmas morning, when you're driving home. Whenever you make the time, commune with Christ this Christmas.

As noted throughout my suggestions to embrace formative traditions, think hard about what matters, and intentionally set aside time for Christ, Christmas ultimately must involve remembering the Good News of Jesus Christ's incarnate arrival on earth. Which leads me to commend that you end the reading of this article with one more Christmas tradition: the reading of the nativity scene from Luke's Gospel.

> *"In those days a decree went out from Caesar Augustus that all the world should be registered. This was the first registration when Quirinius was governor of Syria. And all went to be registered, each to his own town. And Joseph also went up from Galilee, from the town of Nazareth, to Judea,*

to the city of David, which is called Bethlehem, because he was of the house and lineage of David, to be registered with Mary, his betrothed, who was with child. And while they were there, the time came for her to give birth. And she gave birth to her firstborn son and wrapped him in swaddling cloths and laid him in a manger, because there was no place for them in the inn. And in the same region there were shepherds out in the field, keeping watch over their flock by night. And an angel of the Lord appeared to them, and the glory of the Lord shone around them, and they were filled with great fear. And the angel said to them, 'Fear not, for behold, I bring you good news of great joy that will be for all the people. For unto you is born this day in the city of David a Savior, who is Christ the Lord. And this will be a sign for you: you will find a baby wrapped in swaddling cloths and lying in a manger.' And suddenly there was with the angel a multitude of the heavenly host praising God and saying, 'Glory to God in the highest, and on earth peace among those with whom he is pleased!' When the angels went away from them into heaven, the shepherds said to one another, 'Let us go over to Bethlehem and see this thing that has happened, which the Lord has made known to us.' And they went with haste and found Mary and Joseph, and the baby lying in a manger. And when they saw it, they made known the saying that had been told them concerning this child. And all who heard it wondered at what the shepherds told them. But Mary treasured up all these things, pondering them in her heart. And the shepherds returned, glorifying and praising God for all they had heard and seen, as it had been told them." (Luke 2:1-20, ESV)

Christmas Is About the Cross
George Aldhizer

"Here is a trustworthy saying that deserves full acceptance: Christ Jesus came into the world to save sinners"
1 Timothy 1:15

"This is how God showed his love among us: He sent his one and only Son into the world that we might live through him. This is love: not that we loved God, but that he loved us and sent his Son as an atoning sacrifice for our sins."
1 John 4:9-10

"She will give birth to a son, and you are to give him the name Jesus, because he will save his people from their sins."
Matthew 1:21

Thus begins the explanation of the meaning of the Incarnation to the world, Christ has come to save sinners. And what good news indeed— the God of the universe, though offended by the injustice of the world (see "Christmas is about Ferguson") and the wickedness of our hearts, has decided to bring salvation in his incarnate son Jesus.

Within this article, I want us to see with the eyes of the Reformed confessions, that the birth of Christ is not an end in and of itself,[1] but

---

[1] One can read this article as a Reformed addition and supplementation to the discussion in this month's Round Table. The writer appreciates the many insights of the Anglican, Methodist, Orthodox, and Catholic writers within that space. One could also read this article as a response to some comments within the Round Table against the Reformed understanding of the Incarnation. Ben Cabe's argues that the Orthodox view, in contrast to the Protestant view, of the Incarnation is "not viewed as a reaction to man's fall but rather a plan in accordance with the eternal will of the Father." This article sees this comment as presenting a false dichotomy. The eternal will of the Father has always been to redeem broken humanity out of sheer grace through the person and work of Jesus Christ, applied through the drawing of the Holy Spirit. Further, one may read this article as a response to Drew McIntyre's comment that the Methodist view of the Incarnation, in contrast to Calvinism, "is thus not good news for an elect few, but for all humanity

is part of a Trinitarian mission to reconcile a broken world to God. I hope that this Christmas season our imaginations can be shaped and stretched to see the Christ child as the very man who would eventually die as a ransom for many, saving us from the wrath of God.[1] Christmas and Good Friday, though separated by four months on our calendars and thirty or so years in the life of Jesus, are in fact intimately connected in the will of God for the salvation of the world.[2] The following will survey of three Reformed confessional documents, the *Heidelberg Catechism*, *Westminster Larger Catechism*, and the *Westminster Confession*.

The *Heidelberg Catechism*, honored by a number of Reformed denominations worldwide, contains a series of questions and answers, ordered under the headings of Misery, Deliverance, and Gratitude.[3] The *Catechism* sees a direct connection between the birth of Christ and his death, putting them side by side in questions 36 and 37. I quote them below:

Q&A 36. Q. How does the holy conception and birth of Christ benefit you? A. He is our mediator and, in God's sight, he covers with his innocence and perfect holiness my sinfulness in which I was conceived.[4]

---

and indeed the whole of creation." This article also sees this comment as presenting a false dichotomy, for the salvation of God's elect is good news for humanity and the whole of creation. That God would choose to save (much less resurrect within a redeemed New Heavens and New Earth) any is truly good news.

[1] Mark 10:45 and Romans 5:9.

[2] Though the Incarnation of Christ is bound up in the death of Christ, I do not want the reader (as many evangelicals are wont to do) to neglect the life of Christ and the Kingdom he came to establish. There may be a serious danger in doing what the Reformed confessions do, and what I do within this article, if one sees the mission of Christ as merely coming to earth to die. No. The good news of the gospel is grander, though most certainly not less, than atonement. Part of the reason why I wrote "Christmas is about Ferguson" is to recognize the bigness of the Incarnation in reconciling the entire world to God. See Footnote 14 for more of this bigness.

[3] "Heidelberg Catechism." Christian Reformed Church. N.p., 04 June 2012. Web. 20 Dec. 2014.

[4] 1 Tim. 2:5-6; Heb. 9:13-15, Rom. 8:3-4; 2 Cor. 5:21; Gal. 4:4-5; 1 Pet. 1:18-19.

Q&A 37. Q. What do you understand by the word "suffered"? A. That during his whole life on earth, but especially at the end, Christ sustained in body and soul the wrath of God against the sin of the [1]whole human race. This he did in order that, by his suffering as the only atoning sacrifice, he might deliver us, body and soul, from eternal condemnation, and gain for us God's grace, righteousness, and eternal life.[2]

In the *Heidelberg* we see a God who was conceived and born with the intent and purpose to die, to rid humanity of their condemnation before a just God, gaining "for us grace, righteousness, and eternal life." The *Westminster Larger Catechism* echoes this connection, emphasizing the humility of Christ in his conception, birth, life, and death.

Q&A 47. How did Christ humble himself in his conception and birth? A. Christ humbled himself in his conception and birth, in that, being from all eternity the Son of God, in the bosom of the Father, he was pleased in the fullness of time to become the son of man, made of a woman of low estate, and to be born of her; with divers circumstances of more than ordinary abasement.[3]

Q&A 48. How did Christ humble himself in his life? A. Christ humbled himself in his life, by subjecting himself to the law, which he perfectly fulfilled; and by conflicting with the indignities of the world, temptations of Satan, and infirmities in his flesh, whether common to the nature of man, or particularly accompanying that his low condition.[4]

Q&A 49. How did Christ humble himself in his death? A. Christ humbled himself in his death, in that having been betrayed by Judas, forsaken by his disciples, scorned and rejected by the world, condemned by Pilate, and tormented by his persecutors; having also conflicted with the terrors of death, and the powers of darkness, felt and borne the weight of God's wrath, he laid down his life an offering

---

[1] Isa. 53; 1 Pet. 2:24; 3:18, Rom. 3:25; Heb. 10:14; 1 John 2:2; 4:10, Rom. 8:1-4; Gal. 3:13, John 3:16; Rom. 3:24-26.
[2] "Westminster Larger Catechism." ORTHODOX PRESBYTERIAN CHURCH. N.p., n.d. Web. 18 Dec. 2014.
[3] John 1:14,18.
[4] Gal. 4:4, Matt. 5:17, Ps. 22:6, Isa. 53:2-3, Heb. 12:2-3, Matt. 4:1-11, Luke 4:13, Heb 2:17-18, Heb. 4:15, Isa. 52:13-14.

for sin, enduring the painful, shameful, and cursed death of the cross.[1]

Christ's birth, life, and death are all connected by humility for the *Westminster Larger Catechism*. In birth, Jesus is born of a poor peasant woman within "divers circumstances of more than ordinary abasement" (I love this, who writes like this anymore?). In life, God becomes a Jew within an oppressive Roman world, confronts temptations that each of us go through daily, and fulfills the law. In death, the God of the universe enters into the great terror of this broken world, "laying down his life" for the very humanity who crucified him.

Like the *Heidelberg Confession* and the *Westminster Larger Catechism*, the *Westminster Confession*, specifically within Chapter VIII, "Of Christ the Mediator," connects the birth and death of Christ.[2]

II. The Son of God, the second person of the Trinity, being very and eternal God, of one substance and equal with the Father, did, when the fullness of time was come, take upon Him man's nature, with all the essential properties, and common infirmities thereof, yet without sin; being conceived by the power of the Holy Ghost, in the womb of the virgin Mary, of her substance. So that two whole, perfect, and distinct natures, the Godhead and the manhood, were inseparably joined together in one person, without conversion, composition, or confusion. Which person is very God, and very man, yet one Christ, the only Mediator between God and man.[3]

V. The Lord Jesus, by His perfect obedience, and sacrifice of Himself, which He through the eternal Spirit, once offered up unto God, has fully satisfied the justice of His Father; and purchased, not only reconciliation, but an everlasting inheritance in the kingdom of heaven, for those whom the Father has given unto Him.[4]

---

[1] Matt. 27:4, Matt. 26:56, Isa. 53:2-3, Matt. 27:26-50, John 19:34, Luke 22:44, Matt. 27:46, Isa. 53:10, Matt. 20:28, Phil. 2:8, Heb. 12:2, Gal. 3:13.
[2] "Westminster Confession of Faith." *Reformed.Org*. N.p., n.d. Web. 20 Dec. 2014.
[3] John 1:1, 1 John 5:20, Phil. 2:6, Gal. 4:4, Heb. 2:14, Heb. 4:15, Luke 1:27,31,35, Gal. 4:4, Luke 1:35, Col 2:9, Rom 9:5, 1 Pet. 3:18, 1 Tim. 3:16, Rom. 1:3,4, 1 Tim. 2:5.
[4] Rom. 5:19, Heb. 9:14, 16, Heb. 10:14, Eph. 5:2, Rom. 3:25,26, Dan. 9:24,26, Col. 1:19,20, Eph. 1:11, John 17:2, Heb. 9:12,15.

The coming of Christ, the Reformed understand, is one part in the eternal plan of God to reconcile his chosen people to himself. God from eternity past decided to create the world, knowing that it would fall into sin, to then bind himself to people in the form of covenants, to then enter into this sinful world as a human being, thus fulfilling the promises he had made to his people, and then to ultimately die for these people, thus purchasing their salvation by his blood. The Incarnation, rather than being a stand-alone celebration, proceeds from an eternal will that precedes it, and results in a death that reconciles. The celebration of the coming of Christ is far grander (though certainly not less) than a recognition of God-made flesh, pointing toward a humble life, shameful death, and purchasing of an inheritance for God's chosen people. May we this Advent season place ourselves in the waiting anticipation of the Jews, awaiting a Messiah who will come to save us from our sins.[1]

---

[1] Please also read Derek Rishmawy's "Christmas is About the Eschaton". A great Reformed read on the eternity of Christ's Incarnation–truly God is in communion with his people for eternity.

Faith Across Traditions

Christmas Is About the Incarnation
Benjamin Cabe

In a recent Conciliar Post article entitled, *Christmas is about the Cross*, George Aldhizer presented the Reformed understanding of the Incarnation as a means to an end. The end being the death of Jesus Christ on the cross and the salvation of the elect; a salvation that needed to be "purchased" in order to "fully satisfy the justice of [the] Father".[1] George explained the purpose of the article in footnote 1 as,

> a response to some comments within the Round Table against the Reformed understanding of the Incarnation. Ben Cabe argues that the Orthodox view, in contrast to the Protestant view, of the Incarnation is "not viewed as a reaction to man's fall but rather a plan in accordance with the eternal will of the Father." This article sees this comment as presenting a false dichotomy. The eternal will of the Father has always been to redeem broken humanity out of sheer grace through the person and work of Jesus Christ, applied through the drawing of the Holy Spirit.

George mentions in his first paragraph the article's main points: 1. The Incarnation was not an end in itself but was rather meant to restore broken humanity to God. The cross of Christ and the Incarnation are intricately connected to accomplish the salvation of the world. At first blush, these may sound reasonable when applied to postlapsarian (fallen) mankind. Human beings today are certainly plagued with a fractured human nature. The Incarnation and the death of Christ on the cross do, together, accomplish the salvation of the world. However, the purpose behind George's article, while propounding the Reformed understanding of the Incarnation, also seeks to refute the claim that Christ would have become Incarnate even if man had not fallen into sin. As a result of this de-emphasis on the unique accomplishment of the Incarnation, it is marred beyond recognition; it is reduced to having little or no significance for mankind in its own right. George implicitly states that the

---

[1] George Aldhizer, *Christmas is About the Cross*. Conciliar Post. Web. 22 Dec. 2014. https://conciliarpost.com/theology-spirituality/christmas-is-about-the-cross/.

Incarnation is meaningless without the death of Christ on the cross. With this, I could not disagree more.

A Brief Critique of George's Article
First, George argues his points solely with regard to postlapsarian human nature, and thus fails to address prelapsarian (pre-fallen) mankind. Second, he does not speak of the man's creation in the image and likeness of God, that is, of the Incarnate Logos. Third, he does not present the *telos* of prelapsarian man and creation.

Concerning the second, I can only assume that George does not connect man's creation in the image and likeness of God with the Incarnate Christ—who, as the Archetype, came to fulfill the human person.

Finally, George's understanding of salvation does not have a positive aspect. Hear me out here. Surely being "saved from damnation" is positive, but the reality is that we were not just saved from damnation but to salvation *in Christ*. To participate fully in the life of Christ. But I'm getting ahead of myself.

The questions lingering behind George's article must be addressed. Did pre-fallen man have something to aspire to? What was the state of his communion with God? What did the Incarnation uniquely accomplish for man's relationship with God? And, ultimately, what is salvation?

Response
In response to George's article, I will offer a few thoughts:

Within the Orthodox Tradition there is a rich emphasis on the fulfillment of all things in Christ. In contrast to the Reformed idea that "the eternal will of the Father has always been to redeem broken humanity," Orthodox Christians understand creation, in accordance with the eternal will of the Father, as an act of love. "For God so loved . . ." could be rightly added as a prefix to every movement of the Holy Trinity. This is the Orthodox starting point: God *is* love.[1] Christos Yannaras, in *Relational Ontology*, explains that,

---

[1] 1 John 4:8.

> [the word] *Love* here does not mean a form or quality of behavior that is usually in evidence in expressions such as to be "full of love," or to "show love," and so forth. In spite of its semiologically given referential (relational) character, the word *love* functions in this particular proposition as a definition: it defines the *is*, the reality of being, before any manifestation of activity or determination of behavior.[1]

The question of the eternal will of the Father must address the question behind God's creation. From my limited understanding, the Reformed tradition claims that God created human beings to glorify Himself through the salvation and damnation of select individuals. In stark contrast to the idea of glory by damnation, the Orthodox maintain that the Holy Trinity created out of their "unceasing movement of mutual love".[2] The glory of God is not the damnation of man, but rather the fulfilment of man in himself; the human being made fully alive.[3] God did not create *in order to* redeem, he created in order to deify—to give all of himself to man in *ecstatic* love; to grant the life of the uncreated Holy Trinity to man.

This Divine Love would not be satisfied with anything less than full communion; the pre-eternal will spoken of in scripture is referring to the fulfilment of all things in Christ.[4] But here, several other questions must be asked: what constitutes, and what do we mean by 'full communion'? Why was full communion necessary? What was the status of prelapsarian mankind with relation to this communion?

These questions are tied to the creation of mankind which is, in turn, tied to the *telos* of man. We are told in Genesis one that human beings were made according to the image and likeness of God; and in Colossians 1:15-18 we see that the image of God *is* Jesus Christ, who is the *firstborn* of all creation and the firstborn from the dead.[5]

The fact that Adam was created in the image of Christ implies that it was his vocation to be raised up to the Archetype or, more precisely,

---

[1] Panayiotis Nellas, *Deification in Christ*. Crestwood: St. Vladimir's Seminary Press, 1987. Page 35.
[2] Ibid.
[3] Ibid.
[4] Ibid., 37.
[5] Andrew Louth, *Introducing Eastern Orthodox Theology*. Downer's Grove: InterVarsity Press, 2013. Page 84.

to be purified and to love God so much that God would come to dwell within him, that the Logos would enter into a hypostatic union with man, and thus appear in history as the Christ, be manifested as the God-man. The 'entry of the firstborn into the world' (Heb 1:6) fulfils the eternal will of God, the highest mystery 'hidden from ages and from generations' (Col 1:26).[1]

The very creation of man in the image and likeness of God presupposed the Incarnate Christ, the Archetype. For the *telos* of man is his perfection—or completion—in Christ.
The fact that Christ did not exist historically at the time of Adam's creation is of no significance. It is a fundamental biblical teaching that on the level of supra-temporal reality of God, Christ is 'the firstborn of all creation' (Col 1:15-17). If man, for whom all the material creation was brought into being, rose last of all creatures from the earth, it is surely logical that Christ, who is the goal of the whole of the material and spiritual creation, should be later than Adam, since all things are led from imperfection to perfection. Christ, as the highest realization of man, naturally constitutes the goal of mankind's upward journey, the beginning but also the end of history.[2]

The very image according to which man was created is "not simply the Logos but the incarnate Logos."[3] Man's creation in the image and likeness of God is not a small matter; it enables mankind to receive the Incarnate Logos who, in turn, is the *telos* of man.

'in the image' implies a gift within man but at the same time a goal set before him, a possession but also a destiny, since it really does constitute man's *being,* but only in potentiality. The 'in the image' is a real power, a pledge, which should lead to marriage, that is, the hypostatic union, the unconfused but real fulfilling mixture and commingling of the divine and human natures. Only then does the iconic or potential being of man become real, *authentic* being. Man finds in the Archetype his true ontological meaning.[4]

---

[1] Kallistos Ware, *The Orthodox Way*. Crestwood: St. Vladimir's Seminary Press, 1999. Page 27.
[2] St. Irenaeus, *Against Heresies*.
[3] Ephesians 1:10: "that in the dispensation of the fullness of the times He might gather together in one all things in Christ, both which are in heaven and which are on earth—in Him."
[4] Colossians 1:15-18 is striking: "He is the image of the invisible God, the firstborn over all creation. For by Him all things were created that are in

Man's perfection in Christ is something that Adam was called to achieve, not a static reality imposed on him. Once again, man's creation in the image and likeness makes this quite clear.

The word translated 'likeness', *homoiosis,* suggests something more precise in Greek: the ending, *-oisis,* implies a process, not a state (the Greek for Likeness as a state would be homoioma). The word *homoiosis* would moreover have very definite resonances for anyone who had read Plato, who envisages the goal of the human life as *homoiosis* — likening, assimilation — to the divine.[1]

What George is uncomfortable with is the idea that the Incarnation is a reality that accomplishes something in its own right—and thus for prelapsarian man. In one of our conversations, he mentioned that he does not see this idea anywhere in scripture. The scriptures, however, make it quite clear that man's goal is perfection in Christ—one that is accomplished in man's assimilation and recapitulation in him, through the union of the divine and human natures in the hypostasis of Jesus Christ. Scripture also clearly states that Christ is the firstborn of all creation.

The reality is, that human nature does not have to be broken in order to need fulfillment. Certainly man's sin in the garden mentally complicates the issue. But God did not miss a beat. Out of love he exiled man from the garden so that he would not eat from the tree of life, and live eternally in his state of spiritual sickness. Salvation from damnation is the negative aspect of salvation that entered the scene after man's sin. The positive aspect of salvation, that of full communion with God, constituted the eternal will of the Father and the *telos* of man—a reality fully accomplished through the Incarnate Christ.

George uses 1 Timothy 1:15 and Matthew 1:21 in the beginning of his article to prove that the reason for the Incarnation is *only* to save men

---

heaven and that are on earth, visible and invisible, whether thrones or dominions or principalities or powers. All things were created through Him and for Him. And He is before all things, and in Him all things consist. And He is the head of the body, the church, who is the beginning, the firstborn from the dead, that in all things He may have the preeminence."

[1] Kallistos Ware, *The Orthodox Way.* Crestwood: St. Vladimir's Seminary Press, 1999. Page 28.

Faith Across Traditions

from sin. But this argument does not work. Orthodox Christians have never denied the fact that Christ came to save sinners (postlapsarian man). Every Sunday we confess that, "Christ came into the world to save sinners, of whom I am chief." But this aspect of Christ's Incarnation does not automatically exclude all other aspects. The facts that we are saved to something, and as a result, from something, are not mutually exclusive. The *telos* of man has always been union with God.

The final end of the spiritual Way is that we humans should also become part of this Trinitarian coinherence, or *perichoresis,* being wholly taken up into the circle of love that exists within God. So Christ prayed to his Father on the night before his Crucifixion: 'May they all be one: as thou, Father, art in me, and I in thee, so may they also be one in us' (John 17:21).[1]

Concerning this fact, George fails to see that creation *ex nihilo* requires the God-man, the Incarnation, in order to make this union possible. The creature has, "no ontological foundation either in itself (for it is created from nothing), nor in the divine essence, for in the act of creation God was under no necessity of any kind whatever."[2] This is what the creation of man in the image and likeness and the proclamation of Christ as the firstborn of creation means for the *telos* of man. That we might have "life more abundantly."[3] The Incarnation enables us to be "partakers of the Divine nature."[4] Created man is dependent on his creator, and without "the hypostasis of the Logos, [human nature] was in some way without real hypostasis—it lacked real 'subsistence'.[5]

---

[1] Vladimir Lossky, *The Mystical Theology of the Eastern Church.* Crestwood: St. Vladimir's Seminary Press, 1991. Page 98.
[2] John 10:10: The thief cometh not, but for to steal, and to kill, and to destroy: *I am come that they might have life,* and that they might have it more abundantly.
[3] 2 Peter 1:2-4: "Grace and peace be multiplied to you in the knowledge of God and of Jesus our Lord, as His divine power has given to us all things that *pertain* to life and godliness, through the knowledge of Him who called us by glory and virtue, by which have been given to us exceedingly great and precious promises, that through these you may be partakers of the divine nature, having escaped the corruption, *that is* in the world through lust."
[4] Panayiotis Nellas, *Deification in Christ.* Crestwood: St. Vladimir's Seminary Press, 1987. Page 38.
[5] Andrew Louth, *Introducing Eastern Orthodox Theology.* Downer's Grove: InterVarsity Press, 2013. Page 37.

I have had conversations with George centered around this topic he has refused to accept the given *fact* that, because the uncreated God created out of nothing, the "fundamental division within reality [is] not between the spiritual and the material, but between the created and the uncreated."[1] Perhaps it is not this fact that he refuses to accept but rather the thought that this division must be overcome in prelapsarian man, if at all.

This is the great hidden mystery [viz., the mystery of the Divine Incarnation]. This is the blessed end for which all things were created. This is the preordained divine goal of the origin of beings, which we define as the preordained end for the sake of which all things exist, although this end itself depends on nothing. It was with a view to this end [Christ, the hypostatic union of divine and human nature] that God brought forth the essence of all beings.[2]

The Incarnation is deeply related to the creation of man *in the image* which is also related to the *telos* of man: perfection in Christ. These two realities were givens before the fall; it stands to reason, then, that the Incarnation was also a part God's original plan for creation.

Christ is the first perfect man—perfect, that is to say, not just in a potential sense, as Adam was in his innocence before the fall, but in the sense of completely realized "likeness". The Incarnation, then is not simply a way of undoing the effects of original sin, but is an essential stage upon man's journey from the divine image to the divine likeness. The true image and likeness of God is Christ himself; and so, from the very first moment of man's creation in the image, the Incarnation of Christ was in some way already implied. The true reason for the Incarnation, then, lies not in man's sinfulness but in his unfallen nature as being made in the divine image and capable of union with God.[3]

Scripture attests that the *telos* of man is to be made perfect in Christ; this is a perfection in actuality, not merely through some sort of imputation. To be "made perfect in Christ" was the calling of Adam in the garden, not merely a reactionary clause referencing the "reversal

---

[1] St Maximus the Confessor, *To Thalassios: On Various Questions*.
[2] Kallistos Ware, *The Orthodox Way*. Crestwood: St. Vladimir's Seminary Press, 1999. Page 71.
[3] St. Maximus the Confessor, *Letter 21*.

of the fall." God created man for communion—and communion with an infinite God is infinitely realized.

"Ineffably the infinite limits itself, while the finite is expanded to the measure of the infinite."[1]

Created human beings are called to participate in the uncreated life of the Holy Trinity. And by participation, man is made by grace everything that God is by nature thereby superseding natural necessity and createdness. This allows for real and total communion in ecstatic love and has always been the *telos* of man—this can be seen by the gift, in man, of the divine image.

Instead of addressing the question of man's goal in life, the Christocentric nature of creation, and the indelible event of the Incarnation as *fulfillment*, George presents a view of the man, creation, and the incarnation that falls radically short of what we read in scripture and in the teachings of the early Christians. One that, does not exhaust the mystery of the Incarnation of Christ but rather does the complete opposite.

What does it really mean for the creature, for the creation, that the second person of the Trinity became man? What does it mean that the immaterial God indwelled creation? The implications of the Incarnate Logos are staggering; He sanctified and fulfilled creation and united for the first time the divine and human natures in His hypostasis.

To claim that the Incarnation was a means to the end of the cross, and thus has no significance in its own right, is unreasonable. Such thinking leads to an impoverished Christianity—because the Incarnation touches all of Christianity. It informs how we worship and makes possible literal transformation by participation in the life of Christ, the realization of man's calling. How does man achieve the goal for which he was created? How is he perfected in Christ? How do all things find their true end and fulfillment? It is all made possible through the Incarnation.

Conclusion

In conclusion, man's creation in the image and likeness of God points directly to, and is fulfilled by, the Incarnate Christ—who is the

---

[1] St. Athanasius, *On The Incarnation*.

firstborn of all creation. The Incarnate Christ makes possible the *telos* of man—union with God through participation in the life of the Holy Trinity—by overcoming in the person of Christ the division between the uncreated God and created man: a fundamental division that cannot be denied without denying creation *ex nihilo*. When man sinned in the garden, human nature was fractured and death entered the world. The death of Christ, the immortal God, on the cross destroyed death and opened the way for the resurrection of mankind. For us today, these two realities make possible the reality of salvation—not one without the other. When we journey toward fulfillment in Christ (salvation) we are at the same time journeying away from damnation. The second, negative aspect of salvation—salvation from damnation—entered the scene only after man's sin. However, the positive aspect of salvation—salvation as fulfillment, communion with the infinite God in Trinity—existed before the fall. This is why we say that prelapsarian man needed salvation, because prelapsarian man needed the Incarnation. The Incarnation, then, is certainly of great significance in its own right. And today, December 25, we celebrate the birth of Incarnate Logos; Christmas is about the Incarnation.[1]

Merry Christmas, Christ is born! I would like to leave you with this quote by Kallistos Ware.

> St. Isaac urges [that] God's taking of humanity is to be understood not only as an act of restoration, not only as a response to man's sin, but also and more fundamentally as an act of love. An expression of God's own nature. Even had there been no fall, God in his own limitless, outgoing love would still have chosen to identify himself with his creation by becoming man.
>
> The Incarnation of Christ, looked at in this way, effects *[sic]* more than a reversal of the fall, more than restoration of man to his original state in Paradise. When God becomes man, this marks the beginning of an essentially new stage in the history of man, and not just a return to the past. The Incarnation raised man to a new level; the last state is higher than the first.

---

[1] This article was not meant to assume that I know everything about George's beliefs (or Reformed Christians in general). Neither it is an attack on George. It is my attempt to explain why I believe the Incarnation is, indeed, of great importance in its own right.

Only in Jesus Christ do we reveal the full possibilities of our human nature; until he is born, the true implications of our personhood are still hidden from us.[1]

---

[1] Kallistos Ware, *The Orthodox Way*. Crestwood: St. Vladimir's Seminary Press, 1999. Pages 70-71.

Remembering Christmas
AJ Maynard

Inevitably, come each December, Christians experience the "war" on Christmas. An ostensible form of oppression seemingly pushing us ever so precariously toward the edge of a slippery slope—leading directly toward the extinction of religious freedom, as we currently know it. Donald Trump and the conservative media flood our ears with a call-to-arms, "Proclaim Merry CHRISTMAS!" And many are only too happy to oblige. The utterance "Happy Holidays" becomes pejorative, a proverbial four-letter word. "Christ is the reason for the season," we are told.

But, what does that mean? Doubtless, Christ IS the reason for the season; but what does that look like? Does it mean taking a stance against red cups, or taking offense to those proclaiming happy holidays, or something different—something more?

While Christmas is the celebration of the birth of Christ, Christmas does not compel us to extol ONLY the birth of Christ. We also champion peace on earth and good will toward humankind. We, at times, offer gifts to those we dislike and pay-it-forward at the grocery line; we celebrate the SPIRIT of Christmas, which raises the question, "What IS the spirit of Christmas?"

The answer seems obvious: Christ.

But this raises another question: What does it look like for one to both embrace and live out the spirit of Christmas?

Making Christ the "reason for the season" is to make Christ's ministry a reality both in your life and the lives of others. It means sharing your food with the hungry and giving shelter to the homeless. It means giving clothes to those in need and not hiding from troublesome relatives (cf. Isa 58). It means freeing yourself from a haze of indifference that muddies the reality of white privilege, social injustice, racism, and misogyny. It means shedding a worldview that equates poverty with laziness and delegitimizes the cries of abused women. It means seeking out the downtrodden and "opening wide your hand to your brother, to the needy and to the poor" (Deut 15:11). It also means offering more than mere "thoughts and prayers." It means working to assuage the sufferings that often give rise to our proclamations of "thoughts of prayers."

Making Christ the reason for the season means, in part, serving, as best as one can, as Christ served.

Is such a momentous task even possible?

Yes.

Consider the book of Exodus, for example, which displays God bringing Israel out of bondage not through an overwhelming act of divine power but rather through the commissioning of a single individual: Moses. "Look! The cry of the people of Israel has reached me, and I have seen how harshly the Egyptians abuse them. Now go, for I am sending YOU to Pharaoh. YOU must lead my people Israel out of Egypt" (Ex 3:9-10 NLT). This passage represents merely one of many examples in which God answers the prayers of His people through the works of normal human beings like you and me.

Considering this, the argument could be made: YOU are meant to be the answer to the poor man's prayer for money. YOU are meant to be the answer to the starving man's cries to God for a meal. YOU are meant to be the answer to the cries for justice by people of color across the country. Thus, the unanswered prayers of the downtrodden, as I see them, are not GOD'S failures so much as they are OUR failures.

Notice what making Christ the reason for the season does NOT mean: it does not mean demanding others proclaim, "Merry Christmas," nor does it mean bashing coffee companies or (dare I say) going to church. It means meeting both the spiritual AND physical needs of others. Merely thinking and praying about the downtrodden will not help them; offering trite aphorisms and feel-good Facebook posts will not help them. Demanding that one attend church more often or pray harder or work harder or report abuse sooner or be a better (fill in the blank) does NOT extol Christ as the "reason for the season." And to champion such things alone is to place oneself in the company of the men Jesus spoke of in Matthew 23: 4-6 when he stated, "They crush people with unbearable religious demands and never lift a finger to ease the burden. Everything they do is for show. On their arms, they wear extra wide prayer boxes with Scripture verses inside, and they wear robes with extra-long tassels. And they love to sit at the head table at banquets and in the seats of honor in the synagogues."

Christ did not debate the merits of giving free food to the hungry; he fed them. Christ did not ask the sick to pay their share; he healed them. Moreover, the Bible does not extol rugged individualism but rather proclaims power amid community (cf. Ecclesiastes 4:12).

Therefore, when awakening Christmas morning and considering what changes to implement in the New Year, consider REALLY making Christ the reason for the season. Follow a POC activist, read outside your bubble, listen to those with whom you disagree, and love those deemed unlovable.

Christmas need not have a monopoly on Christ or even the Christmas spirit. Indeed, Christ is the reason for every season, and to fight for Christ is not to fight over ridiculous red cups and silly salutations. Rather, it is a call to fight for what God fought—and ultimately died— for: this planet, the animals, and, perhaps most importantly, those who do not have the luxury of ignoring the subject of their own discrimination.

Merry Christmas, and may your New Year be filled with the Christmas spirit.

Faith Across Traditions

God Is With Us
Johanna Byrkett

Christmastide is here. Here. Now. *This* is Christmas. Though the world is weary and rejoicing to have limped through 'the holidays', many traditions have just begun celebrating Christmastide after forty days of darkness and fasting. The season of light has dawned, culminating in a day whose very name means *manifest* or *revelation*. Light does that very thing, it shows us what we would have walked right past in the darkness; it reveals the shapes we feared in the night as friendly, familiar things; it makes manifest God's gift of himself to us.

God gives himself to us...The Incarnation still staggers my mind and heart, sometimes to the point where I give up thinking it through. To be honest, near the end of the year work and friend-gatherings reach a raucous tilt and I hold out hard for the airport. I slide into my window seat with a sigh, watch the night glide past, and take a break. The problem is, I take a break from my habits and routines because I am away from home. I often go to bed late and rise late, skip quiet time and journalling, get easily nettled, and skimp on self-control in just about every area. The last week of Advent and most of Christmastide are often spent in self-inflicted semi-darkness. Sure, there are starlight points in the dark skies of my soul, but it often seems like the sun of revelation is suffering a prolonged eclipse.

Unlocking the front door of my cabin the first week of January seems to coincide with the shadow passing from between me and the Light of the world. I slip back into my own skin, my own home, my own habits. The new year stretches before me like a glorious sunrise—I don't know what the day will hold, but it opens bright and full of hope. Amidst my dim Christmastide and my looking forward to a fresh year, someone I love dearly mentioned how bleak the coming year looks from this vantage point. She said it seemed like she was stuck in an unyielding cycle that someone else chose for her. There isn't an end in sight. Now, I can see only hope that the coming year will be better than the last for this beloved friend, as this year reeked for her. Perhaps I am young and naive, but in my mind, there is an irresistible hope in new years and seasons.

Mid-conversation, I suddenly wondered about the Children of Israel, those between the Old Covenant and the New, those deafened by nearly four hundred years of silence—did they ever lose hope? Did the Messiah seem impossible to them? Obviously they passed down their long-held prophecies and expectations. Mary readily received her role from God, knowing there was to be a Messiah. All of Israel seemed to be peering about for their Saviour throughout the gospels, uncertain if the Man from Galilee could really be the One foretold. They all knew the history, but did they ever get furious that the prophecy sat there, unfulfilled? Did they consistently beg God to defend his name and bring forth the Saviour for these promised people? How many generations were snuffed out in darkness, never seeing the coming Light?

What if my friend never sees the dawn of change, of salvation from this rotten situation in her lifetime? Does God not care? Is God not powerful and kind enough to bring redemption and resolution into a very fractured situation? We talk theology often on this site, but do we believe God intervenes for the unjustly accused, the abandoned, the orphans and the widows? Do we live like *God is with us*? For the in-the-quiet-darkness Israelites, the Incarnation was hoped for, was yet-to-come, but was never fulfilled. However, we know—we know that God *is* with us, he has come. He is here and he is not silent. He does not stand aloof nor remain indifferent to our plight. But what is he doing when nothing changes? Theology fails to comfort the abandoned and hurting. Heady discussions aren't the equivalent of the Holy Spirit changing hearts and healing brokenness. All our comments and platitudes don't end that bleak feeling of the sucking, downward spiral of depression when nothing changes, even though a person has remained faithful to Jesus. If God is with us, why is hope often invisible for the steadfast, God-honouring believer?

I want answers for my friend; for myself. Yet all I have is questions. I still see the Light rising in hope, but how do I give my vision to my friend? How can I be her eyes and impart God's hope to her? How can I bear her burdens and share my joys? Reality sometimes presses us hard with its weight—how do we hold on to real, robust hope that makes our souls buoyant? When we trust God to stand up for himself, to stand up for what is right, how do we not lose hope in the waiting? I don't have solid answers. I don't have something tangible that keeps depression at bay. I know God is with us. My friend knows he is with us. She wants to see him with us. To see him move. To see his power.

To see the Light dawn in the pitch black she's been living in...But what if she is in the middle of a kind of "four hundred years of silence" history with God? What if the coming hope is so bright that it must be preceded by inky silence to contrast just how mighty God is? That's not a query my friend can cling to; not the light at the tunnel's end that she needs to see by. But it may be the truth; it may be reality. I believe she will trust God, even if redemption doesn't come in her lifetime. It will be a continual, exhausting choice—but God with her and in her will help her walk in the starlight. And I believe that her prayers and obedience will advance the dawn in all its glorious brilliance, even if she never sees the Dayspring.

The Fast Before the Feast
Aphrodite Kishi

The Lenten fast is often neglected or misunderstood. But this season offers the time and place to make us freer and stronger.

There's a reason why fasting sounds exhausting. There's a reason why people feel uncomfortable just envisioning a forty-day stretch of abstaining from certain foods or activities. The Lenten season is, after all, a long and tiring period for its participants.

It's hard. That becomes clear in the last days of Lent—the days of final effort—when your body is craving your usual meats and foods and when your mind is ready for that activity you have gone so long without. By the time you hit those last couple weeks, you are physically tired.

Lenten fasting is training: an exercise of discipline, endurance, and patience that is beautiful because of the freedom, strength, and virtue it reaps. It is an opportunity to free us from the bondage of the flesh—a refusal to accept our fallen natures as normal. But this effort is difficult and tiresome. We discover that the desires of our flesh so easily control us.

Our bodies, after all, are accustomed to getting what they want. But even in our increasingly secular age, the ancient practice of fasting is still relevant. At least a quarter of Americans made the decision to fast during Lent last year, a LifeWay Research study found—sixty-one percent of Catholics, along with twenty-eight percent of Protestants (a percentage that increased by twelve percent since 2014). Dietary regulations, whether church-imposed or self-imposed, are enforced for six weeks. Meats and fats are most commonly avoided, and through this long and patient practice of abstinence, man finds that he does not live by bread alone.

Most everywhere, however, society gives people reasons not to fast. We should have it all—and get it when we want it. Restricting the appetites is deemed unnecessary, even viewed as a barricade in our effort to assert our autonomous wills. Fulfilling our most primal desires becomes our mantra. Society tries to convince us that we *do* depend on bread alone.

This is the ideology of instant gratification. It focuses on impulses and our desire in order to quench our natural thirsts. It accepts this dependency as law. But by embarking on a diligent and purposeful period of fasting, and rejecting the things that so often sound delicious or appealing, one slowly learns how to combat an oppressive ideology of our times. To practice moderation and asceticism, and to experience the struggle of doing so, means that we are denying ourselves and refusing to participate in a culture that celebrates indulgence without limits.

Some people view Lent as a season of suffering. They think they need to suffer in order to achieve this independence from their passions. They think that they need to 'give up' or 'sacrifice' things. In this view, fasting becomes a sort of dark sadness. But this is not what Christ intended. Instead, He said, "Whenever you fast, do not be like the hypocrites, with a sad countenance."

Therefore, we should practice Lent with a 'bright sadness.' We should meditate on the life of Christ and see the fast as a time of holy recovery. We should find the beauty, both in the struggle and renewal, of practicing virtue. While fasting from certain foods, we also fast from our love of material things, pleasures of the body, comparison and envy, arrogance and pride. We reclaim our humanity.

We are all controlled by the desires of the flesh through one way or another. They crush us, but Lent renews us. Our passions should not be our master, but we should be the masters of our passions—and by giving serious attention to this struggle, we can then seek to moderate them. The exercise and struggle for Christlikeness is never-ending.

The first commandment Adam received in the Garden of Eden was the divine law of fasting and self-control: he *shall not eat* from the tree of the knowledge of good and evil. Even Adam, who had not yet been exposed to the consequences of sin, was instructed to practice restraint.

Then Christ—the Second Adam—spent forty days in the wilderness, fasting and praying before he started his public ministry. For hundreds of centuries thereafter, Christians have sought to imitate

Christ's fast during the Lenten season. Today, Catholics have Lenten fish fries. Eastern Orthodox avoid meat and dairy. Others give up sweets or their favorite television shows. It is through this season of abstinence from the desires of the flesh, that one sees the extent to which he or she is alive to the surrounding culture.

In this season of endurance, there is an opportunity for grace. Fasting, like all other paths of virtue, is exercised in a world where it is increasingly difficult to imitate the Divine. The Lenten lifestyle—one of patience, restraint, and perseverance—is an opportunity for us to learn to use the power over our bodies well.

Despite this season of fasting, food, drink, and pleasure are gifts. We should, in fact, celebrate them. But the ancient practice of fasting teaches that through discipline comes freedom. It grows into something better, and provides the opportunity to live more freely and abundantly. Lent culminates with the Crucifixion and Resurrection of Christ. *The fast ends with a feast.* It is a celebration of Christ destroying death through his death—and restoring life.

Faith Across Traditions

Holy Week
Daniel Hyland

This week there is another,
one more child lost within
the darkness of my womb.
How I have tried to care
for them, and carry them,
my life's portion, delicate
burdens, slowly forming
crosses to bear–or prove
unable to bear.
As Mary watched
her womb's fruit, ripe
in its own blood, fall
on the road to Golgotha–
once, twice, a third time, cords
lashing around His
crippled form, until
it was impossible to tell
if He was human;
so I watch the third one
fall, and sound the silent
words, the names I would
have used, the boy names
and the girl names, all
my dreams of them, my dear
unspoken hopes of taking up
their hands when they fall,
of teaching them to run,
to let their burdens go.
Where they have gone
I want to follow,
and I'm swept into the corner
between hope and death.
Like a child, I bury my head
in my hands and lay the stone
across the grief that others
will not share with me or help

me carry, who say
my child will come back
in a new pregnancy—saying
in all they say only that they
can't see why I would say
the names, the boy names
and the girl names. Unwilling
to give my grief its name, many
refuse to call my child *human*,
so unripe in its own blood.
But give it time, they say
give it to God, another one
will come along soon enough.

My soul waits for the Lord,
and for my child's voice—tired
of watching, guarding against
new loss, my soul waits
for the Lord—thirsting
for peace, the first words
of my child, yes, my soul
waits for the Lord.

What Day Did Jesus Die?
Jacob J. Prahlow

"When students are first introduced to the historical, as opposed to a devotional, study of the Bible, one of the first things they are forced to grapple with is that the biblical text, whether Old Testament or New Testament, is chock full of discrepancies, many of them irreconcilable.... In some cases seemingly trivial points of difference can actually have an enormous significance for the interpretation of a book or the reconstruction of the history of ancient Israel or the life of the historical Jesus."
Bart D. Ehrman[1]

As this statement from contemporary (and popular) New Testament scholar Bart D. Ehrman indicates, there those who study Christianity—its scriptures and history—who argue that the canonical gospels[2] do not present a historically accurate account of the life, death, and resurrection of Jesus of Nazareth. Around Easter every year, scholars and journalists of this perspective often pen pieces on the "Why the Resurrection Story is a Myth" or "Did Jesus Really Rise from the Dead?" In more nuanced versions of these discussions, the credibility of early Christian accounts of Christ's passion and resurrection is called into question, even on facts as seemingly mundane as the day on which Jesus was crucified.[3]

Such is the position of Ehrman, who argues that the Synoptic gospels (Matthew, Mark, and Luke) and Gospel of John portray Jesus as being killed on two different days, thus revealing their historical inaccuracy and untruthfulness.[4] In this post, I will examine this claim

---

[1] Bart. D. Ehrman. *Jesus, Interrupted: Revealing the Hidden Contradictions in the Bible (And Why We Don't Know About Them)*. San Francisco: HarperOne, 2010. 19.
[2] Matthew, Mark, Luke, and John.
[3] For a historic overview of this problem, see Massey H. Shepherd, "Are Both the Synoptics and John Correct About the Date of Jesus' Death", *Journal of Biblical Literature* 80, 2 (1961): 123-132.
[4] Ehrman, *Jesus, Interrupted*, 19-61.

and explain why the canonical gospels indicate that Jesus died on the same day, what has been historically called Good Friday.

Traditionally, the date of Jesus' death has been derived from the dating given by the Synoptic Gospel accounts in relation to the Jewish festival of Passover. More recently, however, some scholars have argued that the Matthew, Mark, and Luke portray Jesus as being killed *on* Passover, whereas John's Gospel shows Jesus being killed the day *before* Passover, on the so-called "Day of Preparation," the day that the lamb was killed in preparation for the Passover meal.[1]

While some have attempted to explain this apparent contradiction away by suggesting that John changed his narrative to better fit his "Lamb of God" theology, this explanation remains unsatisfying. *Does the Bible really say that Jesus was killed on two different days?* To address this question, let us turn to what the gospels of Mark[2] and John say about the day of Jesus' crucifixion and death.

Context

Before trying to interpret these passages, we need to grasp their basic context. First, the events surrounding Jesus' death occurred around the time of a Jewish festival called the Feast of Unleavened Bread. In today's context, we call this festival "Passover" and then, as now, this holy day is a commemoration of the plague against the firstborns of Egypt recorded in Exodus 12-13.[3] While the people of Israel were not always the more diligent in observing the Passover, the Jews of Jesus' day were quite observant when it came to celebrating the Feast of Unleavened Bread.

Second, we need to be aware of how the Jewish people understand a "day." Notice how time is construed in Genesis 1:
> *"God called the light Day, and the darkness he called Night. And there was evening and there was morning, the first*

---

[1] It should be noted that—theologically speaking at least—some have explained this apparent discrepancy away by arguing that the Fourth Gospel portrays Jesus as crucified on the Day of Preparation for the Passover in order to better fit his "Lamb of God" theology.

[2] The Synoptic Gospels roughly follow the same outline in telling the story of Jesus' life, death, and resurrection. For the sake of time (and my editor's sanity), we will not look at all three of the Synoptics, only the Gospel According to Mark, which is often viewed as the earliest gospel written.

[3] More specifically Exodus 13.3ff.

> day.... And God called the expanse Heaven. And there was evening and there was morning, the second day.... And there was evening and there was morning, the third day."[1]

Here we see the pattern of "evening and then morning" of the {number} day. Based on this passage, the Jewish people reckoned days as beginning at sundown and continuing (what is about 24 hours) until the next sundown. While we gauge days as beginning and ending at midnight, in the ancient world there were no atomic clocks to let you know when it was midnight and a new day had begun. Instead, they relied on the sun: when the sun goes down, the day is over and a new day begins. Therefore—and this is important—what we call Thursday night would actually be Friday evening for Second Temple Jews.

The Crucifixion according to Mark
Mark has the following to say about the chronology leading up to Jesus' death:
> "And on the first day of Unleavened Bread, when they sacrificed the Passover lamb, his disciples said to him, "Where will you have us go and prepare for you to eat the Passover? And he sent two of his disciples and said to them, "Go into the city, and a man carrying a jar of water will meet you. Follow him, and wherever he enters, say to the master of the house, 'The Teacher says, Where is my guest room, where I may eat the Passover with my disciples?' And the disciples set out and went to the city and found it just as he had told them, and they prepared the Passover."[2]

In Mark's chronology (and Matthew and Luke's as well), the sequence of events leading to the crucifixion chronology beings during the daylight hours of the "Day of Preparation" for the Passover, the day "when they sacrificed the Passover lamb." Now, the "Day of Preparation" includes the daytime hours of the 24-hour period during which Passover is eaten after dark. That is, if *we* are going to eat the Passover meal after the sun goes down today (April 2), today's daylight hours are part of the "Day of Preparation" and tonight is the Passover feast. According to this chronology, Mark describes the Last Supper scene as the Passover meal, a celebration of the Old Covenant at which Jesus institutes the New Covenant. Therefore, using our

---
[1] Genesis 1:5, 8.
[2] Mark 14:12-14, 16.

chronology of days, Mark presents the passion of Christ in the following way: Last Supper (Passover) Thursday night, crucifixion during the day on Friday, burial Friday before sundown, and subsequent resurrection Sunday morning.

The Crucifixion According the John

There are a number of passages used to try and demonstrate the chronological differences between Mark and John, including John 13.1, 18.28, and 19.14. The starting point for the Johannine chronology of Christ's death is 13.1, where some argue that John indicates the events which follow occur *before* Passover. Look at John 13.1-4, however:

> *"Now before the Feast of the Passover, when Jesus knew that his hour had come to depart out of this world to the Father, having loved his own who were in the world, he loved them to the end. During* **supper***, when the devil had already put it into the heart of Judas Iscariot, Simon's son, to betray him, Jesus, knowing that the Father had given all things into his hands, and that he had come from God and was going back to God, rose from supper."* (Bolding mine)

The reference to "supper" in verse two seems to be a direct reference to the previous verse, where John speaks of the "Feast of the Passover." It would follow, then, that John is not speaking of a supper before the Passover, but rather that he is talking about the Passover itself (like Mark).

This interpretation is further reinforced by events which occur later at the supper. For example, following the departure of Judas, the remaining disciples wonder why he has left. John writes that, *"Some thought that, because Judas had the moneybag, Jesus was telling him, 'Buy what we need for the feast,' or that he should give something to the poor."*[1]

This explanation only makes sense if they were celebrating the Passover feast for two reasons. First, if Jesus and his disciples are not eating the actual Passover meal, thinking that Judas is going to purchase materials for the duration of the feast makes no sense. They could purchase whatever they needed the next day—the Day of Preparation. If they are in the midst of a multi-day feast, however, going out for more supplies make more sense. Second, a traditional

---

[1] John 13:29.

facet of the Passover celebration involved almsgiving. This explains the alternate explanation John provides, that some thought Judas departed in order to give money to the poor; but this too only works if the Passover had just been celebrated. Reading John 13 contextually thereby suggests that John writes of the Last Supper as happening the night of Passover, just like Mark's Gospel.

A second passage often used to argue for different chronologies of Jesus' death comes from John 18.28, which reads: *"Then they led Jesus from the house of Caiaphas to the governor's headquarters. It was early morning. They themselves did not enter the governor's headquarters, so that they would not be defiled, but could eat the Passover."* At face value the simple reference to the Passover seems to indicate that the Jews had not yet eaten the Passover meal.[1]

To fully understand this passage, however, we must consider the traditions of Passover week and Jewish ceremonial law. Leviticus 15.5-11—and the ceremonial laws derived from that passage—indicate that certain forms of ritual defilement end at sundown. According to this statute, any Jew who entered the home of a Gentile would be considered clean (and thus able to eat the Passover meal) that night. Therefore, the meal that the Jewish leaders are worried about being defiled for (and thus unable to eat) cannot be the Passover itself.

What they could not have eaten if they were unclean was the *hagigah*, a ceremonial meal eaten at noon on the *day* of Passover. Remember, Passover starts in the evening and then continues until the next evening. Thus when John writes that the Jewish leaders would not enter Pilate's headquarters because of Passover, he uses the term colloquially, to indicate that entering the house of a Gentile would make them unclean for the *hagigah* meal. This is much the same way that my wife and I will be busy on this April 6th celebrating Easter; it will not actually be "Easter" on that day, but that's when we are getting together with family to celebrate that holiday. Again, this

---

[1] In trying to make sense of what is going on and unify the gospel accounts, some commentators write that perhaps different sects of Judaism would celebrate Passover on different days. And in fact the historical record seems to indicate that this did occasionally occur. However, no record indicates that different celebratory days were observed in the same city, but that different days were used by when different sects of Judaism were in control. As all of the events being described are going on in Jerusalem, clearly this is not what is happening.

interpretation suggests a uniformity of chronology between John and Mark.

The third passage used to argue for differences between the Synoptics and Fourth Gospel is John 19.14: *"Now it was the day of Preparation of the Passover. It was about the sixth hour. He said to the Jews, 'Behold your King!'"*

Note the grammatical structure of this translation: is it the day of Preparation *for* the Passover? No. It's the day of Preparation *of* the Passover.[1] I point out this distinction because in the Jewish world, Friday is *always*—without exception—*the day of Preparation for the Sabbath*.

Thus, for John to say that the day Jesus was being crucified was the "day of Preparation of the Passover" suggests to his readers that the day he is describing is in fact Friday—the day of Preparation, not for the Passover, but for the Sabbath. Indeed, if we keep reading, John makes this distinction clear in 19.31: *"Since it was the day of Preparation, and so that the bodies would not remain on the cross on the Sabbath (for that Sabbath was a high day), the Jews asked Pilate that their legs might be broken and that they might be taken away."*

According to John 19 (as with John 13 and 18), Jesus was portrayed as crucified and buried the day before the Sabbath (Friday) during the week of Passover. This accords perfectly with the Markan account of the crucifixion, where Mark explains that Jesus was taken down from the cross and hastily buried because it was the Day of Preparation (though Mark here clarifies by noting it was the Day of Preparation for the Sabbath).[2]

Conclusions

Although these three passages from John may, at first glance, appear to contradict the chronology of the passion as outlined in the Synoptic Gospels, this article has shown that a contextual and historically informed approach to John's Gospel indicates there are no such

---

[1] For those curious concerning the Greek in this passage, the word being translated here is *tou*, the genitive article governing the next word *pascha* (Passover). Genitives are often translated "of". If John had used the dative form of the article (in this case *tw*), we could take his meaning to be "for."

[2] Mark 15:42.

contradictions. This means several things. First, the four canonical Gospel accounts present the death (and resurrection) of Jesus following the same chronology; there is no internal canonical confusion on this matter. Second, we may infer that due to the theological construction of John's gospel (namely, his portrayal of Jesus as the Lamb of God), his emphasis may be more theological rather than historical in nature. This does not mean that John is necessarily less accurate than the Synoptics, but rather helps explain why that Gospel employs obfuscating language where the others are more explicit. Third, we may conclude that the traditional Christian chronology of the passion, death, and resurrection finds no reason for historical unreliability. The implications of this historical exercise should call us toward a remembrance of Christ's sacrificial suffering and death for the forgiveness of sins and eternal life, lead us to celebrate (later this week) his defeat of death and resurrection from the death, and spur us on to the hope of his second coming and the future general resurrection of the dead.

To step back from interpretation for a brief moment and offer some more practical conclusions, I make two suggestions. First, I hope this exercise has demonstrated something about the importance of context in understanding and interpreting a passage. The accounts recorded in the Bible were written in and about specific contexts, we must make context king in order to understanding the meaning of anything. This means that we need to read and understand the Old Testament before we can truly make sense of the New Testament. For without understanding the context of Jesus' life, death, and resurrection, how can we fully understand the significance of those events? Second, if we think that Christian faith or the Bible are (in any way) important, we need to try and understand what the Bible says and how we can apply it to our lives. This does not mean forcing what we think to be true onto the Biblical text or reading a passage a certain way because it has "always been" read that way. Rather, this means we should spend time engaging the scriptures in order to continue growing in our faith.

As we remember Christ's death tomorrow and celebrate Easter this Sunday, remember that the canonical gospels present a unified account of Christ's passion, an account which calls us to follow Christ ourselves.

Through the Rain
J.D. Grubb

The wind howls;
People cower
As doors sigh then clang shut,
Metal latches loud and angry;
We feel safe indoors, unaware
That time thus drains our alkaline train
Of thoughts battered with each gusty grey sky
Colliding water and heat, steaming brains.

Yet not all storms are tears, pain, fears;
In years they can grow crops of stronger
Rain, a cleansing rest:
The mud, the Flood, the waking
lungs, expanded chest —
Close your eyes, open hands,
Breathe in, listen, exhume
The tension of excess thought —
Imagine

That breeze and showers whisper 'Hush'
And empty cloistered air, stale office rush —
Inhale again the deep, damp, lush soil —
So much beyond the walls, havens from toil;
That heaven can be touched, smelt, seen
Now go, go, echo the chorus
If not for you, for us

Run, run, run
Through, not in the rain,
For true flesh is waterproof

Faith Across Traditions

Ethics and the Christian Life

The first article published on *Conciliar Post* opened with a reminder from Stephen Covey about the necessity of listening in a culture full of talking. Since that moment, our authors have routinely reflected on how to listen and live as faithful followers of Jesus, both in a divided church and in a difficult culture. These essays offer reflections on justice, enchantment, community, work, entertainment, and prayer—all crucial aspects of the Christian life.

Essays

The Sermon on the Mount and Christian Ethics, *Prahlow*

Let Justice Roll Down, *Justice*

What Re-Enchantment Really Means, *Ehrett*

John Wesley and Small Groups, *Dickey*

Recovering *Koinonia*, *Walker*

Toward a Spirituality of Christian Work, *Aldhizer*

A Christian Defense of Video Games, *Casberg*

Confessions of a Single Mom, Barrett

The Insufficiency of Spontaneous Prayer, *Landsman*

The Sermon on the Mount and Christian Ethics

Jacob J. Prahlow

Questions of an ethical nature dominate headlines, classrooms, and pulpits across the world. In an era where formulations of morality often spring from what "feels right" rather than any sort of foundational principles, many commentators have rightly noted the necessity of carefully considered ethics. For contemporary Christians, ethical thought remains clouded by ongoing disagreements about from where our moral systems arise and how authoritative those sources are in a technologically advanced world of complexity and disagreement. One relatively common location for ethical source material comes in Jesus' Sermon on the Mount, that famous stretch of material which begins with the Beatitudes and includes the Lord's Prayer.

Yet even the practices within this collection of the Savior's sayings remain highly contested: to *whom* was Jesus speaking these words and how applicable are they to modern life? Many readers of the Bible have concluded that these are not simple questions with easy answers. For the duration of this article, I will trace the five primary ways in which Christians have interpreted and utilized the ethical imperatives found in the Sermon on the Mount, arguing that one of these interpretations offers a fruitful basis for formulating Christian ethics in today's world.

For the Perfect
One of the oldest interpretations of the Sermon on the Mount suggests that the words of Jesus found therein are applicable only for those who have vowed lives of perfection. Such was the perspective of Tertullian of Carthage (c. 160-240 CE) and Origen of Alexandria (182-254 CE). This view proved highly influential throughout the medieval period, when the words of the Lord were understood as applicable for members of monastic communities and among the clergy. Not surprisingly, this interpretation convinces few readers of Matthew's Gospel today, often for the simple reason that Jesus

appears to be speaking to a large number of people (Matt. 5:1-2; Matt. 7:28-9), not just a select few whom he called to be perfect.

Pedagogical Instruction
In response to the view that the ethics commands of the Sermon on the Mount applied only to the perfect, the Protestant Reformers (and many of their theological heirs) argued that Jesus spoke to all people despite the fact that no human being can actually meet his demands.

In this view, the Sermon—in much the same way as Old Testament law—highlights human sinfulness and weakness, continually calling Christians toward greater perfection in Christ and emphasizing the need for God's mercy. While this view speaks to one aspect of ethical systems existing in a fallen world—that no one will ever fully satisfy the requirements of perfection—this too remains an unsatisfactory reading of the Matthew 5–7. Jesus admonishes his listeners to hear and obey, to be wise doers. Jesus speaks without qualification or hesitation about the morality he expects his followers to exhibit. There is more going on here than claims of human imperfection.

Interim Ethic
Some readers of Matthew's Gospel—most notably Johannes Weiss (1863-1914)—argue that Matthew wrote down Jesus' commands for a short interim period (the time between his ascension and Second Coming). In this view, Matthew expected Jesus-Followers to heroically adhere to these ethical parameters for a brief period of missional activity. And in light of the fact that Jesus did not return shortly after his ascension to usher in the messianic kingdom, contemporary Christians may rightly modify or update these teachings in order to comfortably live in a non-eschatological age.

There are problems with this interpretation as well, not the least of which is the slippery-slope suggestion of the mutability of Jesus' teachings. Additionally, even within an early dating scheme, Matthew's Gospel was clearly written late enough to already be dealing with the problematic of Jesus' "delayed" return. Thus, an interim ethic perspective fails to adequately explain Matthew's inclusion of this material in his gospel.

New Torah
Interpretations of the Sermon on the Mount which emphasize its place as New Torah situate Jesus' ethical imperatives as the *only* adequate bases for the construction of Christian ethical systems. In

short, Jesus' ethic is the *only ethic*. The Lord's words in the Sermon represent *the* guidelines for Christian piety and practice, with all other biblical sources either rendered antiquated or inaccurately interpreted. Appropriate Christian ethics, therefore, start and end with the Sermon on the Mount.

Yet there are problems with this interpretation as well, foremost of which involves the fact that this view makes the vast majority of the Bible ethically useless. By over-emphasizing these three chapters, the New Torah approach becomes functionally Marcionite—rejecting the theological value of the Old Testament—and truncates even other New Testament ethical sources (such as the Pauline epistles or book of James).

Transformational Ethics
The fifth major way to utilize the ethical imperatives found in the Sermon on the Mount is to interpret this passage as the transformational foundation for Christian ethics. In this view, the ethical imperatives of the Sermon neither supersede the rest of scripture nor do they exist only for limited persons or purposes. Rather, Jesus' words stand as a source of radical transformation anticipating the kingdom of God. Here, Jesus turns ethical conventions ("an eye for an eye") and interpretation ("you have heard it said") on their heads, intensifies the heart of Torah (love of God and neighbor), and calls his followers to radical selflessness and sacrifice ("In everything do to others as you would have them do to you; for this is the law and the prophets."). Torah has not passed away, but has been transformed into a condition of the heart.

Of course, this reading offers a more complicated situation for the formation of Christian ethics than the other viewpoints we have examined, requiring prayerful and faithful integration of other canonical sources rather than "one size fits all" interpretations. Consider the example of a woman being abused by her husband. A transformational reading of the Sermon on the Mount encourages her to pray for her husband (acting here as her enemy), but by no means requires her to simply "turn the other cheek." Instead, she rightly seeks the protection of her community (Deut. 10:18) and the governing authorities (Rom. 13:2-4) in order to rectify the wrongs that her husband commits.

Sorting through difficult ethical issues is no easy task and Christians do themselves no favors by presuming otherwise. The Sermon on the

Mount has long been—and should remain—an important source for Christian reflection upon and formation of ethics and morality. In utilizing this important section of Jesus' teaching, we would do well to take a balanced approach, one which recognizes the importance of Jesus' words without rejecting the rest of the scriptures while at the same time taking seriously the transformational nature of what the Lord says.

In this way, we may become wise followers of Christ, for
> *Everyone then who hears these words of mine and acts on them will be like a wise man who built his house on rock. The rain fell, the floods came, and the winds blew and beat on that house, but it did not fall, because it had been founded on rock. And everyone who hears these words of mine and does not act on them will be like a foolish man who built his house on sand. The rain fell, and the floods came, and the winds blew and beat against that house, and it fell—and great was its fall!* (Matt. 7: 24-27)

Let Justice Roll Down
David Justice

The words of Amos 5:24, "But let justice roll down like waters, and righteousness like an ever-flowing stream," have been inscribed on the American mind through our annual remembrance of the Rev. Dr. Martin Luther King Jr. and his speech on the steps of the Lincoln Memorial. This favorite verse of King's presents a beautiful image.

However, because King is generally thought of primarily as a civil rights leader and not a Christian theologian, in King's speech this verse is often reduced to a platitude and taken out of its Biblical context. King surely knew that in the verses preceding his now famous quotation God denounced the nation of Israel and informed them that, despite what the Israelites might think, the coming of the Lord would mean not their salvation. Rather, it would herald their destruction. Let us examine this passage in the broader context of Amos chapter 5, beginning with verse 6:

> *Seek the Lord that you may live, Or He will break forth like a fire, and it will devour Bethel, with no one to quench it. Ah, you that turn justice to wormwood, and bring righteousness to the ground!... Therefore, because you impose heavy rent on the poor, and exact a tribute of grain from them, though you have built houses of well-hewn stone, yet you will not live in them; You have planted pleasant vineyards, yet you will not drink their wine. For I know your transgressions are many and your sins are great, you who distress the righteous and accept bribes and turn aside the poor in the gate...Alas for you who desire the day of the Lord! Why do you want the day of the Lord? I hate, I despise your festivals, and I take no delight in your solemn assemblies. Even though you offer me your burnt offerings and grain offerings, I will not accept them; and the offerings of well-being of your fatted animals I will not look upon. Take away from me the noise of your songs; I will not listen to the melody of your harps. But let justice roll down like waters, and righteousness like an ever-flowing stream.*

Within this broader context, it becomes clear that Amos' message to Israel is that they are bringing down judgment upon themselves. While they may say that they desire the coming day of the Lord, when that day comes they will be destroyed unless they cease oppressing the poor and righteous in their midst. The religious festivals and offerings that were supposed to turn their hearts to God clearly have failed to do so. Evil and sin, rather than righteousness, rule the land. Given the original meaning of this text, King is not merely trying to provide pleasant visuals for those listening to him speak; instead, King suggests through the prophetic words of Amos that unless America makes justice and righteousness a reality, America will be destroyed in the coming day of the Lord. Much like Israel in the time of Amos, King saw that in America the poor were trampled and the rich stored up more than they could possibly use in many lifetimes. Additionally, through its international influence, America had exported its systematic oppression of the poor to the world, trampling on God's children across the globe.

Because King was firmly rooted in the tradition of the Black Church, King knew that Amos' words had meaning for those attempting to realize justice and righteousness in the present. As an institution "born in protest [and] tested in adversity," the Black Church has historically seen the need to make the gospel matter in the spiritual and material realms and work to make social justice a reality.[1] King loved America and he devoted much of his life to bringing America in line with the ethical demands of the Beloved Community, which for King was synonymous with God's coming Kingdom. However, King also was painfully aware that America was far from meeting its obligations to the oppressed—that it was locked in the jaws of oppressive systems such as white supremacy, militarism, and extreme materialism. Thus, like Dives, the rich man, who ignored the poor man Lazarus at his gate, King saw that America was headed towards destruction. In a sermon in the final year of his life, King preached against America stating:

> Dives finally went to hell because he sought to be a conscientious objector in the war against poverty. And I come by here to say that America, too, is going to hell if she doesn't use her wealth. If American does not use her vast resources of wealth to end poverty and make it possible for all of God's

---

[1] Diana Hayes, *Forged In The Fiery Furnace: African American Spirituality* (Maryknoll, NY: Orbis Books, 2012), 93.

children to have the basic necessities of life, she, too, will go to hell.[1]

Shortly after warning America of her impending damnation, King ends this speech by returning to his famous quotation of Amos 5:24, though this time with additional urgency, "Now is the time for justice to roll down like water and righteousness like a mighty stream. Now is the time." In other words, America must soon transform itself into a nation in line with the coming of God's kingdom—the day of the Lord—or America will be destroyed by the cleansing conflagration that accompanies the Beloved Community.

King's words preached more than 50 years ago are sadly relevant in America today, where extremism is on the rise, racism and misogyny are increasingly mainstreamed, and power and wealth are sequestered by a tiny elite class while many at the bottom of society struggle to access what they need to survive. So, if you remember King fondly today, know that his was a voice of prophetic fire, condemning America and the world for failing to respect the dignity and worth of human beings. King's dream is far from realized. To change that, much of what America holds dear, including the lies we Americans value regarding our collective righteousness, must be committed to the flames, and a new world founded on justice and love must come into being.

If you're interested in learning more about King's dream and making it a reality, I've included a couple links below:
1. The King Center has training courses in nonviolence and activism that can be completed online: https://thekingcenter.org/nonviolence365-education-and-training/
2. Throughout his life, King was committed to ending the exploitation that accompanies capitalism and moving society towards democratic socialism. The Institute for Christian Socialism is recruiting members to participate in working towards a more just economy: https://christiansocialism.com/membership/

---

[1] Martin Luther King, Jr., "All Labor Has Dignity: American Federation of State, County, and Municipal Employees (AFSCME), Memphis, Tennessee, March 18, 1968," in *All Labor Has Dignity*, ed. Michael Honey (Boston, MA: Beacon Press, 2011), 173.

Faith Across Traditions

What Re-Enchantment Really Means
John Ehrett

Out of all the Christmas presents I've received over the years, none so far can hold a candle to what showed up under the tree when I was ten: a thick paperback set of J.R.R. Tolkien's *The Hobbit* and *The Lord of the Rings*. I'd been raised on (and loved) C.S. Lewis's *Chronicles of Narnia*, and Tolkien's intricate cosmos felt just like that, but *more*. Here was a sprawling world with its own languages and legends and histories, charged with the possibility that every new page might hold a fresh clue to unlocking an ancient mystery.

That was just the beginning. After plowing through the box set, I turned to *The Silmarillion*, Tolkien's doorstopper compendium of the mythology underpinning the better-known books, and after that to the endless volumes of draft material—*The Book of Lost Tales, The Lays of Beleriand, The Shaping of Middle-Earth*, and on and on—painstakingly edited by his son. And then it was on to other fantasy: Lloyd Alexander, Susan Cooper, Terry Brooks, Robert Jordan, R.A. Salvatore, and countless others. With each new writer, a whole new expanse of mystery and wonder opened up.

The enchantment phrase didn't last, though. Eventually, I concluded that real-world girls were more interesting than fictional elf-princesses, and my reading tastes shifted accordingly. By the time my teenage years rolled around, I'd managed to convince myself that Michael Crichton and Clive Cussler and Louis L'Amour were more grown-up stuff. And as the years passed, I largely moved out of reading fantasy altogether—though I still dipped into the genre occasionally just to see how long-running book sagas ended. (Or so I told myself.)

Not everyone I knew made the shift, though. At my small evangelical college, there were plenty of "friends of Narnia" to go around—indeed, I often wondered if they'd read any books *other* than Lewis and Tolkien. Some adopted full-fledged Renaissance Faire getups, spending their spring afternoons swanning around the retention pond students had christened "Lake Bob," while others were quite determined to be the next generation of Christian fantasy writers.

All of this, of course, was eye-rolling stuff for those of us who had decided that adulthood meant cynicism, and in particular cynicism about fantasy. After seeing one too many ex-homeschoolers post that "Aslan is on the move!" a friend of mine took to posting a rather grisly Discovery Channel GIF of a lion bringing down a gazelle. Naturally, my friends and I were early fans of *Game of Thrones* and its deeply misanthropic take on the genre.

If Bard College professor Maria Sachiko Cecire is to be believed, all this cynicism is entirely justified. In *Re-Enchanted: The Rise of Children's Fantasy Literature in the Twentieth Century*, Cecire builds out a far-reaching intellectual genealogy of what she terms the "Oxford School" of fantasy literature—meaning, of course, Lewis and Tolkien and their artistic heirs.

Well before they were household names, Lewis and Tolkien were deeply enmeshed in a series of battles over the literary canon that would be taught to Oxford undergraduates. At the time, some members of the Oxford faculty favored excising older materials to make room for more contemporary literature in the program, as was the practice at Cambridge—a modernizing impulse that, Cecire hypothesizes, helps explain the mélange of anachronistic material present throughout Cambridge graduate T.H. White's *The Sword in the Stone*, and which Lewis himself derisively described as "fashion."

By contrast, Lewis and Tolkien stressed the retention of classics, particularly the Old and Middle English literature—*Beowulf, Sir Gawain and the Green Knight*, and so forth—from which the great texts of the Middle Ages eventually emerged. These wellsprings of English identity and culture, for Lewis and Tolkien, offered enduring wisdom as bulwarks against the encroachment of an ever-more-unstable modernity.

Placing the accent on Lewis and Tolkien's *Englishness* is a deliberate move, and it forms the lodestar of Cecire's overarching point—which is that Lewis and Tolkien were, to be blunt, flat wrong about the reality of timeless truths. Cecire is concerned, like any good follower of Foucault, primarily with power and the social constructions informing its deployment. If all social features inevitably reduce down to power relations, entirely untethered from any moral order woven into the fabric of creation, even fantasy-world talk of "legitimate authority" or "kings and queens" can only be a fig leaf for defending the power distribution of the status quo. Lewis and Tolkien, in Cecire's telling, are to be defined less by their theological commitments than by their allegedly reactionary politics—a move that allows her to call into question whether the premodern cosmologies of their stories really reflect a fear of God, or instead merely a fear of losing hegemonic power.

Re-Enchanted argues that Lewis and Tolkien's works, for all their power to delight generations of children, work as a kind of opiate of the masses—perpetuating a toxic "racial innocence" in not foregrounding real-world racism as a central narrative concern, and even trafficking in reactionary nationalist agitprop. For Cecire, "Lewis and Tolkien's backlash against linear notions of progress and modern disenchantment coincided with a powerful Anglophilia that celebrates Britain's medieval origins in ways that build on colonialist sentiments and tend toward (typically unthinking) white supremacy." Most notably, in Cecire's hands *The Voyage of the Dawn Treader* an extended apologetic for British colonialism, complete with "tax collection and the oversight of regional governors" and "learning how to rule over Indigenous peoples in spite of seemingly nonsensical local practices."

Notably, the plot motifs Cecire associates with the Oxford School—medieval politics, exploration, discovery, battle, and so forth—are all hallmarks of the modern fantasy genre, such that Cecire's hermeneutic of suspicion calls into question virtually the entire canon of well-known fantasy literature. And Cecire is explicit about that goal, explaining from the start that a principal purpose of her work is to "challenge[] individuals to complicate their own pleasure in medievalist children's fantasy by facing down the genre's exclusionary aspects."

What might an appropriate alternative be? Cecire makes only a few remarks on that, admiringly noting that some contemporary fantasy eschews grand narratives of cosmic order in favor of "locat[ing] enchantment in the achievement of inner happiness and love through overcoming the wounds of childhood," "engaging in the never-ending process of self-making," and "finding inspiration within themselves and their relationships with others." The ideal future of fantasy, on this account, is a kind of magical self-care; knights and fair maidens need not apply

All told, Cecire's indictment is far more lacerating than any ever leveled against the *Harry Potter* books by evangelical parents. In *Re-Enchanted*, cynicism about the fantasy genre reaches its apex: Cecire's book invites us to feel *good* about ourselves in turning to other texts, in rolling our eyes at those still clinging to their Tolkien and Lewis and dismissing them as not simply juvenile, but politically retrograde.

That invitation, however, is undermined by the fact that many of Cecire's gotcha examples simply do not ring true. *Dawn Treader's* lengthiest treatment of colonial governance culminates not in the subjugation of a local population, but rather in the abolition of the slave trade enacted by an illegitimate governor. And the Oxford School's silence on race is completely explicable in context: it would make no narrative sense to transpose contemporary racial conflict into a fantastical society not marked by the same past scars. After all, Lewis and Tolkien were writing fantasy—not history with some names changed.

Furthermore, the fact that Lewis and Tolkien were self-consciously critical of modernity is obvious to the point of banality—one need consider only Lewis's indictment of scientistic humanism in *That Hideous Strength*, or Tolkien's broadsides against industrialization in the contentious "Scouring of the Shire" chapter of *The Lord of the Rings* (an episode left out of Peter Jackson's film trilogy). If Lewis and Tolkien meant their works to serve as a covert endorsement of existing power structures, they seem to have had an unusually shameless way of going about that goal.

Finally, it bears mention that readers turn to fantasy to contemplate alternatives to the way things are, rather than to read their current situation comfortably affirmed. What springs forth from the pages of *The Return of the King* or *Prince Caspian* is not an endorsement of monarchy or authoritarianism as a political model, but rather the glory of *eucatastrophe,* the reality of things ultimately going right when all hope seems lost. Cecire's critique, by and large, seems to reflect a fundamental disdain for imaginative storytelling as such and a preference for hard-nosed didacticism—a claim, ironically, often directed at the overtly Christian elements of the Narnia books.

Indeed, when viewed from a different perspective, *Re-Enchanted* powerfully exemplifies how deeply impoverished the Foucauldian interpretive paradigm really is. Latent within Cecire's withering critique of the Oxford School's metaphysical vision is the presumption that Cecire herself enjoys an epistemically privileged vantage point, a place from which she can conclude that Lewis and Tolkien's books were *really and truly about* cultural anxiety and the glories of British empire. And yet the moral logic that animates her argument—that the world ought to be principally understood in terms of a struggle against oppressive power—is a time-bound, historically conditioned narrative all its own, one that excludes *a priori* the possibility of *legitimate* exercises of power or *genuine* cosmological order. As John Milbank observed decades ago in *Theology and Social Theory*, "the normative perspective of modernity allows one to think that there is always a dimension of pure 'social action,' pure 'social power,' occurring between the individual and the social, and separable from its ritual, symbolic or linguistic embodiment." Any ensuing attempts to reframe "enchantment"—a fundamentally theological matter—in Foucauldian terms simply amount, as Milbank notes, to "a secular policing of the sublime. Deconstructed in this fashion, the entire subject evaporates into the pure ether of the secular will-to-power."

What if, in short, Lewis and Tolkien's vision is in fact truer than Cecire's? *Re-Enchanged* offers no reason to conclude otherwise.

This is an argument, though, of the head and not the heart: it's one thing to feel the analytical force of Milbank's reasoning, and quite another to internalize it. Here's a more difficult question: what would it mean to read Tolkien and Lewis and their successors again, but without cynicism? For those of us in whom the poison of endless irony has festered for years, is such a thing even possible?

Perhaps. And perhaps it need not require that we turn back the clock to childhood naïveté, switching off our critical faculties altogether. Like the jaded dwarfs of Lewis's *The Last Battle*, wandering helplessly through a sunny field while believing themselves trapped inside a pitch-black stable, the real challenge may simply be to see what's always already been there from the start.

As a child, I didn't know why *The Lord of the Rings* was jammed with so many songs, some of which span multiple pages. As a college student, I made fun of it. But Lisa Coutras's volume *Tolkien's Theology of Beauty: Majesty, Splendor, and Transcendence in Middle-Earth* offered a different perspective. Tolkien's primordial creation myth, the *Ainulindale*, depicts the shaping of the world as a great symphony, a play of interlocking melodies and harmonies through which the ordering of the cosmos was accomplished. Within Tolkien's Middle-earth, song is a truer way of getting in touch with the essential makeup of the world than speech—both an inversion of and an homage to the traditional Christian claim that God's Word summoned the creation into being. Song is *natural* to Middle-earth in a way that spoken words are not.

Similarly, I once read the Narnia books as primarily adventure stories with spiritual lessons attached—which is, indeed, what a whole legion of Narnia imitators have turned out to be. But Michael Ward's *Plant Narnia: The Seven Heavens in the Imagination of C.S. Lewis* invites the reader to contemplate that, perhaps, each of the books stands for one of the heavenly realms of traditional Ptolemaic cosmology: *The Magician's Nephew* is identified with the fecundity and new life of Venus, *The Lion, the Witch, and the Wardrobe* is identified with Jupiter as the locus of royalty and power, and so forth.

And so, in the end, I have come to see that I was wrong. For too long, I thought I could dismiss these books as simply the stuff of childhood, volumes to be put away until my own children came of age. But beneath all the straightforward good-versus-evil storytelling, which so many successors have adopted, lies a theological vision of great depth and sophistication—even if it takes time and effort to fully uncover. The touchstones of the Oxford School may have far more to say to an adult than they do to a child.

Cecire is right about one thing: on the other side of cynicism and critique is, indeed, a kind of re-enchantment—but it is not the enchantment that comes with wearing medieval dresses on the shores of Lake Bob or peppering one's speech with inapt Narnia references. Nor does it have anything to do with self-actualization or the individual generation of individual meaning. Rather, it has everything to do with better apprehending what is *given* in the first instance. And what could inspire more wonder than that?

John Wesley and Small Groups
Jarrett Dickey

As one raised in the United Methodist Church, I was always familiar with the radical ministry of John Wesley, hearing stories in Sunday sermons or learning the history of the Methodist revival in confirmation class. In my final year at the Candler School of Theology, I had the privilege of exploring Wesley's life and thought in more detail in a course entitled: "John Wesley's Theology and 18th Century Epistemology." For my final assignment in the course, I wrote a 22-page paper on the small group organizational structures of early Methodism. To get historical perspective, I examined how Wesley's historical encounters with the Moravians, a group of pious Christians from Germany, shaped his understanding of small group structures. It was a fascinating study, and I was truly impressed with Rev. Wesley's organizational genius. He developed an intricate system for creating Christian disciples that is still relevant today. It was a three-part system consisting of societies, class meetings, and bands, which will be explained in further detail below.

The Society
Society meetings were like small congregations. There could have been anywhere from fifty to several hundred members involved with a society. They met on Sunday evenings for hymn-singing and preaching/teaching. One element of traditional Christian worship noticeably absent, at least at first, were the sacraments. Wesley encouraged persons to attend their local Anglican church on Sunday mornings to receive the sacraments. Wesley was adamant that the Methodist movement was not a separatist movement. Of course it would later split off from the Anglican church and become a separate denomination, but that was not John Wesley's original intention.

The societies were mainly geared towards education. The Methodist movement was successful in evangelizing lower class persons because of Wesley's field preaching. Societies became the places where these new converts were educated in the faith. But John Wesley was not content to merely educate new-Christians so each member of the Methodist societies was also required to attend a weekly class meeting.

The Class Meeting
Class meetings met weekly and consisted of about 12 persons, with a mixture of gender and marital status. The group was led by a class leader, who was appointed by the society leadership. The meeting would begin with prayer and hymn-singing. After that, the class leader shared an orderly account of the week, focusing on personal spiritual growth. After the class leader shared, the rest of the group would take turns answering the question, "How goes it with your soul?"

All Methodists were required to attend these meetings and were given tickets to get in. If a person missed too many meetings in a quarter, they would lose their ticket and not be able to participate. It was very much a high commitment style of Christian discipleship and nurture! The class meetings were also places where offerings were collected to support the work of the Methodist movement. Whereas the societies were focused on education, the class meetings were much more focused on spiritual nurture, spiritual direction, and mutual encouragement.

The Band
The deepest level of commitment in the Methodist movement was the band. Unlike the class meetings, these gatherings were entirely voluntary and homogeneous (same gender and marital status). These were also the smallest groups, 3-4 persons. These groups focused on intimate sharing of temptations and confession of sins. They were in essence accountability groups. As one might imagine, these groups were not very popular. No more than about 25% of Methodists participated in the bands.

What Can We Learn From John Wesley Today?
Wesley's small group system has much to teach us today. For example, the model provides for both education (a focus on the mind) and nurture (a focus on the heart). At times we pick one or the other, but the early Methodist system shows a way to unite them in a context of Christian growth. Additionally, the system offers several levels of commitment and depth. People who want to go deeper in their discipleship can voluntarily join a band. However, it makes discipleship a requirement for everyone (class meeting). Too often we make discipleship optional in our churches. It's interesting how people tend to respond favorably to high-commitment Christianity. In many of our churches we assume people don't want to be bothered

much, but that may not be the case. They may actually be looking for a church that asks them to be committed Christians rather than nominal ones.

Yet, the Wesleyan system also provides a realistic perspective on the nature of spiritual growth and discipleship. Not all believers are either able to join high-commitment accountability groups or interested in them. While pastors and priests may desire that all members of their congregation progress toward the highest level of discipleship, the reality is that a church will always contain a mixture of believers with a range of interest levels. The Wesleyan system, in a pragmatic way, creates spaces for both types of Christians–the new believer and the high-commitment longtime disciple.

If you want to learn more about the Wesleyan small group system consider reading *A Model for Making Disciples*, D. Michael Henderson and *The Early Methodist Class Meeting*, David L. Watson.

Recovering Koinonia
Wesley Walker

"And they devoted themselves to the apostles' teaching and fellowship, to the breaking of bread and the prayers."
Acts 2:42 (RSV)

According to Acts 2:42, the primitive church dedicated itself to four practices: apostolic teaching, fellowship (*koinonia*), breaking of bread (Eucharist), and prayer. In some way or another, most Christian traditions maintain these practices despite disagreements concerning their meaning and shape. Yet, of the four, *koinonia* is the least understood. Is it a mutual association flowing from affinity? Is it just "doing life together?" *Koinonia* is deeper than that; it is a theological reality before it is a pragmatic one.

In his significant book *Christ, the Christian, and the Church*, E.L. Mascall invites us to contemplate which comes first: the Church or the Christian. The assumption made by many moderns would no doubt be that the individual Christian comes first; the Church comes into being through a network of relationships with like-minded people who also identify as Christian. Mascall points out that the reality is actually the opposite: individuals cannot precede the Church. As the domain of grace, the Church is where the individual becomes a Christian. It begs the question: if the Church is not dependent on individuals, what is its basis for existence? The answer is Christ himself, the head of the Body (Rom 12:5; 1 Cor 12:12-27; Eph 3:6, 5:23; Col 1:18, 24). Further, he is the one who appointed the apostles and gave them their authority (John 20:23). The Church, then, is divinely instituted.

Within modernity, our conceptualization of community has become warped. In his article "Authenticity, Community, and Modernity," Kenneth C. Bessant discusses how, in social theory, the forces of urbanization, industrialization, and rationalism are credited with creating a shift away from the village as an authentic expression of community towards a more fragmented, impersonal, and artificial understanding of how we are to live together. The Church has mirrored the larger culture in this shift. Parish life was, at one time, a microcosm of the rural village, but has undergone changes as modernity has progressed. Robust community life has been replaced by the shallow "worship-industrial complex" and a program-driven church mentality. Worshippers are treated as consumers to be satiated, rather than as humans to be formed. Authentic *koinonia* in such a system is only ever an abstract ideal to which lip service is paid, rather than a lived reality.

The remedy to our modern malaise and return to a biblical and traditional sense of *koinonia*, we must return to the starting point that the Church is the divine organism "in Christ," with him at its head. According to L.S. Thornton, "Christians are specifically united neither by material good, nor by cultural interests, nor even by rational ideas." *Koinonia*, rather than being merely affinity-based, is derived from and energized by the Sacraments. Properly understood, it is the self-sacrificial participation of redeemed persons with each other and God on the basis of the incarnation, death, and resurrection of Christ. What is common to the members of the Church is cruciformity. This is true from the moment of Baptism where one dies with Christ (Rom 6:3-4) to weekly celebrations of the Eucharist where we present ourselves as "living sacrifices" at the altar (Rom 12:1). Christ's work is the basis for *koinonia*. Thornton observes that, as a result of the suffering and glory which characterized the messianic life, the messianic community can expect the same pattern to compose our common life. Further, as we become who we are called to be, we must be keenly aware that we are becoming in mutuality with the other members of the body. The Church, far from being a place for individuals to voluntarily associate is a place where its members are increasingly conformed to the Messiah through cruciformity.

Colossians 1:18 reminds Christians that "He [Christ] is the head of the body, the church." Thornton observes, "Partnership in the Gospel creates a common mind." What is this "common mind?" The answer can be found in what Michael J. Gorman calls his "master story," Philippians 2:5-11:
> Have the mind among yourselves, which was in Christ Jesus, who, though he was in the form of God, did not count equality with God a thing to be grasped, but emptied himself, taking the form of a servant, being born in the likeness of men. And being found in human form he humbled himself and became obedient unto death, even death on a cross. Therefore God has highly exalted him and bestowed on him the name which is

above every name, that at the name of Jesus every knee should bow, in heaven and on earth and under the earth, and every tongue confess that Jesus Christ is Lord, to the glory of God the Father.

The Christian *koinonia* is the domain whereby we live out Romans 12:1-2 by becoming living sacrifices and are transformed as a result of offering ourselves on the altar. *Koinonia* is the place where the sacramental benefits bestowed in Baptism and the Eucharist come to fruition.

The Church is in desperate need of recovering its purpose. We need sacraments, preaching, and prayer, but without recovering a robust conception of *koinonia* we will remain stuck in the doldrums of a world where fragmented community is the norm. By recovering the true *koinonia* of the Church, we can recover an ecclesiology that is thoroughly cruciform and engage in a space where we become what we are supposed to be.

Faith Across Traditions

Toward a Christian Spirituality of Work
George Aldhizer

"Follow your passion!" Rings out perhaps the most popular piece of career advice for high school and college students. Simply figure out and follow what you most love, the section of the bookstore you gravitate towards, or what gets you out of bed in the morning, and you will have a meaningful and fulfilling career. "Choose a job you love," so the saying goes, "and you will never have to work a day in your life."

There appears to be a cottage industry of critiques against this notion. A quick Google search of "follow your passion" reveals a myriad of articles *against* the claim, not apologetics for it. Cal Newport at *CNN.com* notes that there is little scientific evidence that workplace satisfaction is connected with a "pre-existing" passion.[1] Mike Rowe, star of the television series "Dirty Jobs," raises the problem that one cannot tell another to follow their passion, without first knowing if the passion is good or not.[2] Caroline Beaton at the *Huffington Post* argues that discourse about immediate "passions" blinds us to seeking long-term "purpose."[3]

I certainly agree with all of these criticisms; "Follow your passion" is specious career advice for the reasons mentioned above. However, I'm not convinced that the current preoccupation with finding the right career should be the name of the game. What if the most important question is not "What should I do with my hands?" But, "How does the work of our hands affect our souls?" Perhaps what is most important is not getting to the destination of a good job, but of

---

[1] Newport, Cal. "Why 'follow your passion' is bad advice", CNN.com, August 29, 2012, http://www.cnn.com/2012/08/29/opinion/passion-career-cal-newport/
[2] "Don't Follow Your Passion", PragerU, June 6, 2016, https://www.youtube.com/watch?v=CVEuPmVAb8o
[3] Beaton, Caroline. "What No One Told Me About Following My Passion", The Huffington Post, August 8, 2016, http://www.huffingtonpost.com/caroline-beaton/what-no-one-told-me-about_2_b_11618730.html

loving God and neighbor regardless of the job(s) we have. Maybe our macro-reflection about finding satisfying work neglects the hour-by-hour and minute-by-minute on-the-job realities that offer opportunities for our flourishing.

These are the premises of the fabulous book *Taking Your Soul To Work*, written by R. Paul Stevens and Alvin Ung. The book seeks to answer a profound question, "How do I grow spiritually when I work?"[1] The answer to this question, the authors point out, is not to be in a religious vocation, as if God is only concerned with the spiritual growth of pastors. Nor is the answer to the question to merely evangelize to coworkers or set aside time for prayer during the workday, for these responses assume that *actual work* cannot be pleasing to God. The animating answer to the question that fuels the book is, "We long to take our souls to work, to be attentive to God's presence in the midst of a busy and intense work life, and to be gradually transformed into loving and holy persons while we work."[2]

The rest of the book operates under the assumption that God cares deeply about our daily lives at work, for it is an opportunity for us to either serve ourselves or to glorify God. This fact is not to be taken lightly, as the introduction of the book proclaims starkly, "The workplace is a major arena for the battle of our souls."[3] Speaking from my own experience of work, I initially recoil at this statement, finding it awfully hard to believe. For one, my job is not very contentious or competitive, nor does it seem as if I have much opportunity to sin against others or myself. As an accountant, it doesn't seem as if the numbers on the screen have any relation to humans in the real world. And seriously, can working in a cubicle on a computer really be all that spiritually important?

Reading *Taking Your Soul To Work* is a practice in beginning to take the workplace seriously as an opportunity for spiritual growth. The urgency for this consciousness, the authors argue, is due to the fact that the converse is also true–our work is an opportunity for spiritual degeneracy. The book outlines nine "deadly work sins" including pride, greed, lust, gluttony, anger, sloth, envy, restlessness, and boredom, each of which have the power to "produce a habitual

---

[1] Stevens, R. Paul and Ung, Alvin. Taking Your Soul to Work: Overcoming the Nine Deadly Sins of the Workplace, (Grand Rapids: Eerdmans, 2010), 2.
[2] Ibid., 3.
[3] Ibid., 11.

pattern that gains control of our will, our desire, our character, and our lives."[1] Said another way, the intentions of the nine work sins are to permeate and pervert our motivations, our relationships with coworkers, the thoughts of our head, the emotions of our heart, and the output of our work.

Perhaps the most convicting chapter in the book for me was chapter 2, "Greed: The Desire for More." In this chapter, greed is defined as "the drive to achieve and acquire more, in the shortest time possible."[2] Greed is a restless grass-is-always-greener mentality, causing us to "feel discontented with what we have and obsessed with what we do not yet have."[3] The authors quote the fourth-century Christian monk Evagrius of Pontus who describes greedy people as those who are always "thinking about what does not yet exist."[4] The other side of the greed coin, a personal struggle of mine, is stinginess, a "fear and aversion to risk" that hinders us from being generous with what God has given us.[5]

The parallel chapters to the deadly sin of greed are the fruit of "Goodness" and the outcome of "Persistent Gratitude". In order to grow spiritually as we work, we must become those who "give rather than take, who share rather than hoard."[6] This will result in certain practices such as giving some of our wages to the poor, "loving God over all competing loves," and performing our work with "faith, hope, and love." In cultivating gratitude, we will recognize that all we have is a gift from God, leaving no room for pride. This gratitude, if persistent, will result in giving thanks to God for such things as our co-workers' success, a challenging task, a coffee break, a successful (or failed!) project, and even the ability to work.[7]

One might read the above descriptions of the necessity to recognize our sinfulness, and the need to cultivate the fruits of goodness and gratitude, as potentially exhausting. Doesn't this just add more work to my work? The good news, however, is that we aren't alone in becoming good and grateful people. If we were, our goodness could

---

[1] Ibid., 11.
[2] Ibid., 22.
[3] Ibid., 22.
[4] Ibid., 22.
[5] Ibid., 24.
[6] Ibid., 76.
[7] Ibid., 79-80.

be an opportunity for further pride and faux autonomy. As the authors write, "Christian spirituality is the Spirit of God working to transform us from within; our inner transformation then affects everything we do and why we do it."[1] As we work, the Holy Spirit is also working to make us more like Christ, the supreme exemplar of a good worker.[2]

To conclude, the wisdom of the Christian tradition leads us to believe that all of life is left untouched by our sinfulness. "Follow your passion" is bad advice for a myriad of reasons, not least of which is that our passions are often the problem. A Christian spirituality of work will mean confronting our own sinfulness at work, how it can creep into our thoughts, emotions, relationships, and outputs. It will also require resting in the God who is faithful to forgive and transform us hour-by-hour and minute-by-minute. It will lead us to believe that all of God's world is left untouched by his grace—even the workplace.

---

[1] As a brief aside for Conciliar Post readers, the book is perhaps best viewed as an ecumenical devotional. Each chapter utilizes the wisdom of a prominent Christian figure, from Martin Luther to Mother Teresa to Matthew the Poor. The writers do not operate as if "faith and work" conversations are the exclusive right of Protestants, but draw from Protestants, Catholic, and Orthodox equally. Each chapter is an exercise in gleaning from the wisdom of the Christian tradition, and seeking to apply it to one's life.

[2] Ibid., 172.

A Christian Defense of Video Games
Chris Casberg

Friends, family, fellow writers, and dear readers: I have a secret that I fear I can no longer hold in. Though we have long peacefully sipped our tea here in this ecumenical garden of theology and philosophy and literature, quoting our Chesterton and Tolkien as we read our Milton and laugh gaily together about the foibles of our denominations and, yea, even of the world, an unspoken darkness lingered just below the surface of this otherwise innocent and endearing young man from the Midwest.

I pray that you are seated, my brothers and sisters in Christ, for the unveiling of this secret may render your knees weak. Your legs may wither away altogether. I do not confess this without shame; indeed I am both very afraid and deeply abashed. The psalmist declares "The sacrifices of God are a broken spirit; a broken and contrite heart, O God, you will not despise" (Psalm 51:17). I bring my confession to you with a humble, heart-filled sorrow.

You see, I play video games. Please forgive me.

Wow! I can hear the weeping and gnashing of teeth from here. Whoever is crying "But you were such a good Christian boy!" is exceptionally shrill. However, there is a typical baritone element missing from the outcry that I'm hearing. Ah, wait, there it is: the chorus of grey-haired salesman of wisdom divorced from cultural shifts crying out, "Real men don't waste their time with video games!" I should have expected the delay; I'm told one tends to slow down as one gets on in years.

I recognize that, for some, being an adult male who plays video games is a sin whose magnitude lags only slightly behind blasphemy of the Holy Spirit. Now, I understand the gravity of the transgression; I truly do. However, if it is not too unpardonable, I would like to take the remaining space to offer a justification for my actions, as scant and tepid as it may be.

The first thing I want to address is really a small tangent about Christian manhood and manliness, a topic which I am genuinely afraid will someday, in a very literal sense, bore me to death. It is a struggle to keep my eyes open when someone speaks on this topic, and I fear the consequences of someone chattering on about Christian manhood and manliness while I drive down the interstate will be nothing less than catastrophic. This is why I only listen to NPR or the rock station while in the car, by the way.

I have two issues with the Christian manhood and manliness (henceforth "CMM") approach, as ventured by say, Eric Metaxas, the author of *Seven Men: And the Secret of their Greatness*. One: this conception of manliness is an anachronism; it's a view of masculinity ripped from an idealized, myopic version of the mid-20th century, when America was on top and capitalism fought the good fight against communism. Gosh darnit, back then men were men, and it was great, even though African Americans couldn't use the front door. It's an arbitrary historical fiction with Bible verses stapled to the manuscript. Honestly, it is no surprise to me that an ideology rusted to an imagined bygone era is incapable of a judicious approach to a technologically advanced medium like video games.

Second, singling out video games for some sort of transgression against manliness does not quite jibe with reality. Allow me to share a small example. My experience in the United States Marine Corps may be comparatively limited—I was only on active duty for five years—but in my experience, most Marines played video games. Our Master Gunnery Sergeant, a man whose musculature I am convinced was made entirely of steel or some other ferrous metal, was a notorious fan of World of Warcraft. The author of the comic Terminal Lance, a former infantry Marine, often writes about playing video games in the Corps.

As I said earlier, the CMM conversation bores me terribly, so I will abstain from further discussion on the matter. However, if Eric Metaxas or anyone else would like to discuss the manliness of playing video games, I cordially invite them to take up the issue with the United States Marine Corps.

Let's move on to the interesting part of this conversation, which is to ask, "Why *shouldn't* good Christians scorn you and every other indulger of video games and cast you all out of our congregations like the Satan worshippers you are?" That is an excellent question, and I'm glad I asked it. The answers, of course, are legion.

Perhaps that was a poor choice of words.

Video games are a medium, not a message. As today we largely have the good sense not to automatically cry anathema when we discuss the merits of film, photography, or the novel, we must understand that video games are an art form, and that the form itself is neutral. It cannot be dismissed wholesale. As a vehicle of meaning, video games aren't inherently good, bad, wasteful, or emasculating. The meaning, or at least the symbolism, is supplied by the creator *through* the form. There are admittedly many distasteful, reprobate examples of video games; I have personally enjoyed many of them.

However, we do not throw the baby out with the bathwater. We don't abandon the novel because Harlequin Romance churns out stinkers at a supernatural rate. We don't give up on film because of Ed Wood. We do not wash our hands of sculpture just because teenage boys given a lump of clay will inevitably make the same oblong shape. The poor craftsmanship or immature subject matter of one or more artists is not a strike against the medium.

Fantastic work is being done in the field of video games, and there are a great many games worthy of critical analysis for their interpretation and implementation of themes. *Gone Home*, for example, is an exploration of identity and acceptance. *Braid* ingeniously weaves the themes of regret, alcoholism, and broken relationships into a game where the player literally tries to turn back the clock. *Everybody's Gone to the Rapture* is a meditation on loss, loneliness, and reconciliation at the end of all things. Today's games are rich and artful, and they have the ability to hammer the player with great emotional force. There is simply no excuse to dismiss them so off-handedly.

Last year, I heard a lecture on the history of television in the context of American Christianity. (I don't recall the name of the lecturer and I don't have my notes, so you'll have to bear with my imprecision.) The lecturer painted a picture of Christians scorning television and resisting it, preferring instead to stick to the radio waves. Fast forward to the dawn of the 21st century, authentic Christianity has almost zero presence in mainstream television, despite it being the predominant faith of the country. If Christians can't get over the mental hurdle of appreciating video games, we risk losing our presence and influence in another medium destined for ubiquity.

Finally, if you are a believer who is unimpressed with my justification and still repulsed by video games, I resort to this: have a heart. Don't be dismissive, and don't rush to judgment. Be quick to hear and slow to speak (James 1:19). You might not like them, but I bet you love somebody who does. Condescend to their level and engage with them there. This should be a familiar model to Christians.

Art is beautiful. It connects us to one another and it connects us to God. Art is also something we can offer up to God in praise and service. I believe that video games are an art medium, and it's my hope that Christians are able to understand them as such, even if they don't play them themselves. Maybe the medium hasn't matured enough to make its worth self-evident. Maybe the generation of cranky old gatekeepers of art and culture must retire first. Maybe both are true, or neither are. Whatever the case, I think it's high time more Christians took video games seriously.

Confessions of a Single Mom
Rebecca Barrett

You know that feeling of knowing that serious pain is coming and there is no way out of it? Like knowing throughout a pregnancy that labor pains are coming one day and there is no way to make it out without feeling them? The type of situations that you dread but know deep down you're just going to have to get through them? The ones where trying to think things through and analyze and rationalize how you are going to handle them only makes them worse? Then ones you dismiss and say, "I'll cross that bridge when I get there"?

Mine was knowing that there would be a day when my beautiful little girl realized that our family was not complete. That her friends at school all had something that she did not: a father. "Why don't I have a daddy?" haunted my thoughts and followed me to sleep at night. I was paralyzed by the fear of how she would respond and terrified that I would not know how to answer her. The more that I thought about it and the vast assortment of answers I could give, one thing was unavoidable: that moment when I would have to tell the most precious little girl in the world her daddy abandoned her. There was no ending that I could foresee in which her heart did not get broken. So, in my weak attempt to cope, I just quit thinking about it. Sure enough that day came, and sooner than later.

Shortly after leaving all of my family and friends to pursue an incredible job opportunity in New Mexico, we were invited to dinner with a family who were members of the church we were attending. We had completed the meal and were sitting around the table talking when my darling little Paizley with two other girls came up to the dinner table, interrupted the conversation and asked "Mommy, I don't have a daddy. Why don't I have a daddy?" Before I could respond one of the other little girls instantly chimed in "Is Paizley's daddy dead?" Oh, how badly I wanted to say yes! That would have been an easy answer invoking sympathy from everyone around the table rather than the true answer that is directly connected to the most painful memories of my life. Memories that I definitely did not want to share with a group of people I did not know. Although I cannot remember verbatim my answer, I clearly remember Paizley taking my hand, looking me in the eye and saying "That's okay. God is my real daddy anyway."

Being a single mom is hard. Having to fill the role of protector and provider as well as nurturer is difficult. The most painful part of the struggle is the fact that I can be the best mother ever who does everything right all the time (which I am so very far from) and it still would not be good enough. Paizley has needs which, no matter how hard I try, I can never, and will never, meet. Though it has only been three years since my divorce, it feels like an eternity. There are days when it seems like there is no end in sight. I find myself waiting to be rescued by prince charming. Waiting for the struggle to end, for the exhaustion to end. To not feel like I am in this alone. This is when the Lord reminded me that there is only one man who can save me. There is only one man who can meet every need that Paizley has. And he already did it.

I am learning what it means to find satisfaction in Christ alone. To walk in His protection and provision. To love Him with everything in me and desire Him above all else. And although I have the incredible opportunity to experience Him in such a personal way, there is something far more magnificent that He is showing me. The presence of Jesus Christ in Paizley's life is undeniable. Words simply cannot explain the power of witnessing the grace of Christ completely enveloping my child, protecting her from my bad decisions, from her father's bad decisions, from consequences she should never have to pay. She talks to Jesus nonstop—as if He were flesh and blood holding her hand, walking her through life.

So yes, my car smells like spoiled milk. Yes, when told to get dressed the other morning, Paizley put on a clean set of pajamas and I did not notice until I was dropping her off at school. Yes, we eat between eight and ten meals a week in the car (most of which are fast food). Yes, the highlight of my Friday nights is watching animated movies. Yes, my dryer is full of clothes that were washed two weeks ago. And yes, I have not done dishes in over a week and I grocery shop once every two months. But, I also hear a sweet voice in my house clearly singing "holy, holy, holy is the Lord Almighty" or "by your grace I'm saved, by your grace I'm saved."

It is true, I am no super mom. I am not a sufficient substitute for a dad. But that is what makes our lives so beautiful. I cannot do it. But Jesus can. I do not have to do it, because Jesus does. Where I fall short, where I can go no further, Jesus carries us through. In the most broken parts of our lives, He is there doing a mighty work. Being a single parent is hard. It is not what God intended a family to look like. But I have learned that what I have destroyed He can make beautiful. In what I have caused shame, He can work for His glory. He is the husband to the husbandless and the father to the fatherless.

The Insufficiency of Spontaneous Prayer
Michael Landsman

"Now if we imagine that we can sustain spontaneous prayer throughout our life, we are in childish delusion."
Anthony Bloom[1]

In the Charismatic Tradition there are generally two ways of prayer echoing the words of St. Paul in I Corinthians 14:15: praying with the Spirit and praying with the understanding (or mind). Praying with the Spirit is understood as praying in tongues, or as praying in a private prayer language given upon reception of the Baptism of the Holy Spirit subsequent to the salvation experience. Praying with the understanding is understood as praying with the mind, or as praying in human language(s). In this system there are many different types of prayer: intercessory, faith, agreement—but the method of those types of prayer falls into one of the two mentioned above—Spirit or understanding (though this can be a bit amorphous in practice).

One method of prayer that was frowned upon, while being instructed on how to pray, was praying prepared or pre-written prayers—unless of course it was the Our Father or St. Paul's prayers in his Epistles. Even then, the Our Father was taken as more of a prayer guide instead of an actual prayer one should pray. I can still remember my lessons, breaking down the Lord's prayer line by line as an instruction for how to pray, because to pray it as an actual prayer would be vain repetition, an action performed by rote rather than relationship. In other words we were taught, using the Lord's prayer as a guideline, to structure spontaneous prayer. This type of spontaneous prayer has a definite structure to it and we were encouraged to follow this general structure in our own prayer life. One of the great ironies was that in following a structure our spontaneous prayers became, in a way, prepared prayers as the patterns we utilized were dependent on knowledge of biblical texts we would use when we prayed. In the Charismatic Tradition, then, the purest form of spontaneous prayer would be praying in tongues. There is no structure, no pattern, and

---

[1] Bloom, Anthony. *Beginning to Pray* (Mahwah: Paulist Press, 1970), 57.

Faith Across Traditions

no order as the mind is not engaged since the practice is seen as communicating directly with God.

So what good are spontaneous prayers if spontaneous prayers aren't actually spontaneous? What does spontaneous prayer even look like? In his book *Beginning to Pray*, Metropolitan Anthony Bloom writes that spontaneous prayer is only possible in two situations:

> *"Either at moments when we have become vividly aware of God, when this awareness calls out of us a response of worship, of joy… or when we become aware suddenly of the deathly danger in which we are when we come to God, moments when we suddenly shout from the depths of despair and dereliction."*[1]

I find it fascinating that he notes that true spontaneous prayer comes either from a response of joy or from the exact opposite, despair. If Metropolitan Anthony is correct then true spontaneous prayer may be something wild and unstructured, something that rises from the deepest place within us as we become aware of God's presence, his grace, or experience the depths of his love. It also arises from the place where we feel his absence, sense our unworthiness, or the realization that our sinful actions drive us from him. At this point Charismatics would probably say that this is where speaking in tongues comes into play, since speaking in tongues is seen as direct communication with God. Speaking in tongues needs no priming, it has no form to it, it simply arises as needed. But if actual spontaneous prayer functions differently than how speaking in tongues functions, then that means that speaking in tongues cannot be substituted for actual spontaneous prayer. And spontaneous prayer should occur in actual known languages.

At this point Charismatics may appeal to Romans 8:26, where St. Paul speaks of the Spirit groaning within us, but this text says that the Spirit is the one doing the praying—not the person whom the Spirit abides within. In addition to this, the Spirit is doing so with inexpressible groanings, and praying in tongues is not unintelligible speech but a personal prayer language. With this in mind, true spontaneous prayer should be intelligible. And true spontaneous prayer—since it stirred by powerful positive or negative experiences of God's presence—should lead us to gratitude for his goodness and joyful celebration of life in Christ, or should drive us to our knees in

---

[1] Bloom, Anthony. *Beginning to Pray* (Mahwah: Paulist Press, 1970), 56.

repentance as we seek to be cleansed of wicked in our hearts. We cannot live on those two extremes of prayer, we would burn out, but as we incorporate the expression of spontaneous prayer into a robust prayer rule or personal discipline we may have glimpses of God's active care and presence in our lives.

Faith Across Traditions

A Sonnet on the Occasion of Super Tuesday
Chris Casberg

For this pack of wolves, it is now the time
To the cameras howl and bear shiny teeth
All are future kings, if just in their minds
But none are better than a common thief
I'll be at my desk away from all the din
Fighting ignorance, which is our disease
Not with sword and shield, but the humble pen.

Let us not forget holy charities
Love the Lord thy God with mind, soul, and strength
Remember how far the Lord went for you
Even down to the blackest hellish lengths
He's the one who said, Love thy neighbor, too.

Hatred and despair are what mark this year,
But recall: perfect love casts out all fear.

Faith Across Traditions

Faith in the Public Square

It is often said that in polite company, you should avoid discussing religion and politics. The essays in this section resist that tactic, instead opting for the prophetic witness of faith in the public square. Conservatives, progressives, the politically homeless, those outside the American political sphere—all can find a home in Christ's Kingdom.

Essays

Could Liberals and Conservatives Follow the Same Christ, *Tillman*

An Open Letter to Christian Bakers in Indiana, *Johnson*

Dear White Christians, It's Time for Us to Listen, *Quick*

Social Justice Without Resurrection Is Dead, *Aldhizer*

Gnostic Anthropology and Identity Politics, *Ehrett*

CRT and Its Dissidents, *Walker*

Faith Across Traditions

Could Liberals and Conservatives Follow the Same Christ?
Micah Tillman

If you worship the Jesus-Who-Lived, you end up voting like a liberal Democrat. To become a conservative Republican, in contrast, it helps to worship the Jesus-Who-Died and/or -Is-Coming-Again. That is what I argued in a previous article time. Today, I'd like to explore four possible paths for achieving political unity.

First, if we could prove that the other side's Christ was a fraud, we might be able to convert them to our political point of view. Second, if we could demonstrate that the three Christs were one—even without reinterpretation—we might be able to blend our two sides together. Third, if we could find some new principle for reinterpreting all three Christs, we might be able to move everyone to a new side. And fourth, if we could show that one Christ was key to reinterpreting the other two, we could undermine the other side and perhaps get them to adopt our way of voting.

Let's start with option 1.

Proving a Fraud
If we could show that the Jesus-Who-Lived simply does not exist, the conservatives would win and we'd all have to join the Republican party. If we could show that the Jesus-Who-Died simply did not exist, however, we would undercut the worries about immorality and divine judgement behind so much of the Republican "values voter" platform. To do either, we would need to appeal to Scripture—at least if we are going to satisfy *sola scriptura* Protestants. We would need to show that you just don't find one of these three Christs in the Bible.

Unfortunately, however, each Christ has a pretty well-defined home in Scripture, as we saw last time. All three are interpretations of well-attested biblical data. We *might* be able to get rid of the Jesus-Who-Is-Coming-Again, since it relies so heavily on the book of Revelation and that book is both historically-contested and notoriously-difficult to interpret. But even if the Church Fathers debated whether it really belonged in the Canon, we seem stuck with it now.[1]

Instead of throwing out one book, of course, we *could* follow a certain strand of "Higher Criticism" and reject the historical reliability of the entire New Testament. With the primary scriptural bases for all three Christs gone, however, most of Protestant Christianity would disappear and I'm not sure how erstwhile Protestants would vote. We tend to think of those who leave mainstream Christianity via "Higher Criticism" as theological liberals, but I'm not sure if that branch of liberalism is connected to the political variety.

Uniting the Three
We might, therefore, want to try the opposite approach. Instead of throwing out one or more of the Christs, perhaps we should add the other side's Christ(s) to our own. The Jesus-Who-Lived had to come from somewhere and go to somewhere, after all, and the Jesus-Who-Died (and thus -Who-Was-Born), gives us that.

Even if we combine multiple Christs into one, however, we still are left with the question of how to tell the story. What was the moral? Was Jesus born in order to show us how to live, even though this new way of life got him killed? Or was Jesus born in order to die, and had to live thirty-three years waiting in between?

When I think of using personal history to unite the three Christs, I tend to think of Thomas Reid's objection to John Locke's theory of personal identity. The objection goes roughly like this:

Locke believes that memory is what makes a person the *same* person over time. If you can remember your earlier life, then the person who lived that life is the same as you. So, if you-as-an-adult remember being a child, then your child self is the same as your adult self. "A = B." And if you-as-a-senior remember being a younger adult, then your younger adult self is the same as your senior self. "B = C." But what if you-as-a-senior do not remember being a child? In that case, it seems

---

[1] To start, see the Wikipedia articles for "Antilegomena" and "Luther's canon", as well as the section on the book's "Canonical history" in the Wikipedia article on the book itself. Then, of course, you'll want to move on to more scholarly sources.

that your child self is not the same person as your senior self. A = B, and B = C, but A ≠ C.[1]

That's a technical objection to one philosophical theory, but compare it with how we often think of musicians. "If you want to hear what they *really* sound like, you have to listen to their albums before x; x was their first album on a major label—after they sold out." We do the same thing with our heroes when we find out they "went bad" at the end—and thus conclude they were not *really* worthy of our respect all along. And we do the opposite with political leaders and loved ones when we excuse their past actions in light of "the person they have become."

In our attempt to follow the *full* Christ, in other words, we would slide quite easily into debates about which phase of Christ's personal history was the *real* Christ. You might say we *could* treat all three Christs as coequal, but I don't think this is possible, given the incompatibilities I discussed last time. In trying to put the Christs together, we will be forced to reinterpret at least one of the three to create a coherent whole. It's time, therefore, that we ask what principle we ought to use to interpret our various Christs.

An Outside Principle
If you've hung around *Conciliar Post* for long, you will have noticed that Christendom and Protestantism are not coextensive. There are other ways of being Christian, and perhaps we could find in them a way of seeing Jesus that would revamp and reconcile the three Protestant Christs.

Catholicism
The most obvious place to begin would be Catholicism, since it is "closest to home" for Protestants. Alas, however, you find the same three Christs in Catholic history. If one Catholic tradition didn't focus on the Jesus-Who-Died, the medieval Catholic Church could never have used indulgences or excommunication like it did. If another Catholic tradition didn't focus on the Jesus-Who-Is-Coming-Again, medieval Catholicism could never have spent so much blood and effort trying to impose the Kingdom of God. And if a third Catholic

---

[1] See Rebecca Copenhaver, "Reid on Memory and Personal Identity," *Stanford Encyclopedia of Philosophy*, https://plato.stanford.edu/entries/reid-memory-identity/.

tradition didn't focus on the Jesus-Who-Lived, medieval Catholicism could never have produced Sts. Benedict and Francis.

Protestantism inherits the three-Jesus problem from Catholicism, in other words. Having spent years studying in a Catholic university, furthermore, I know that Catholics also divide politically along the liberal/conservative line. If Catholicism hasn't solved the problem of division for those inside, therefore, I doubt it is going to help us Protestants who are standing outside.

Eastern Orthodoxy
It would make sense, therefore, to turn to the East and ask for their wisdom. I've heard, for example, that Eastern Orthodoxy lacks the Augustinian notion of original sin—or at least, original guilt.[1] That might imply that the Eastern Church doesn't focus so much on the Jesus-Who-Died. Alternatively, it might imply that the Orthodox understanding of the Jesus-Who-Died is not that Jesus fulfilled the Law to save us from being damned for breaking the Law, but that Jesus did something else by dying. But what else?

It has been suggested to me by an Orthodox friend,[2] for example, that we might choose to follow "the Jesus-Who-Heals." Referring to Isaiah 53:5, St. Peter writes: "He himself bore our sins in his body on the cross, so that, free from sins, we might live for righteousness; by his wounds you have been healed" (1 Pet. 2:24, NRSV). Wasn't healing what the Jesus-Who-Lived was all about (Matt. 4:23–24; 8:16; 9:11–13, 35; 10:1–8; 14:14; 25:35–45), and might the Jesus-Who-Is-Coming-Again have the mission of finally healing the whole of Creation (Rom. 8:18–25; cf. Is. 65:17; 2 Cor. 5:17, 2 Pet. 3:13; Rev. 21:5)?

How would we vote if we really believed that Jesus is primarily about healing? Could we vote to repeal the ACA, for example, or environmental regulations? Would we vote to expand funding for defense, or to put the same money into the work of reconciliation (e.g., the Peace Corps; cf. Rom. 5:11, 2 Cor. 5:18–19)? How would we approach caring for mothers and the unborn? What about food

---

[1] See, for instance, the Q&A on "Original Sin" at the Orthodox Church in America website: https://oca.org/questions/teaching/original-sin.
[2] Protestants don't have relics or shrines they can appeal to for healing, for instance.

stamps and low-income housing? How would we ensure the health of markets, or demand that our legal system interact with criminals?

Unfortunately, I can't answer those questions by pointing to how the Orthodox vote here in the States. I simply don't know enough either about Orthodox theology or Orthodox political demography. Since *Conciliar Post* is a forum for dialogue, therefore, I would like to ask those of you who belong to Orthodoxy for your input. If your congregations had to fill in the blank in "the Jesus-Who-_____," how would they do it? What was Jesus *actually* all about? And how do your fellow congregants tend to vote in response?

Reinterpreting the Two in Light of One

I think reinterpreting all three Christs in terms of healing is very promising. It adopts an interpretive principle that Catholics have historically been more comfortable with than Protestants,[1] but it also fits with the healing-focus often seen in the Charismatic branch of Protestantism. So, it is not entirely foreign to the West.

However, while we await rescue from the East, I would like to point out one other approach to reinterpretation. This approach relies on hermeneutics, as practiced both in biblical studies and Continental philosophy.[2]

Where We Start Reading

Last time, I pointed out that the three Protestant Christs live in different parts of Scripture. A corollary of that point is the following: where you begin reading the Bible determines which Christ you adopt. That is, the portion of scripture through which you read the other passages determines how you understand Jesus.

Some churches start with the Sermon on the Mount and read the New Testament forward. This gives you the Jesus-Who Lived. Others start in the Book of Revelation and read backward. This gives you the Jesus-Who-Is-Coming-Again. Still others start in the Epistle to the Romans, and read out in both directions. This gives you the Jesus-Who-Died.

---

[1] See C. Mantzavinos, "Hermeneutics," *Stanford Encyclopedia of Philosophy*, https://plato.stanford.edu/entries/hermeneutics/.

[2] See Aristotle, *Politics* I.2, See C. Mantzavinos, "Hermeneutics," *Stanford Encyclopedia of Philosophy*, https://plato.stanford.edu/entries/hermeneutics/.

Sometimes, of course, a church will start in a particular place and simply stay there, spinning its wheels. Conservative "End Times" churches do this, but so do liberal "Social Justice" congregations. However, I don't think this is common. In my experience, churches tend to read the whole of Scripture. It's just that if you read one passage through the lens of another, you may get something completely different out of it than a person who did not have that lens.

Where Should We Start?

So, where *should* we start reading the Bible? Which passages ought to be the lens through which we read the others? You might say we ought to read each passage on its own terms—but this cannot mean reading without context. And you might say that we ought to start with the whole of Scripture—but our finite minds mean we always enter the Bible at a particular spot. So, we must choose our entry point carefully.

I think starting in Revelation and reading the Bible backward is obviously wrong. However, any good Aristotelian will tell you that you *have* to understand a thing's end in order to properly comprehend it.[1] I similarly think that starting in Romans and reading out is wrong. Romans is an interpretation of the data provided by the Gospels, and interpretations are secondary to data. However, any good biblical scholar will tell you that Romans was written before the Gospels,[2] and any good philosopher of science will tell you that your interpretations can also determine the data you collect.[3]

In spite of all this, I can't escape the feeling that when reading Scripture, you should begin at the beginning, either of the Old Testament or of the New. Since we Christians are Christ-followers, specifically, I think this means we ought to start with Matthew. We should then read the Old Testament the way Jesus did, and read the Pauline and Johannine literature through the lens of the Gospels.

---

[1] See the Wikipedia article on the subject, as a place to start: https://en.wikipedia.org/wiki/Dating_the_Bible#Table_IV:_New_Testament.
[2] See Jim Bogen, "Theory and Observation in Science," *Stanford Encyclopedia of Philosophy*, https://plato.stanford.edu/entries/science-theory-observation/.
[3] See Aristotle, *Nicomachean Ethics*, http://classics.mit.edu/Aristotle/nicomachaen.html.

That is, I side with the Jesus-Who-Lived. Where I depart from those who would *exclusively* follow this Christ is in insisting on the inescapability of the other two. It's just I think those Christs have to be reinterpreted in light of the Christ who came to give us life more abundantly (John 10:10). I think Jesus came to usher us into a new way of living that begins now (Luke 17:21) and reaches its perfection when Creation is renewed. Tying the Jesus-Who-Lived to the Jesus-Who-Is-Coming-Again then gives us a context for interpreting the Jesus-Who-Died. Ethics—understood in an Aristotelian sense—of entering into the life of Christ (cf. Gal. 2:19-20), taking his yoke upon us (Matt. 11:28–30), lays the groundwork for soteriology.

Conclusion

The approach I suggest is, in essence, a reinterpretation of the notion of eternal life (cf. John 17:3), which extends it backward into the present and forward through the resurrection.[1] To cite my sources, I believe it is an approach inspired by Thomas Aquinas,[2] C. S. Lewis,[3] and N. T. Wright,[4] on the one hand, and Aristotle,[5] Kant,[6] and

---

[1] See my previous article for *Conciliar Post*, "The Resurrection and Nietzsche's Wager," https://conciliarpost.com/theology-spirituality/the-resurrection-and-nietzsches-wager/.

[2] See his *Treatise on the Virtues* in *Summa Theologica*. This is qq. 48–67 of the *Prima Secundae Partis* in the *Summa*, which can be found in the "Habits" section at this link: http://www.newadvent.org/summa/2.htm.

[3] Perhaps I should point to Lewis's *The Great Divorce* here, but I'm sure many of his essays have influence me as well.

[4] See Wrights work both on the Resurrection (*The Resurrection of the Son of God* [Minneapolis: Fortress Press, 2003]) and Paul (you can start with his lecture, "New Perspectives on Paul," at http://ntwrightpage.com/2016/07/12/new-perspectives-on-paul/).

[5] I find his view of ethics so compelling. See, as noted above, his *Nicomachean Ethics*, at, http://classics.mit.edu/Aristotle/nicomachaen.html.

[6] Specifically, Kant's view of the Kingdom of Ends has significantly impacted the way I think about the Kingdom of Heaven, what it would mean for the Kingdom to be "among us" (Luke 17:20–21). To read about Kant's Kingdom of Ends, do a ctrl-F/cmd-F search for "kingdom of ends" on this page: http://philosophy.eserver.org/kant/metaphys-of-morals.txt. If you have Kant's *Groundwork for the Metaphysics of Morals*, you can read the relevant passage there. It is in the Second Section, starting on p. 432 of the Akademie edition, where Kant is introducing the third formulation of the Categorical Imperative.

Nietzsche[1] (surprisingly), on the other. In making *life* its principle, furthermore, I think it works well with the suggestion we saw before: that Jesus was primarily about healing.[2]

However, I know of no single systematic theology text that has adopted this point of view—perhaps N. T. Wright has written one?[3]—so I do not know how viable it ultimately is. And that means I do not know how convincing it could be made to anyone who does not already feel its pull. Until I have the time to read the rest of Wright's works, or the money to get a second Ph.D. from a seminary and write the required text,[4] therefore, I welcome your input and suggestions. If we are ever to achieve theological and political unity, surely it will be through dialogue.

---

[1] Life—that is, *lively* life (healthy, vigorous life)—is the source of all value. See his *On the Advantage and Disadvantage of History for Life* (or *On the Use and Abuse of History for Life*, depending on your translation). You can find one translation here: https://records.viu.ca/~Johnstoi/nietzsche/history.htm.

[2] That is, I think it is one of history's great ironies—indeed, great tragedies—that Nietzsche could come so close to true Christianity without realizing it. See note 4, above.

[3] In a comment on the previous article (https://conciliarpost.com/philosophy/liberals-conservatives-follow-christ/#comment), Peter Schellhase suggests that N. T. Wright might have already done the work. I suspect he is right, given what I've read of Wright.

[4] Or, rather, to collect Wright's various writings into a systematic theology, like Peter Lombard did with his *Sentences*. Perhaps we could start with Wright's essay, "Historical Paul and 'Systematic Theology'," http://ntwrightpage.com/2017/02/24/historical-paul-and-systematic-theology/.

An Open Letter to Christian Bakers in Indiana
Russell Johnson

Dear Bakers,
You have been getting a lot of attention recently, especially since the new law passed that would likely allow you to refuse to make cakes for gay weddings. It's certainly worth asking how to interpret the First Amendment on this issue, but perhaps first we should ask what the gospels say.

As you may remember, Jesus's first miracle was at a wedding party. He provided wine for a bunch of people who were already drunk. Not exactly where you'd expect a Messiah begin, but His mom told him to, and it's not wise to argue with a Jewish mother.

Did Jesus grow out of this partygoing phase? By all accounts, no. At every stage in the gospels we find him with prostitutes, tax collectors, Roman soldiers, and anarchists. I know what you're thinking—Jesus didn't approve of their lifestyles. And you're right. But that didn't stop Him from spending time with them and caring for them. Jesus never let the fact that people are sinners keep Him from meeting them where they are, sharing food with them, laughing and crying with them. His "No" to people's self-destructive behaviors and the lies they trapped themselves in always came from within a full-blooded "Yes" to their identity as beloved children of God. It's one note of condemnation within a grand symphony of compassion.

If we see it this way, Jesus's bringing the booze to the wedding party fits in perfectly with the rest of His life. This is the same Jesus who taught us to give our cloaks to those who steal our tunics. The same Jesus who healed the ear of one of his captors. The same Jesus who got down on his knees and washed Judas's feet the night He was betrayed.

God doesn't have to approve of our lifestyles in order to go out of His way to serve us. That's not just a footnote in the gospels—it's the whole good news. And I am thankful for it every day because God does not fully approve of my lifestyle—my pride, my apathy, my hardheartedness—but He stays with me. He supports me. And He loves me. We have a God who wanders with those who are wandering... and parties with those who are partying.

So what about gay people asking you to make their wedding cake? I'm not saying you have to condone their behavior, nor that you have to pretend to. But you have to serve them with the same messy, humble, all-forgiving love that Jesus shows you. My advice: regardless of the laws, bake the cake. Bake the biggest, tastiest, gayest cake you can, and do it for the glory of God. Because Jesus's first miracle was at a wedding, and according to Revelation 19, His last miracle will be at a wedding too. He will look at a mess of sinners like us and once again say, "It is good." As we live between those two weddings, we should take every opportunity to celebrate. We can rejoice with those who rejoice, because we know God is bringing new wine to the reception.

Peace,
Russell

Dear White Christians, It's Time for Us to Listen
Jacob Quick

Saying that the last few months in America have been horrific and tragic is an understatement. America is, once again, confronted with the needless deaths of innocent people. The racial tensions in America have been laid bare for all to see again, whether we acknowledge them or not. But where do we go from here? I want to say what so many have already said before, and are still saying today, but is all too often ignored: it's time for white Christians in America to listen.

Racism is Alive and Well
It's unfortunate to see that so many firmly believe that racism is, for the most part, a bygone part of American history. "Sure", you might say, "there are still racists. But systemic racism? That went away with Jim Crow." Those who adopt this belief then chastise people who bring race into the conversation, claiming that they are just "race baiting," "racemongerers," or "playing the race card." But behind this belief is a misunderstanding of sin and an unloving posture toward non-white Americans.

Sin is Generational
The toxicity of sin is prevalent in the stories of Jacob and his sons (Gen. 27, 37). Jacob, motivated by jealousy and covetousness, slaughtered a goat and used its fur to deceive his father, Isaac, into giving to Jacob what belonged to Jacob's older brother. Many years later, Jacob's sons, motivated by jealousy and covetousness, slaughtered a goat and used its blood to deceive Jacob into believing that his favorite son, Joseph, had been murdered. Thus Jacob the deceiver was deceived. The literary irony in these stories demonstrates the degree to which sin is ingrained and perpetuated from generation to generation.

In *Not The Way It's Supposed to Be: A Breviary of Sin*, Cornelius Plantinga uses the analogy of pollution to describe sin.[1] Sin infects and alters the very fabric of our families, relationships, and societies. Surprisingly, defining sin as "missing the mark" misses the point. Sin does not merely concern an individual failing to live up to a certain standard (although that is a part of it), but it infiltrates communities, rupturing the very love and peace which God intends. *My question is this: if sin is a pollutant, a toxin which infects and perpetuates evil, then how can we legitimately claim that racism is no longer an issue in the United States?*

To use one example, it wasn't until 1964 that the US outlawed racial discrimination. This means that every category of opportunity—whether financial, educational, or any other—that was available to whites in the 1960s was not available to so many non-white Americans at that time. *Believing that government-sanctioned discrimination against certain races 60 years ago has no systemic impact on their descendants today underestimates the toxicity of sin.* No, America still has a long way to go before it can claim any semblance of the equality of opportunity.

Here's another example. The war on drugs has been widely recognized as having an explicitly racist agenda, targeting black communities. The evidence suggests as much.[2] Recently, an old interview was published in which one of Nixon's top advisors explained that the United State's War on Drugs was initiated in order to disrupt black communities. Here's a portion of the article about the interview,

> "The Nixon campaign in 1968, and the Nixon White House after that, had two enemies: the antiwar left and black people," former Nixon domestic policy chief John Ehrlichman told Harper's writer Dan Baum for the April cover story published Tuesday.
>
> "You understand what I'm saying? We knew we couldn't make it illegal to be either against the war or black, but by getting the public to associate the hippies with marijuana and blacks with heroin. And then criminalizing both heavily, we could disrupt those communities," Ehrlichman said. "We could

---

[1] Plantinga, Cornelius. *Not The Way It's Supposed To Be: A Breviary Of Sin* (Grand Rapids: Eerdmans, 1995), 39.
[2] See http://www.drugpolicy.org/race-and-drug-war.

arrest their leaders. raid their homes, break up their meetings, and vilify them night after night on the evening news. Did we know we were lying about the drugs? Of course we did."[1]

The significance of this cannot be overstated: Nixon's domestic policy chief stated that, in 1968, *the federal government deliberately issued a decree with the specific intention of targeting, disrupting, and destroying black communities.* This "war on drugs" was only denounced by the US government in 2011. The systemic racism of the war on drugs is blatant, undeniable, and, unfortunately, still in effect today. The US is attempting to mitigate and alter this dreadful policy, but it's difficult to unearth and overturn four decades of deliberately racial persecution carried out by one of the most powerful governments in the world. After all, we still have at least one vocal and unashamed white supremacist in congress and a former KKK leader running for Senate.[2]

As an additional but important point, white Americans take an individualistic approach to race, which misconstrues the entire issue. Racism is not only concerned with the conscious beliefs of individuals, but the systemic prevalence of oppression. As Robert DiAngelo explains, "Social scientists understand racism as a multidimensional and highly adaptive *system*—a system that ensures an unequal distribution of resources between racial groups. Because whites built and dominate all significant institutions, (often at the expense of and on the uncompensated labor of other groups), their interests are embedded in the foundation of US society."[3] Racial oppression is written into our laws and sewn into our soil.

Don't take my word for it. Recent studies have shown that Americans display a widespread preference for white people, over and against other races.[4] The more empirical data pours in, the more we realize

---

[1] See http://edition.cnn.com/2016/03/23/politics/john-ehrlichman-richard-nixon-drug-war-blacks-hippie/.
[2] See http://www.nytimes.com/2016/07/19/us/politics/steve-king-nonwhite-subgroups.html and http://edition.cnn.com/2016/07/22/politics/david-duke-senate-race/
[3] See https://goodmenproject.com/featured-content/white-fragility-why-its-so-hard-to-talk-to-white-people-about-racism-twlm/
[4] See https://www.washingtonpost.com/news/wonk/wp/2014/12/08/across-america-whites-are-biased-and-they-dont-even-know-it/

how racism is deeply ingrained in America, whether we acknowledge it or not. This should not be surprising if, after all, sin does not happen in a vacuum. *The belief that centuries of deeply embedded and enforced racism can disappear by the addition of an amendment to the Constitution requires one to have a biblically uninformed understanding of sin and a skewed interpretation of systemic racism in US history.*

The Denial of Sin
On July 4th, the Christian rapper Lecrae caught some fire for posted this tweet:

> Lecrae @lecrae · Jul 4, 2016
> My family on July 4th 1776.

Much of the response, while predictable, was disgusting.[1] Many equivocate between the acknowledgement of American racism with hate speech. Apparently acknowledging and mourning the horrific injustices faced by African-Americans is unnecessarily divisive. However, the fact that white Americans want to silence African-American voices brings up an interesting point: *The denial that racism is still a reality in the US itself constitutes evidence for the fact that racism is alive and well. The fact that Lecrae cannot bring up legitimate, undeniable historical facts because they do not align with a white-washed history shows how calloused white Americans are to the suffering of non-white victims.*

The Path of Repentance
The first step toward repentance is acknowledging sin. We cannot turn from sin that we pretend does not exist. Bryan Stevenson brought up the fact that, in Berlin, *acknowledgement* of the holocaust

---

[1] See http://thegrio.com/2016/07/05/lecrae-christian-rapper-angers-some-fans-with-his-fourth-of-july-tweet/

is everywhere.[1] Such an acknowledgement recognizes the severity of the atrocities committed, and serves as a reminder of the commitment to not repeat the sins of the holocaust. Unfortunately, America does not have the same philosophy regarding our past sins. In fact, even reminding Americans of past atrocities is a surefire method of being ostracized and denounced as treasonous. *We are ignorant of systemic racism today because we are numb to the racism in our history.* The first step is to call out evil for what it is for the sake of healing, love and justice.

After that first step, however, comes a new way of being. Unfortunately, America persistently refuses to engage in the *ongoing process* of repentance for racism. We have failed to honestly and contritely repent of racism, and, as a result, racism continues to permeate our society. The repentance required for these sins is not an event that transpires in one moment—it is not the emancipation proclamation. It is not a piece of legislation. It is not the end of the war on drugs. Repentance is a continual process. A slow, arduous process of examining the past and understanding the way it shapes our present. That process should never end.

Quick to Listen

So what does this new way of being look like for those of us who are white Christians in America? Perhaps we should take James's advice to be slow to speak but quick to listen (James 1:19). We have been on the side of the oppressors, and continue to reap the benefits. Instead of lecturing non-white Americans about how to think and talk about their own suffering, perhaps we should take a more empathetic, caring approach. Have we actually sat down and listened, without interrupting, to a fellow human being describe the racism they experience on a daily basis? Have we sat down to hear a mother who lost her child in a neighborhood shootout describe the opportunities that are closed off to her and her family merely on the basis of their racial profile? I am confident that, were we to do so, we would think twice about throwing "black on black" crime statistics in her face just to silence a voice that's been smothered for centuries. Perhaps, we may even learn the meaning of what it is to weep with those who weep. Have we wept with someone who has experienced racial degradation? Have we sat in proximity to this pain? *Or does this pain merely represent a challenge to our political ideologies?*

---

[1] See http://www.charlotteobserver.com/news/local/article61649457.html

The refusal, on the part of white Americans, to listen and learn about racism shows the relevance of Dr. Martin Luther King Jr.'s keen observation, "Whites, it must frankly be said, are not putting in a similar mass effort to reeducate themselves out of their racial ignorance. It is an aspect of their sense of superiority that the white people of America believe they have so little to learn."[1]

This is a plea—to my fellow white American Christians—to stop and truly consider whether our posture is Christ-like. We are called to bear one another's burdens. We are called to be fellow sufferers. *Perhaps we should first seek to bear the burden and pain of fellow image-bearers, and then, afterward, frame our understanding of and approach to race through these shared tears.*

Where should we go from here? What's the best action to take in order to have a more loving and just society? I don't need to know. As the story of Socrates goes, he was the wisest man in Athens not because he knew the answers, but because he was the only one aware of his own ignorance. Let's embody that wisdom. Let's love. And, perhaps for the first time, let's listen.

---

[1] King, Martin Luther. *Where Do We Go from Here: Chaos or Community?* (Boston: Beacon, 2010), 10.

Social Justice Without the Resurrection Is Dead

George Aldhizer

In today's cultural climate, much is thrown around concerning the term "social justice." Many are passionate about seeing the many injustices and oppressions of this world reversed into true human flourishing, and seeing the way the world is as different from the way the world ought to be. The primary worldview used as the foundation and motivation for this term is a notion of "progress," fueled by a passion to make the world better. While I believe that the social justice impulse is in many ways a good one, I want to argue that the dominant worldview supporting this ideology is insufficient. The Christian worldview, by contrast, offers a foundation and eternal significance for social justice work in this world.

Foundation

The Christian story begins with an eternal God fashioning the world out of nothing, declaring it to be truly "good." It continues with a God who then culminates His creation in humanity, male and female, of God's own likeness and image, to then care for and have dominion over creation.[1] Much has been written concerning the theological significance of this "image of God," but in this article I want to highlight one facet of this Image. Yale philosopher Nicholas Wolterstorff in his article, "How Social Justice Got to Me and Why it Never Left," interprets the Image of God as meaning that "persons are regarded as having a worth that requires of us that we treat them in certain ways."[2] Thus, the foundation of social justice in the Christian tradition is in the recognition of the worth of each human being, imbued by the God of ultimate worth.

---

[1] All scripture quotations, unless otherwise noted, are taken from The Holy Bible, English Standard Version® (ESV®) Copyright © 2001 by Crossway, a publishing ministry of Good News Publishers. All rights reserved. ESV Text Edition: 2011.

[2] Nicholas Wolterstorff. "How Social Justice Got to Me and Why It Never Left," *Journal of the American Academy of Religion*, Vol. 76, No. 3 (2008): 672.

In contrast, the worldview of progress contains no such foundation, simply assuming that the human being has worth. The claim of the dignity of the human being thus rests on assertion, "unable to specify what it is about them on which that dignity supervenes."[1] Without the foundation of the Image of God, the progress narrative relies on the malleable spirit of the times. Wolterstorff sees this conclusion not as an opportunity for a zinger against secularism, but as an opportunity for viewing the most vulnerable in our society (he cites the Alzheimer's patient lacking rational capacity) as worthy of infinite dignity.

Eternal Significance
Contrary to some "Christian" (read: Gnostic) views of the afterlife, which posit that the afterlife consists of disembodied existence, the New Testament view of eternity is one of resurrection of the body. Those in Christ are to be raised from the dead to life imperishable, free of sin, death, decay, and mourning. Paul in **1 Corinthians 15** explains that "death [will be] swallowed up in victory," for those that are in Christ share in His victory over sin and death, they will be raised as he was raised from the grave.

Thus, the Christian hope of eternity is one in which God continually declares His creation to be good. It is not to be abandoned with the introduction of sin and death, but it is to be recreated to new life. The God who in the garden called humanity to reflect His image, is now calling and equipping His people, through Christ's work and in the power of the Holy Spirit, to care for creation once again. This work of racial reconciliation, economic justice for the poor, care for the elderly, and other social justice concerns, modeled after Christ's life, is not done away with in death but will last into embodied eternity. As N. T. Wright summarizes, "God's recreation of his wonderful world, which began with the resurrection of Jesus and continues mysteriously as God's people live in the risen Christ and in the power of his Spirit, means that what we do in Christ and by the Spirit in the present is not wasted. It will last all the way into God's new world."[2]

By contrast, narratives of progress or a disembodied heaven do not posit an eternity in which our social justice work in the present will come to fruition. Under these two worldviews, we can have no confidence that our care for the poor will continue in ultimate release

---

[1] Ibid., 674.
[2] N. T. Wright. *Surprised by Hope* (New York: HarperOne, 2008), 208.

of the poor from bondage. In both, the tool of the oppressor, death, has the ultimate victory. The awful reality without Christ's resurrection is a world free of hope, free of ultimate social justice. Truly, social justice without the resurrection is dead.

To conclude, the Christian framework for social justice, founded on a good creation and humanity's image of God, motivated by Christ's work and kingdom on Earth, and transformed by the power of the resurrection, offers a better narrative than that of mere progress. In sum, if you have an impulse to be about social justice, then you should be a Christian. For it offers you a more coherent, beautiful, and eternal story to frame and motivate your work.

A few points of clarity:

> (1) What I am not saying is that Christians are able to build the kingdom of God here. Rather, as N. T. Wright helpfully clarifies, we are, with God's enabling, to "build for the kingdom," bringing foretastes of the eternally-just-reality to this world. His book *Surprised by Hope* helped me to understand this distinction.

> (2) Also, what I am not saying is that non-Christians, specifically those of the progress narrative, are not doing good or not doing social justice. In many ways they are, and we should celebrate this. Unfortunately, many non-Christians lack a foundation and eternal significance for their work.

> (3) Yes, I know. Not all Christians are about social justice. Ultimately, Matthew 25 says this is a denial of Christ himself, who identifies with the poor. Christians are called, not to a cheap grace, but to one in which we pray "thy kingdom come, thy will be done, on earth as in heaven," in which we are commissioned to play a role in the kingdom come.

"My friends: Let us listen to the voices and the faces of the wronged. They are everywhere, about us and among us. And let us not harden our hearts." [1]

---

[1] Wolterstorff, 678.

Gnostic Anthropology and Identity Politics
John Ehrett

Within the general framework of contemporary identity politics – a term that I use here to refer to a synthesis between one's personal attributes, or the intersections between said attributes, and one's political preferences – an ancient theological debate may be resurfacing under different conceptual umbrellas.

Recent scholarship has advanced an "intersectional" understanding of how race and gender interact to perpetuate discriminatory structures. Yet where the philosophy of such a movement is concerned, the two schemas developing on axes of race and gender are potentially irreconcilable. Though often treated together as subtypes of an undifferentiated "leftism," these strains fundamentally differ on the issue of philosophical anthropology.

Within the field of African American studies, an important recent contribution has been Ta-Nehisi Coates's book *Between The World And Me*. Coates – a longtime writer for *The Atlantic* – has discussed American racial dynamics for many years, and in this work develops his thoughts more fully. Coates's writing is characterized by a consistent awareness of *embodiedness* – namely, the ways in which the physical bodies of African Americans consistently have suffered, and continue to suffer, diverse indignities. In Coates's framing, race is clearly not a social construct to be elided; it is something bound into the fabric of human biology, driving chasms between persons and stymying human flourishing. His personal identity – and the identity of others whose perceived race does not conform to that of the privileged caste (which, Coates holds, are white Americans) – is inextricably connected to empirically observable biology. I will term this view the *integrationist* (or counter-Gnostic) perspective.

This understanding of personal identity as inevitably connected to human biology clashes with the anthropological understanding exposited in the broad corpus of gender studies literature. For many scholars in this field, personal identity exists on a plane wholly decoupled from the properties of one's biological tissue. Gender is fluid and malleable, and biology is anything but destiny. I will term this view the *gnostic* perspective.

During the time of the early church, controversies rapidly emerged alongside the rise of Gnostic theology. The Gnostics taught that matter was inconsequential or evil, and that the project of human existence was to liberate the soul from crude matter so that it might ascend to heaven. Traditional Christian theology, conversely, taught that the body and soul, while distinct, were both integral aspects of the human person: matter, as something created and sustained by God, was not intrinsically evil, but originally created good. Accordingly, the human person was not just a "soul in a meat-sack" but a holistic image-bearer of God. Ergo, Christ, in taking on human form, did not merely appear as an illusory divine specter, but rather as a man with a cognizable human nature.

The language of the debate over Gnosticism has since changed, but its essential qualities remain the same. In the contemporary gnostic framing, a sense of experienced personal identity serves as a proxy for traditional theological-philosophical conceptions of the human soul. That identity – that soul – exists in a world of physical matter, which may either be *oppositional to* the nonmaterial human property or *intertwined with* it.

Coates offers an integrationist approach: for him, what it means to be African American today is indivisible from the realities of physical existence and the physical properties of one's body. Gender studies theorists argue the opposite: identity exists in a discrete meta-paradigm within which biology is irrelevant. In so doing, Coates aligns himself with the Gnostics' critics, while the gender theorists echo Gnostic arguments under new banners.

In light of this, it is perhaps ironic that some critics have described these types of controversies as heralding a "brave new world." The names and concepts may be superficially different, but at bottom, these debates have surprisingly ancient roots.

CRT and Its Dissidents
Wesley Walker

Given the continued protests and social unrest over structural racism in the wake of George Floyd's murder, many American Christians have found themselves intensely grappling with the issue. In my own Anglican context, it has become a controversial topic as critiques like "Can the Christian Use Critical Theory" by Fr. Matt Kennedy and "Race and Redemption" by Fr. Gerry McDermott have been published in response to a statement on anti-racism put out by some clergy in the Anglican Church in North America. Frs. Kennedy and McDermott contend that the use of "critical race theory" as a methodology is functionally irredeemable. For example, Fr. Kennedy asserts, "CRT does not add anything of substance to a purely biblical analysis using biblical categories and language." Fr. McDermott questions "the mainstream media's account" of race, citing affirmative-action programs as evidence of inclusion and equality. He then accuses church leaders of using "old creation" perspectives that divide people by skin color," which has ultimately led to Mainline Protestantism's decline in numbers. Anti-racism, he contends, creates a new religion that mimics Christianity but lacks any framework for redemption. Without grace, talk of race is reduced to "sinful judgment" that "imputes motives to others based on skin color." Accordingly, Fr. McDermott opposes a "replacement theology" where the Church's theology of forgiveness is replaced by a secular atonement narrative.

My aim is to provide a rejoinder to Fr. Kennedy and Fr. McDermott. I am certainly not a "critical race theorist," nor do I advocate the wholesale embrace of any particular organization or of "critical race theory." I've even previously written about how purely activist iterations of Christianity in the Mainline context are Pelagian, and I have been fairly critical of Dr. James Cone, the founder of Black Liberation Theology. That said, I propose that Fr. Kennedy and Fr. McDermott do not adequately argue against what they call "critical race theory."

The first problem with their critiques is that "critical race theory" is not the monolithic entity it is often made out to be. Not only do voices like Cone's not represent the entirety of the Black Church, but it would also be virtually impossible, for example, to think that his Black Liberation Theology could be compatible with other variations of "critical race theory" like the "Afropessimism" of a figure like Frank Wilderson. The two might share similar starting points, but treating them as the same would be a fallacy of equivocation. Further, Fr. Kennedy frequently identifies Marxism as the starting point for critical race theory as a means of discrediting it. The role of Marxist analysis within the world of critical race theory, however, is debated. This is clear in Edward P. Antonio's analysis of the debate between B. Moore and Sebidi about whether the dynamics of South African conflict should be discussed through a lens of class struggle or racialized ideology. Further, Fr. Kennedy's use of the Marxist label is a genetic fallacy: the fact that certain ideas and grammars may be genealogically connected to Marx does not automatically discredit them. For example, most conservative Christians would appreciate the contribution of Neil Postman's book *Technopoly: The Surrender of Culture to Technology*, which employs some Marxist analysis. From a Christian perspective, while it is important to identify competing metaphysical presuppositions, it would be impossible to say Marxist analysis is universally bad (even though we would certainly agree it is not all good). In *God of the Oppressed*, for example, I think we can affirm Cone's positive citation of Marx on the social embeddedness of ideas, affirming a connection between economic and political power in socio-cultural definitions of truth. At the same time, I have criticized Cone's work, such as *The Black church and Marxism: what do they have to say to each other,* in which he prescribes commingling the "old time religion" of his grandparents with Marxist critiques. In other words, it might be possible to affirm the sometimes insightful diagnoses of Marxism while his prognostication falls short from a Christian perspective. At this juncture, the question becomes whether examples like ACNA's anti-racism statement is a capitulation to something irredeemable, or rather the baptism of insights which can be gleaned through "critical race theory."

Contrary to what seems to be asserted by some in the conversation, Christianity is not hyper-individualistic. The person, after all, is always enmeshed in various social situations that work to form them into who they are. I am *me* because of where I was raised, how I was educated, who I've spent time with, and so forth. I do not wholly precede my environment, nor am I exclusively a product of it—I emerge from my participation in and engagement with various social structures.

If we take Christian anthropology seriously, we believe in universal, inherited original sin. Sin, then, permeates the atmosphere of the City of Man, which our carnal and natural selves help construct. The structures built by sinful individuals will inevitably bear their images. It would be naive and ahistorical, then, to assert that American institutions that perpetuated slavery, Jim Crow, and countless other cruelties could be purged with the stroke of a pen. The fact that activism is a kind of Pelagianism cuts both ways then. Approaches that emphasize only incremental progress in the face of urgent demands for transformation recapitulate and re-entrench the myths of modernity. The fact is, such structural analyses are hardly anathema to conservative Christianity: abortion perpetuates a culture of disposability, often aimed at minority communities, and the effects of the sexual revolution are common examples (and rightfully so) used to demonstrate the damage wrought by oppressive structures. Biblically, we see similar rhetoric used in the depiction of the Tower of Babel (Gen 11), a project remarkably similar to that of modernity, which warrants collective punishment.

Likewise, collective social injustice is one of the three major sins for which the Israelites were constantly chastened by their prophets (cf. Isa 1:16-31; Jer 22:3; Amos 5:11-15). The question is not whether structures of Sin and violence exist; they certainly do. The question is how an individual who inhabits them should orient themselves in relation to those structures. Perhaps this is why many reflexively react with the common objection "But I didn't own slaves." On one level, such retorts are fair—except that they function as red herrings. The goal of the Christian in this situation is not the litigation of individual white people's culpability, 150+ years after the fact, so much as an interrogation into how we got here, into a world where police brutality, ghettoization, ecclesial segregation, and so forth are very real problems.

And here is where some of the tendencies in Fr. Kennedy and Fr. McDermott's articles get closer to the truth by asking the question of redemption and grace. But, it should be noted, the question remains fraught and complex. That God is merciful and does not desire the death of a sinner (Ezek 18:23) is hardly up for debate. The question then becomes one of cheap grace and legalism. "Cheap grace," as Bonhoeffer defines in *The Cost of Discipleship*, "is the preaching of forgiveness without requiring repentance, baptism without church discipline, Communion without confession, absolution without personal confession. Cheap grace is grace without discipleship, grace without the cross, grace without Jesus Christ, living and incarnate."

To name one example, holding up largely ineffectual affirmative-action programs as proof that the problem of racism has been ameliorated is the way of cheap grace. On the other hand, legalism—which could be defined as the foreclosure of reconciliation—is a serious problem we see manifested in the unrelenting rise of cancel culture. The Christian must walk a narrow *via media* here: God's mercy is new every morning (Lam 3:22-23), but it is in no way a means for self-justification, license, or presumption. Redemption—individual and collective—can not be devalued by easy answers or self-absolutions. Yet, as Cone notes in *God of the Oppressed,* too often the pattern is whites asking the question about reconciliation *of* blacks as an easy out. Part of any good confession is compunction, and that is precisely what seems lacking in this discussion.

In terms of fleshing out some of the practical implications of all this, I have very little to offer, except to say that the anti-racism statement signed by many ACNA clergy seems to be at least a step in the right direction. I would also commend the statement of the House of Bishops in the Anglican Province of America in the wake of George Floyd's killing, "Notes Toward a Theology of Race" by Fr. Mark Perkins, and the ongoing work of Fr. Esau McCaulley.

However, one proposal I will put forward is that of a robust Christus Victor model of the Atonement. Singular "Atonement theories" are deficient and lack the explanatory power, in and of themselves, to fully express the mystery of Christ's work. Scot McKnight advises us to think of the various theories as metaphors indwelt by God. Each metaphor is the facet of a gem that refracts light in a new way. All facets are essential and point us to a more complete picture of the truth. What we now call Christus Victor functions as a cosmic framework within which we can understand the story of Satisfaction. The Christus Victor model allows us to see humanity both as a victim of and participant in Sin. We are ravaged by Sin so that we have deficiencies, but we are not passive because our nature is "inclined to evil" (Article IX). Racism, we can say, is a demonic tendril of Sin that functions on both social and individual levels. The work of analysis that relies on "critical race theory" is an exercise in hamartiology, an excavation of one aspect of the rather insidious human heart which is "wicked above all else" (Jer 17:9). Does this necessarily entail a wholesale agreement with everything to be found in the pages of works deemed "critical race theory" or Black Liberation Theology? Definitely not. However, it also does not mean stopping up one's ears. It is important to listen, especially to Christians, who are contributing to the discussion.

The Christian tradition rarely provides us with easy answers. Rather, it cultivates in us a sacrificial love for the other, earnest self-examination, and a heart of repentance that prays for souls and for society. The Gospel is only sweet once the Law has crushed our self-righteousness and shocked us into the awareness of our human inadequacy. Have we, as members of the American Church, been properly astonished by our depravity? I don't think so.

Almighty God, who hast created man in thine own image; Grant us grace fearlessly to contend against evil, and to make no peace with oppression; and that we may reverently use our freedom, help us to employ it in the maintenance of justice among men and nations, to the glory of thy holy Name; through Jesus Christ our Lord. Amen.

God Remembers
Tomerot Lambert

What if we are a memory,
in God's mind?
I had this thought
when I was sitting and doing homework.
I remembered something
I did in the past. It got me thinking:
Could God have everything
in my life as a memory, and his remembering
is making present my existence?
I happened
but I am in the present moment
by God pulling me from the past to
here and now.

Scripture and Interpretation

Perhaps no single topic has produced as much dialogue at *Conciliar Post* as Scripture and its interpretation. Indeed, one author went so far as to dub these conversations "the authority wars" given their importance for understanding and differentiating Christian traditions. Should Christians adopt a *sola scriptura* approach, employ *prima scriptura,* rely on Scripture and Tradition, or follow another approach? These essays are the best of a deep and ongoing conversation, so take up, read, and reflect accordingly.

Essays

The New Testament in Order, *Prahlow*

Books Removed From the NT, *Bryan*

Visiting D.C.'s Museum of the Bible, *Ehrett*

Augustine on Biblical Interpretation, *Dickey*

In Praise of the English Bible, *Rebholtz*

Maccabees in the New Testament, *Bryan*

Sola Scriptura's Relevance for the Modern Church, *Hall*

Faith Across Traditions

The New Testament in Order[1]
Jacob J. Prahlow

Begin reading through the New Testament and, in addition to the grand story, you will eventually notice a few things. For one thing, the story of Jesus gets repeated four times, *then* you hear the story of the early church, and *then* you begin to read letters that don't seem to be in any sort of coherent order. *Why is the New Testament organized how it is, and not some other way?* Why is the New Testament canon laid out in the order that it is? Why is the New Testament not arranged in order of its events? Or, to ask yet a slightly different question, why is the New Testament not arranged in the order in which it was written?

In this article, we will look at the major orders in which the New Testament can appear. First, we will consider *canonical order*: the order in which the writings of the New Testament appear in modern, published Bibles. Second, we will consider *chronological order*: the order in which the events of the New Testament are portrayed. And finally, we will consider several different proposals for *the compositional order*: the order in which New Testament writings were actually written down.

As one final prolegomenological note, let me foreground my belief that each of these orders provides insights into the meaning and message of the New Testament. Context matters a great deal—in fact, it governs the meaning of everything. While we often pay close attention to historical context when it comes to questions about the ordering and understanding of the New Testament, *literary* context also matters. In short, where you find a particular book or passage in the collection known as the New Testament makes a difference to and influences the interpretation of that book or passage. Thus, canonical order, chronological order, and compositional order each cast (and recast) the writings of the New Testament in ways that are fruitful for faithful and critical readings of the text.

---

[1] A version of this article appears as an appendix in *Encountering God's Story: A Guide to Better Reading and Understanding the Story of Scripture* (St. Louis: Arise Press, 2023).

Canonical Order

First, let us consider *canonical order:* the order of New Testament books that appears in modern published Bibles. Before diving in, let me first note that not every edition of the New Testament has included precisely the 27 books modern readers are familiar with, nor have those books always been in exactly the order in which we are used to them appearing.

To cite one historical example, *Codex Sinaiticus* (one of the oldest full copies of the New Testament) uses the following order: *Matthew, Mark, Luke, John, Romans, 1 Corinthians, 2 Corinthians, Galatians, Ephesians, Philippians, Colossians, 1 Thessalonians, 2 Thessalonians, Hebrews, 1 Timothy, 2 Timothy, Titus, Philemon, Acts, James, 1 Peter, 2 Peter, 1 John, 2 John, 3 John, Jude, Revelation, Epistle of Barnabas, Shepherd of Hermas.* There are obviously a few key differences there, as well as some familiar patterns.

That said, there are two primary reasons why the New Testament appears in the order it does today. First, the New Testament largely follows the organizational pattern of the Old Testament, with the core story (Torah for the OT, Gospels for the NT), followed by historical accounts and other writings. Obviously, the pattern does not match entirely, but it's relatively easy to notice a three-fold pattern of organization in both testaments.

But a second reason the New Testament looks like it does is because collections of now-New Testament writings circulated in the ancient world centuries before they found their way into the canon of the New Testament. Based on evidence from early Christian writers known as the Apostolic Fathers, it seems that collections of writings were beginning to circulate by the last first century. While we are not 100% certain what these collections initially would have looked like, by the late-second and early-third centuries, several clear groupings had emerged:
- Gospels (often, but not always in the order of Matthew, Mark, Luke, John, and sometimes including a Luke-Acts collection)
- Pauline Epistles (often, but not always arranged largest to smallest, Romans to Pastorals, sometimes including Hebrews and sometimes not)
- General Epistles (typically James to Jude)

There was no uniform standard in the earliest years of these collections, as *usefulness* and *accessibility* often governed what an early Christian community might have in their growing collection of *scriptura*. The Gospels were the most commonly circulated, followed by the works of Paul. Everything else enjoyed a pattern of usage that sometimes varied by geography. Finally, in the early fourth century, we begin to see evidence of the New Testament canon as we have it today:

- Gospels: Matthew, Mark, Luke, John[1]
- Acts[2]
- Pauline Epistles: Romans, 1 Corinthians, 2 Corinthians, Galatians, Ephesians, Philippians, Colossians, 1 Thessalonians, 2 Thessalonians, 1 Timothy, 2 Timothy, Titus, Philemon[3]
- General Epistles: Hebrews, James, 1 Peter, 2 Peter, 1 John, 2 John, 3 John, Jude[4]
- Revelation[5]

This order was popularized by the time of Athanasius of Alexandria's *Festal Letter 39* and eventually became the standard ordering of the New Testament canon.

Chronological Order

A chronological ordering of the New Testament is arranged a little differently, with the main difference being that many New Testament letters find themselves superimposed into the narrative of Acts. Without digging too much into the minutia, it probably looks something like this:

---

[1] The canonical order has traditionally been explained as the order in which the gospels were written, though this was brought into question as seemingly early as Papias and Origen. See Eusebius, *Ecclesiastical History* 6.25 and Augustine, *The Harmony of the Gospels*, I.2.4

[2] As Luke Part II, Acts was never seriously doubted as part of the canon, though it's specifical placement in the canon varied quite dramatically in early canons.

[3] The Pauline canon follows two orderings: epistles to churches and epistles to people (also known as *pastorals*), and longest to shortest (the exception being Ephesians, which is a little longer than Galatians).

[4] The general (or catholic) epistles likewise are arranged in a roughly longest to shortest, with Hebrews bridging the gap between Paul and non-Pauline writers.

[5] Technically, Revelation falls into at least two genres: letters to churches (chapters 1-3) and apocalypse (chapters 4-22, though some interpreters divide these chapters into apocalypse and prophecy sections).

- Gospels[1]
- Acts 1-14
- James / Galatians[2]
- Acts 15-18.18
- 1 Thessalonians
- 2 Thessalonians
- Acts 18.19-19
- 1 Corinthians
- 2 Corinthians
- Acts 20.1-3
- Romans
- Acts 20.4-24
- Colossians, Philemon & *Laodicians*[3]
- Ephesians
- Philippians
- Acts 25-28.29
- 1 Timothy
- Titus
- 1 Peter
- Hebrews
- Acts 28.30-31
- 2 Timothy
- Jude
- 2 Peter
- Revelation 1-3
- 1 John
- 2 John
- 3 John
- Revelation 4-22

There's plenty of debate about some of this, but based on what events are described or assumed to be contemporaneous with these writings and passages, this is a basic outline of a chronological reading of the New Testament.

---

[1] In parallel for long sections of course.
[2] Presuming that these letters are both about the Gentile controversy addressed in Acts 15 by the Council of Jerusalem.
[3] Paul's authentic letter to the Laodicians remains lost, although Paul clearly mentions the letter in Colossians 4:16 and at least some pseudonymous editions appear to have circulated in the ancient world, including (according to Tertullian) in Marcion of Sinope's canon.

Compositional Order

A final way to think about the ordering of the New Testament is in the order in which these documents were written. At first, you might imagine that this would parallel the chronological ordering, but that's not quite correct. Most scholars believe that either 1 Thessalonians, Galatians, or James was the first New Testament document written, all of which speak to events chronologically later than the Gospels. This is largely due to the fact that the Gospels are not media reports or live tweets about Jesus: they are literary biographies, composed by followers of Jesus to tell the story of Jesus as the first generation of Christians got older.

The order in which the writings of the New Testament were composed is a topic of much scholarly debate. On the one hand, many contemporary scholars push the writing of certain documents well into the second century and speak extensively about anonymous and pseudonymous authorship of certain writings. On the other hand, there are plenty of scholars who advocate for much earlier (and more traditional) datings, with some scholars even suggesting that the contents of the New Testament were written before the destruction of the Second Jewish Temple by Rome in 70 CE.[1]

Consider Marcus Borg's listing of the New Testament books in the order they were written in *The Evolution of the Word* (including his likely dates[2]):
- 1 Thessalonians (50 CE)
- Galatians (50 CE)
- 1 Corinthians (50 CE)
- Philemon (mid-50s CE)
- Philippians (mid-50s CE)
- 2 Corinthians (mid-50s)
- Romans (58 CE)
- Mark (70 CE)
- James (70-80 CE)
- Colossians (80s CE)

---

[1] The most influential advocate of this position is John A.T. Robinson, whose *Redating of the New Testament* continues to provide fodder for scholarly conversations about the dating of New Testament documents

[2] Dating ranges are notoriously fickle and circumspect, with most published pieces including appropriate notations that all such dating estimates are necessarily *circa* given the realities of accurately describing history.

- Matthew (80-90 CE)
- Hebrews (80-90 CE)
- John (90 CE)
- Ephesians (90s CE)
- Revelation (90s CE)
- Jude (90s CE)
- 1 John (100 CE)
- 2 John (100 CE)
- 3 John (100 CE)
- Luke (100 CE)
- Acts (100 CE)
- 2 Thessalonians (100 CE)
- 1 Peter (100 CE)
- 1 Timothy (100-110 CE)
- 2 Timothy (100-110 CE)
- Titus (100-110 CE)
- 2 Peter (120-150 CE)

Likewise, consider the "consensus dates"[1] that are often used as a benchmark by New Testament scholars for discussing when the writings of the New Testament were composed:

- Galatians (48 CE)
- 1 Thessalonians (51 CE)
- 2 Thessalonians (51 CE)
- 1 Corinthians (53-57 CE)
- Philippians (54-55 CE)
- Philemon (54-55 CE)
- 2 Corinthians (55-58 CE)
- Romans (57-58 CE)
- Jude (60-110 CE)
- Colossians (62-70 CE)
- Mark (65-73 CE)
- James (65-85 CE)
- 1 Peter (75-90 CE)
- Matthew (80-90 CE)
- Luke (80-90 CE)

---

[1] There's really no such thing as a "scholarly consensus" about such things, let alone a fixed consensus. Scholars are constantly going back and forth about when NT documents were written and how we might know. That said, it remains common in the field to talk about consensus, if only as a foil for whatever proposal or project one is working on.

- Acts (80-90 CE)
- Hebrews (80-90 CE)
- Ephesians (80-90 CE)
- John (90-110 CE)
- 1 John (90-110 CE)
- 2 John (90-110 CE)
- 3 John (90-110 CE)
- Revelation (95 CE)
- 1 Timothy (100 CE)
- 2 Timothy (100 CE)
- Titus (100 CE)
- 2 Peter (110 CE)

One Final Proposal

Alternatively, my own research suggests a much tighter window of writing:
- Galatians (48-49 CE)
- James (48-49 CE)
- *Jerusalem Council* (50 CE)
- Mark (50-60 CE)
- Jude (50-60 CE)
- 1 Thessalonians (51-52 CE)
- 2 Thessalonians (51-52 CE)
- 1 Corinthians (54 CE)
- 2 Corinthians (56 CE)
- Romans (56-59 CE)
- Colossians (58 or 61 CE)
- Philemon (58 or 61 CE)
- *Laodicians* (58 or 61 CE)
- Matthew (~60 CE)
- Luke (60-62 CE)
- Philippians (61-62 CE)
- Ephesians (61-62 CE)
- 1 Timothy (62 CE)
- Titus (62 CE)
- Acts (62-64 CE)
- 2 Timothy (64 CE)
- *Death of Paul* (64 CE)
- 1 Peter (64-66 CE)
- Hebrews (64-70 CE)
- 2 Peter (66-68 CE)
- *Death of Peter* (68 CE)
- Revelation (68-70 CE)

- *Destruction of Jerusalem* (70 CE)
- John (70-80 CE)
- 1 John (70-80 CE)
- 2 John (80-100 CE)
- 3 John (80-100 CE)

There are two driving ideas behind this proposal. First, I find generally compelling Robinson's argument in *Redating the New Testament* (since echoed and expanded upon by countless scholars) that the implications of the destruction of Jerusalem should be noticeable in early Christian writings after its occurrence. Particularly in New Testament writings written for a Jewish audience, the lack of clear signals about this event is extremely telling. The detailed arguments in Hebrews, for example, make little sense if they had been written after Jerusalem has fallen; in that case, why not simply spell out the disastrous implications of Judaism, as later anti-Jewish Christian writers would?[1]

The second driving idea behind my proposal is that *early Christian writing occurs around events*. That is, for a missional and eschatological movement such as early Christianity, there needed to be some clear impetus for taking the time to write something down and then preserve it. Religious movements that expect an imminent end do not typically write much down for posterity's sake. There need to be certain developments, debates, or deaths to drive such a shift. In my thinking, the chart below indicates some of the influences that were likely at work in the composition of New Testament texts.

Writing/Event	Driving Influence
Galatians (48-49 CE)	Debate (Gentile Controversy, pre-council)
James (48-49 CE)	Debate (Gentile Controversy, pre-council)
Jerusalem Council (50 CE)	
Mark (50-60 CE)	Debate (Gentile Controversy, post-council)
Jude (50-60 CE)	Debate (Gentile Controversy, post-council)

---

[1] This is one reason why I find post-70 CE datings of Johannine literature compelling. In contrast to every other New Testament writing, John's use of *the Jews* indicates not a formal parting of the ways (which other historical sources reveal was a centuries-long process), but a differentiation of *the Way* from the Jewish rebels who have just suffered defeat at the hands of Rome.

1 Thessalonians (51-52 CE)	Development (theological questions, post-visit)
2 Thessalonians (51-52 CE)	Development (theological questions, post-visit)
1 Corinthians (54 CE)	Development (theological questions, post-visit)
2 Corinthians (56 CE)	Development (theological questions, post-visit)
Romans (56-59 CE)	Development (theological questions, pre-visit)[1]
Colossians (58, 61 CE)	Development (theological questions, post-visit)
Philemon (58, 61 CE)	Development (theological questions, post-visit)
Laodicians (58, 61 CE)	Development (theological questions, post-visit)
Matthew (~60 CE)	Development (generation shift and/or commenting/building on Mark)
Luke (60-62 CE)	Development (generation shift and/or commenting/building on Matthew and Mark)
Philippians (61-62 CE)	Development (theological questions, post-visit)
Ephesians (61-62 CE)	Development (theological questions, pre-visit)[2]
1 Timothy (62 CE)	Death (Paul's pastoral reflections pre-death)
Titus (62 CE)	Death (Paul's pastoral reflections pre-death)
Acts (62-64 CE)	Development (generation shift and/or continuation of Luke)
2 Timothy (64 CE)	Death (Paul's pastoral reflections pre-death)
Death of Paul (64 CE)	

---

[1] Romans stands out among Paul's letters not only for its length and theological heft, but also as one of the few surviving letters (if not only letter) to have been written to a church *prior* to Paul's presence there.

[2] Based on an understanding of Ephesians as an encyclical to the wider area of churches around Ephesus and not to the urban Ephesian church itself, which Paul would have been quite familiar with by this point.

1 Peter (64-66 CE)	Death (Peter's pastoral reflections post-Paul)
Hebrews (64-70 CE)	Development (theological questions, post-visit)[1]
2 Peter (66-68 CE)	Death (Peter's pastoral reflections pre-death)
Death of Peter (68 CE)	
Revelation (68-70 CE)	Development (theological questions and apocalyptic warning, post-visit)
Destruction of Jerusalem (70 CE)	
John (70-80 CE)	Development (generation shift and/or commenting/building on Synoptics)
1 John (70-80 CE)	Development (theological questions, post-visit)[2]
2 John (80-100 CE)	Development (theological questions, post-visit)
3 John (80-100 CE)	Development (theological questions, post-visit)

Why does the New Testament appear in the order it does? For a variety of reasons, perhaps including reasons influenced by chronology of events or order of composition, but not limited to those factors. Considering alternative orders to the New Testament—especially the chronological and compositional—does provide a useful lens for considering what the New Testament says and means. In fact, there is much to be learned from considering alternative orders. As we take up and read, therefore, let us be aware of how literary context shapes and influences how we engage the Scriptures.

---

[1] Hebrews is probably an edited sermon, sent as theological encouragement to area churches.
[2] 1 John is probably an edited sermon, sent as theological encouragement to area churches.

Books Removed From the NT?
Matthew Bryan

A friend recently asked if any books had been removed from the New Testament. Such questions often come from an intent to discredit the Bible, but she sincerely wondered. For example, some skeptics point to the *Gospel of Judas* as a removed book. National Geographic published the first English translation of it in 2006. This gospel mostly offers conversations between Jesus and Judas. In it, Jesus praises Judas as His wisest disciple and commends him because Judas would sacrifice the man who "clothes" Him. It also offers an unusual creation account; an angel named Saklas created six other angels, who helped him create Adam and Eve.

The *Gospel Of Judas* is just the most recent book to be offered as a "lost" or "removed" book of the New Testament. The most famous of such writings is the *Gospel Of Thomas*. Each time we hear of a newly discovered "gospel," many media outlets sensationalize it as an alternative form of early Christianity. They mourn how the primary form of Christianity supposedly ran roughshod over other legitimate expressions of the faith. In such a view, the "winning" form of Christianity unfairly excluded or even removed several books from the Bible. Some early apostolic Christians actually did consider seven other books to be part to the New Testament, but Gnostic writings like the "Gospel of Judas" and the "Gospel of Thomas" were not among the seven writings that some Christians briefly considered Scripture.

How The New Testament Formed
Contrary to modern claims, the Council of Nicea neither debated nor decided the canon of the New Testament.[1] For a detailed look at that

---

[1] Dan Brown in his book "The Davinci Code" popularized the idea that the Council of Nicea decided the canon of Scripture. His innovative claim relies on a single sentence which the preceding 1600 years never claimed as evidence of a Nicene canon of Scripture. Regarding the Old Testament book of "Judith" (which Protestants reject), Jerome wrote that the Council of Nicea counted it among the number of sacred Scriptures. Jerome did not state that the Council decided which books were canon, nor did his

council according to those who actually attended the council, see Paul Pavao's *Decoding Nicea*. The Christian canon gradually coalesced over several centuries through the collective authority of the "apostolic bishops" across three continents without any bickering and without a single ecumenical meeting on the topic.

The apostolic line of bishops are those who were ordained by other bishops who were ordained by earlier bishops whom the original apostles themselves had ordained. The New Testament canon gradually formed in churches through the authoritative use of Scripture by the apostolic bishops. In contrast with the twenty-seven universally accepted New Testament books, Gnostic writings never enjoyed the approval of an apostolic bishop.[1]

In Book III, chapter 25 of *Ecclesiastical History*, 4th century historian Eusebius of Caesarea listed six books which he said some bishops had received as Scripture:
1. "Acts of Paul"
2. "Shepherd of Hermas"
3. "Apocalypse of Peter" (not to be confused with the "Apocryphal Apocalypse of Peter")
4. "Epistle of Barnabas"
5. "Teaching of the Apostles" (also called "Didache," meaning "teaching")
6. "Gospel of the Hebrews"
7. Not listed by Eusebius is "1st Clement," which was written by Bishop Clement of Rome to the Corinthians.

None of these seven books ever reached universal acceptance in early Christianity, therefore none of them can rightly be accused of ever being part of the Christian Bible. Yet they came far nearer to acceptance in the New Testament than did any of the Gnostic books which the modern media sensationalizes. The following writings have

---

contemporaries, much less those who attended the council. If the council had discussed such an important topic, then the historian Eusebius of Caesarea would have included that fact when he discussed the New Testament Canon. Eusebius, after all, attended the Council of Nicea himself. The most likely explanation for Jerome's statement is that someone at the council simply quoted Judith as Holy Scripture.

[1] Athanasius in his 39th Festal Letter: "...nor is there in any place a mention of apocryphal writings. But they are an invention of heretics..."

tremendous value to the Christian reader, so long as one does not use them for doctrine.

Acts Of Paul

In the order of Eusebius' list, the *Acts Of Paul* comes first, having been written in the second century AD. Among other apostolic Christians, the famous presbyter and scholar Origen of Alexandria accepted "Acts of Paul" as Scripture. He quoted it authoritatively in *De Pascha*, in *On First Principles*, and in *Commentary On John*.[1]

Near the opening, the book portrays the apostle as demanding celibacy even in marriage, a common theme of early non-canonical writings. Chapters three and four of the fourteen chapter book have received inordinate attention. In those chapters, a new convert named Thecla forsakes her wedding engagement in order to devote herself wholly to God. She then escapes several execution attempts before dying "a noble death." The book does not portray Thecla as clearly engaging in public ministry. Nevertheless, so many were the number of readers who interpreted such from AoP, that Tertullian found it necessary to condemn the account in his book *On Baptism*.

Shepherd Of Hermas

Next in Eusebius' list comes the *Shepherd Of Hermas*, dating no later than the second century, thanks to its inclusion as Scripture in the Muratorian Canon. It offers colorful visions, parables, and repeated calls to repentance from every kind of sin. The "shepherd" in the book calls himself the angel of repentance. If a Christian attempts to take the book as doctrine, it will seem harsh and legalistic. As a book for reflection and consideration though, it offers valuable insights into the human heart.

Most of all, *Shepherd Of Hermas* presents a lofty view of the church. It clearly affirms the offices of bishops deacons. The first tower vision of the church is worthy of the time of every Christian reader, although the second tower vision seemed overdone and tedious to this reader. Bishop Eusebius attributed the authorship to the same Hermas whom Paul listed in Romans 16:14.[2] The *Shepherd* was very popular

---

[1] Pervo, Richard, "Acts of Paul," (Wipf and Stock Publishers: Eugene, OR) pp 44-45.
[2] Eusebius of Caesarea, "Ecclesiastical History," III.3.6.

in the early churches, being quoted as Scripture by Bishop Irenaeus of Lyons,[1] Clement of Alexandria, and Origen of Alexandria.

Apocalypse Of Peter

Also included as Scripture in the Muratorian Canon is the *Apocalypse Of Peter*. Bishop Methodius quoted it as Scripture in his *Symposium*[2] around AD 300, as Clement of Alexandria[3] and Origen had done before him. Christian understandings of heaven and hell throughout the dark ages sprang from the *Apocalypse Of Peter*. In hell, the apocalypse portrays each sinner's worst sin as determining the method of his or her torment. This apocalypse along with *Epistle Of Barnabas* and the *Didache* all testify to early Christian condemnation of abortion. The apocalypse reads:

> "I saw another strait place into which the gore and the filth of those who were being punished ran down and became there as it were a lake: and there sat women having the gore up to their necks, and over against them sat many children who were born to them out of due time, crying; and there came forth from them sparks of fire and smote the women in the eyes: and these were the accursed who conceived and caused abortion."[4]

Epistle Of Barnabas

Among those who discussed the authorship of *Epistle Of Barnabas* in the early Church, all of them attributed it to Paul's companion Barnabas, despite modern rejection of that claim. This epistle dates no later than the second century, since Clement of Alexandria quoted it as Scripture.[5] Likewise did Presbyter Origen after him. Compilers included it as Scripture in the 4th century Codex Sinaiticus.

Of the seven books that came nearest to becoming Scripture, *Barnabas* offers the greatest wealth of Christian edification. For one example, the writer exhorts us not to forsake the gathering:
"Do not, by retiring apart, live a solitary life, as if you were already [fully] justified; but coming together in one place, make common inquiry concerning what tends to your general welfare. For the

---

[1] Eusebius, V.8.7.
[2] Methodius, "Symposium," book II, chapter 6, http://www.ccel.org/ccel/schaff/anf06.xi.iii.iii.vi.html
[3] Eusebius, VI.14.1.
[4] Roberts-Donaldson translation, paragraph 25.
[5] Eusebius, VI.14.1.

Scripture saith, 'Woe to them who are wise to themselves, and prudent in their own sight!'"[1]

In chapter 10, *Barnabas* explains the eternal spirit of Mosaic dietary laws. In 15, he deftly defends the Christian celebration of Sunday against the Mosaic Law's Saturday Sabbath. In these and many other ways, *Barnabas* shared Paul's deep burden in the letter to the Galatians, that Christians would not return to the yoke of the letter of the Mosaic Law.

Teaching Of The Twelve Apostles
Fifth in the list of seven books is the *Didache*, meaning "Teaching." Such is the shortened title of *Teaching Of The Twelve Apostles*. The *Didache* reflects portions of Matthew's Gospel, Luke's Gospel, *Shepherd Of Hermas*, *Barnabas*, and several Old Testament books. Scholars debate the dating of this book, some putting it in the first century and others the third or fourth century.

Clement of Alexandria may have referred to the Didache as Scripture in his *Stromata*, but his possible reference lacks clarity. While we do not know who wrote it, the *Didache* is generally honored as an edifying work of the Apostolic Fathers. The Teaching covers a wide range of topics in few words. It refers, for example, to the Eucharist communion as a meal. It also allows holy baptism by sprinkling if one does not have access to immersion. The *Didache* is brief, simple in form, and widely honored.

Gospel Of The Hebrews
Of these seven books, we only lack a copy today of the *Gospel Of The Hebrews*. We can still hope for its discovery since several of the others were not discovered until recent times. If early Christians purposely destroyed all copies, then we can blame that destruction upon the Ebionite heresy. Bishop Eusebius of Caesarea said that the Ebionites made much use of this book.[2] The Ebionites denied the pre-existence of Jesus, clung to the letter of the Mosaic Law, and rejected Paul's writings.

---

[1] Schaff, "Ante Nicene Fathers," http://www.ccel.org/ccel/schaff/anf01.vi.ii.iv.html.
[2] Eusebius, III.27.4.

Bishop Papias of Hierapolis appears to have used this gospel in the second century,[1] but not necessarily as Scripture. Quotes of the book also survive in the writings of Hegesippus, Origen, Jerome, and perhaps Didymus the Blind. In his *Commentary On Ecclesiastes*, Didymus claimed that "gospels" (plural) included the account of the stoning of the adulteress. We are left to assume that he refers to *Gospel Of The Hebrews*, based on what Eusebius attributed to Papias in *Ecclesiastical History*: "And he relates another story of a woman, who was accused of many sins before the Lord, which is contained in the Gospel according to the Hebrews."[2]

First Clement

Finally, we come to the letter of *First Clement*. Bishop Eusebius of Caesarea said regarding *First Clement*, "We know that this epistle also has been publicly used in a great many churches both in former times and in our own.[3] Unlike the previous six books, most modern scholars agree with historic testimony regarding who wrote it. Clement of Rome presided as bishop over the city of Rome in succession to Peter himself, as either the second or third bishop of Rome, depending how one counts the succession.

We call the epistle "First Clement" in order to distinguish it from a later letter, which was falsely attributed to the same bishop. *First Clement* begins by praising the believers in Corinth, then lectures the same audience at length regarding dissensions among them. The epistle famously claimed that the phoenix bird actually exists and reincarnates itself. *First Clement* is nevertheless revered as a work of the apostolic fathers.

Conclusion

When people accuse early Christians of removing books from the New Testament, they offer us an excellent opportunity to testify to the unity of the faith. The apostolic bishops simply and peacefully disagreed about the New Testament canon for centuries until they miraculously came into agreement regarding twenty-seven books. History proves that seven additional books were seriously considered for inclusion in the New Testament, but none of those seven have the scent of Gnosticism, unlike those popularized today. If we Christians will take time to read the six books which have survived, we will edify

---

[1] Ibid., III 39.16.
[2] Ibid., III.39.17.
[3] Ibid., III.16.

ourselves and have personal testimony of the Christian joy presented in them. Let the skeptic investigate them and join us in joyful submission the same King of Kings whom these six writings harmoniously proclaim.

Faith Across Traditions

Visiting D.C.'s Museum of the Bible
John Ehrett

To take certain commentators' reports at face value, the Museum of the Bible in downtown Washington, D.C. is just one small step removed from Ken Ham's Creation Museum and Ark Encounter—an expressly sectarian environment cloaked in pseudo-neutrality. At least, that's the line peddled by Candida Moss and Joel Baden, longtime critics of the project and authors of "Bible Nation: The United States of Hobby Lobby." Echoing Moss and Baden, *Vox* writer Tara Isabella Burton similarly accuses the museum of "routinely disregard[ing] basic principles of academic inquiry" in a way that "should make would-be visitors very, very cautious."

But these commentators would be wrong, and their various grievances likely say more about their own fixations than about the museum itself.

For one thing, the Museum of the Bible definitely isn't the tawdry Smithsonian knockoff these critics describe. Purely as a matter of design, this is a slick, high-tech experience on par with any of D.C.'s other museums, even if its subject matter isn't technically as "glitzy" as the rockets of the Air and Space Museum, or as ancient as the dinosaur skeletons of the Natural History Museum. Laden with touchscreens, video displays, and large-scale effects (the 140-foot screen that spans the ceiling of the main entry hall is particularly eye-popping), the museum is clearly working hard to define itself as a *contemporary, relevant* space. (I wouldn't have minded some dusty glass cases and inscrutable papyrus fragments here and there, but I recognize I'm probably in an old-fashioned minority.)

The museum's permanent collection fills three major exhibition floors—focusing on the impact of the Bible, stories from the Bible, and the history of the Bible, respectively. The "Impact of the Bible" gallery traces the impact of biblical themes and concepts throughout the Middle Ages, the American Founding, and subsequent social movements throughout American history. (Notably, this isn't an unqualified celebration of the Bible's impact; a significant amount of display space is devoted to the pro- and anti-slavery arguments drawn from the text during the Civil War.) The "Stories of the Bible" floor, for its part, relies heavily on theme park-style interactive exhibits (including a life-size reconstruction of Nazareth as it might've appeared in Jesus' day). And last but certainly not least is the "History of the Bible" gallery, which covers the assortment and dissemination of scriptural texts across time.

Perhaps the museum's single most striking exhibit is a massive chamber filled with translations of the Bible into different languages. Nestled beside these existing volumes are shelves of empty notebooks, symbolizing those languages for which translations are still needed. On and on run these rows of notebooks, enveloping the visitor in a cocoon of blank pages—a testament both to the world's profound linguistic diversity and to the need for translation efforts to continue.

But what about those *scathing reviews?*

Speaking as someone who's read Moss and Baden's argument against the museum in "Bible Nation," theirs is not a particularly compelling critique. For instance, Moss and Baden spend many, *many* pages stewing over the museum's importation of certain artifacts through a process that turned out to be fraught with improprieties. (The museum paid a hefty fine and returned the items in question.) Yet one wonders whether Moss and Baden routinely muster the same indignation over the British Museum's longtime (and controversial) possession of the Elgin Marbles, or whether the international sale of artifacts is ultimately preferable to their destruction at the hands of ISIS vandals. Nor does it strike me as inherently objectionable that the members of the Green family—the evangelical owners of the Hobby Lobby craft store chain and principal benefactors of the museum—have their own firm beliefs about what the Bible represents. No one will *ever* be a genuinely disinterested party, particularly on a topic this weighty.

It's not particularly hard to track down the source of progressives' animus; many likely have a bone to pick with the Green family over their non-museum activities. In 2014, the Greens prevailed over the government in a controversial Supreme Court case, *Burwell v. Hobby Lobby*, that held the government could not compel Hobby Lobby to provide certain forms of contraception to their employees through their insurance plans. Hobby Lobby's reticence stemmed from its owners' belief that certain forms of hormonal birth control are potentially abortifacient—a belief that, you guessed it, is grounded in the Greens' understanding of the Bible. The pieces fall into place from there: if you think *Hobby Lobby* was a legal abomination and that the Greens are delusional, how will you feel about anything that appears to promote their notions of the Bible?

At bottom, there's really no need to relitigate old grudges; one can make sound criticisms of the museum that aren't just pretextual grousing against the Greens. For one thing, the museum suffers from a real dearth of material on early Gnostic texts, on the circumstances surrounding the Muratorian Fragment and the Synod of Hippo, and on the many normative debates regarding canonicity. There's a fine exhibit showing the variance between different versions of the Bible across religious traditions (who knew the Ethiopian church's canon included so many different books?), but important questions over the criteria for inclusion or exclusion aren't squarely presented. Moreover, for all the fuss over smuggled tablets, it's a bit jarring to realize that there really aren't that many actual artifacts on display. Many of the display cases are filled with facsimile papyri or glass reproductions of ancient stelae—an understandable move, given that many such items are already prominently displayed in other museums, but a shade disappointing nevertheless. And I'll give Moss, Baden, and their compadres this much: even if the museum doesn't have an explicitly evangelistic bent, it does *feel* rather like a Protestant megachurch (the beige marble walls might have something to do with this).

But none of this is to say that the Museum of the Bible isn't worth visiting (particularly given the low price of admission—free, with a suggested $15 donation). This is a high-quality—if not quite *definitive*—museum that largely accomplishes its mission: highlighting its subject matter and encouraging visitors to engage. And that's worth celebrating.

Faith Across Traditions

Augustine on Biblical Interpretation
Jarrett Dickey

> *"So anyone who thinks he has understood the divine scriptures or any part of them, but cannot by his understanding build up this double love of God and neighbour, has not yet succeeded in understanding them."*[1]

Those familiar with the biography of Augustine will know that after being ordained a presbyter in the African town of Hippo, reportedly against his own wishes and desires, he requested time off to study the scriptures intensely.[2] However a person views Augustine, it must be acknowledged that Augustine was primarily a pastor and an interpreter of the Bible. His rigorous study of the scriptures before embarking upon the journey of ordained ministry proves how central the scriptures were to Augustine's thought and life. As a pastor and teacher of the faithful, Augustine wrote *On Christian Teaching* as a simple guide to biblical interpretation. Like many pastors, Augustine was not simply content to teach the Bible to his congregation. He wanted to equip his congregation to read, interpret, understand, and apply the scriptures on their own.

As the opening quote illustrates, for Augustine, biblical interpretation is always abundantly practical. A correct understanding of the scriptures produces the double love of God and neighbor. A person who does not grow in love does not truly understand the scriptures, even if that person knows a lot about the scriptures. Reading and interpreting the Bible is never meant to be a purely academic or intellectual exercise, although it certainly can be read in that fashion. As Paul says, "All scripture is inspired by God and is useful for teaching, for reproof, for correction, and for training in righteousness, so that everyone who belongs to God may be proficient, equipped for every good work (2 Tim 3:16-17)." Paul and Augustine are making the same point: the truths of the scriptures are meant to be lived out. For Augustine, the Christian life is ultimately a

---

[1] Augustine, *On Christian Teaching*, 1.86.
[2] Augustine. *On Christian Teaching*. Translated by R.P.H. Green (Oxford: Oxford University Press, 1997), vii-viii.

life of correctly ordered loves—loving the things that ought to be loved in the appropriate measure.[1] Therefore, one who truly understands the scriptures will live well and love well.

You Have to Crawl Before You Can Walk

"The most expert investigator of the divine scriptures will be the person who, first, has read them all and has a good knowledge—a reading knowledge, at least, if not yet a complete understanding—of those pronounced canonical."[2]

I teach a basic introductory course on the Bible as a great work of literature at my local community college. Each semester I work with students who have either very little or no exposure to the Bible.[3] Before we even begin to read any selections from the Bible, I start with a series of lectures that explain the history of the composition and formation of the Bible. Then I make sure that my students have a general sense of the books of the Bible and their arrangement. I explain how books are divided into chapters and verses, a topic tedious for my more experienced readers, I know. My reasons for starting this way are simple: you have to crawl before you can walk. If my students do not grasp the basics of the Bible first, they will have a difficult time reading the oracles of the prophets, the poetry of the Psalms, or the parables of Jesus.

In the same way, Augustine argues that the most advanced students of the scriptures begin by gaining a basic reading knowledge of the Bible. They know the arrangements of the books and can identify the various genres of literature. They have a working knowledge of the history of the Israelite people. They can see how biblical law works, and they understand the purpose and symbolism of biblical ritual and worship. As many Bible teachers recommend, Augustine encourages readers to gain understanding of the original biblical languages.[4] If this is not possible, it is best to either consult literal translations or to compare several translations.[5] Of course, as a student progresses on this path, other issues become relevant. Eventually readers of the

---

[1] Ibid., 1.59.
[2] Ibid., 2.24.
[3] I also work with adult students who have been reading the Bible for many years. This creates a challenging classroom dynamic! It is not easy to teach such a wide spectrum of students.
[4] Ibid., 2.34.
[5] Ibid., 2.44, 50.

Bible have to learn how to differentiate between passages meant to be read literally and passages meant to be read figuratively, something that can challenge even the most advanced readers.[1] Augustine recognizes that becoming an expert interpreter is a "laborious task," but it begins with the simple task of committing the Bible to memory or, if nothing else, becoming "not totally unfamiliar" with the content of the Bible.[2]

Dealing With Bad Bible Interpretation
As a pastor and member of a Christian church, I regularly teach my interpretation of the scriptures and listen to others offer their interpretations of the scriptures. At the risk of offending someone, I have to confess that I am routinely disturbed by the amount of bad Bible interpretation floating around. Before it sounds like I am only pointing fingers outward, I must admit that when I look at my old sermon notes I am often mortified by my own preaching. By no means am I immune to misunderstanding a word or expression, overlooking the historical context, or projecting my own issues and baggage onto the text. Clergy and laity are both subject to hermeneutical errors, but this is not the main point I want to make about this issue.

Often times when I hear bad Bible interpretation, I do not know how to respond because I can see that the bad interpretation is bearing a measure of good fruit in the person's life. Maybe the person has misunderstood an expression in one of Paul's letters or has taken the prophets out of their historical context, but their reading of the scriptures has increased their double love of God and neighbor. How am I, as a teacher of the Bible, to respond?

"If, as I began by saying, he is misled by an idea of the kind that builds up love, which is the end of the commandment, he is misled in the same way as a walker who leaves his path by mistake but reaches the destination to which the path leads by going through a field. But he must be put right and shown how it is more useful not to leave the path, in case the habit of deviating should force him to go astray or even adrift."[3]

In the above quote, Augustine offers a somewhat surprising response. Keeping in mind that the goal of the Christian life is to order one's

---

[1] Ibid., 3.20-34.
[2] Ibid., 2.30.
[3] Ibid., 1.88.

loves correctly, the person who has interpreted the Bible wrongly, but loves, has taken a side trail to the right destination. To a certain degree, I find this to be a rather generous attitude toward bad biblical interpretation. Of course, Augustine goes on to say that the person should be corrected and shown both the right path and the right destination, but, as far as it goes, the person's wrong reading of the Bible has produced a good result. However, the person ultimately needs to be corrected so that future interpretative mistakes do not lead to the wrong destination.

Do We Really Need the Scriptures?

"Therefore a person strengthened by faith, hope, and love, and who steadfastly holds on to them, has no need of the scriptures except to instruct others. That is why many people, relying on these three things, actually live in solitude without any texts of the scriptures."[1]

If the goal of reading the Bible is to grow in love, what happens when one reaches the destination? Is there, then, any further need of the scriptures? On a basic level, one might argue that the journey toward love is never fully complete; therefore, the scriptures have continual relevance for the life of faith. However, Augustine makes the provocative statement that a person firmly rooted in faith, hope, and love really has no need for the scriptures. If the purpose of the scriptures is to train a person to live a righteous life and to equip a person to do good works (2 Tim 3:16-17), then I suppose the scriptures cease to have a purpose once a person is living them out. Or maybe it would be better to look at it differently. The person who is living the scriptures has made them a part of their being; at this point there is no longer a need for written texts. As the scriptures themselves prophesy, "I will put my law within them, and I will write it on their hearts; and I will be their God, and they shall be my people (Jer 31:33b)."

In *On Christian Teaching*, Augustine outlines his rules for biblical interpretation so that Christians can grow in the double love of God and neighbor. The process of reading and understanding the Bible begins with baby steps—familiarizing one's self with the content of the Bible—and grows from there. Sometimes readers of the Bible make interpretative mistakes, but it still produces love in their lives. Those readers should be gently corrected and directed back to the right path. Ultimately, if a person grows in their ability to understand the Bible

---

[1] Ibid., 1.93.

so much so that it becomes a part of the fabric of their being, they have no further need of written texts. When we love well, the text is written on our hearts.

Faith Across Traditions

In Praise of the English Bible
Brian Rebholtz

In the Anglican Book of Homilies, the first sermon is entitled, *A Fruitful Exhortation To The Reading And Knowledge Of Holy Scripture*. It begins with simplicity, clarity and power: "Unto a Christian man, there can be nothing either more necessary or profitable than the knowledge of Holy Scripture, forasmuch as in it is contained God's true Word, setting forth his glory and also man's duty."

I've been reflecting on these words as we approach the 504th anniversary of the Reformation. Are my own Scriptural reading habits as robust as they could be? Does the devotional life within my parish *really* reflect the belief that there is nothing "more necessary or profitable" than a deep familiarity with the Bible? I know that we have Bibles in our pews and Bibles on our bookshelves, but are they read, marked and inwardly digested? And if they are, do those of us who read and study the Scriptures honor and cherish the courage, devotion and sacrifice that has placed the Bible in our hands?

There are many ways, of course, to tell the story of the English Bible, but the classic tale begins with a priest and theologian named John Wycliffe (1324-1384). Wycliffe was a student of the Latin translation of the Bible, but the more he read the more he doubted that the teachings of the New Testament were being honored in the Church. His radical treatise *De Veritate Sacrae Scripturae* broke with the settled theology of his day and argued for the sufficiency and primacy of Holy Scripture. Soon, glosses and translations of the Latin Bible into the vernacular began to circulate in England, and these writings quickly became associated with the preaching and teaching of Wycliffe. By the 1370's, Wycliffe and his followers were being denounced as "lollards" or "mutterers" because of their intense focus on reading, memorizing and proclaiming the Bible in English.

Wycliffe was lucky. Despite ecclesiastical hearings and a papal condemnation, he retained his freedom and ministry, dying of a stroke in his parsonage in 1384. His followers, however, were not so lucky. By 1410, owning or copying a "Lollard Bible" was condemned by both Church and Crown, and espousing Lollard beliefs warranted persecution as a heretic. In 1425, even Wycliffe himself was condemned posthumously, and his body was dug up, burned and thrown in a river. Nevertheless, Wycliffe's ideas continued to spread, and the Lollards continued to preach, teach and transcribe copies of Biblical books into English.

By the end of the century, the Lollard movement was on the wane, but in 1494 William Tyndale was born. Like Wycliffe, Tyndale was ordained as a priest and trained as a scholar of the Latin Bible. He too became convinced that the Church he served had drifted from her proper Scriptural moorings, and so he began a project to translate the entire New Testament into English, working not from the Latin manuscripts as Wycliffe and his followers had done, but translating directly from manuscripts written in Greek.

By this time, however, copying and circulating the Bible in English had become highly dangerous and subversive work. The same year Tyndale began translating his New Testament, a young man from Norwich was burned publicly for heresy for the "crime" of owning a copy of the Lord's Prayer in English. Tyndale finished his New Testament and had it printed abroad in 1526, but he was forced to flee to Antwerp in order to continue his work on the Old Testament. Tragically, Tyndale was betrayed by an acquaintance in Antwerp and arrested, tried and convicted of heresy. On October 6, 1536 he was strangled to death and his body was burned publicly for daring to translate the Bible into English.

Thankfully, Tyndale's death did not stop his New Testament from being printed, sold and read. In fact, printings rapidly increased. Soon after Tyndale's execution, Miles Coverdale completed his translation work on the Old Testament and full copies of the English Bible began to be printed, circulated and sold (illegally) in England. Although it has become somewhat standard in historical scholarship to think of England's Reformation as a "top down" affair imposed by clergy, this view underestimates the well-documented desire among the English laity to hear and understand the Bible for themselves. Tyndale did not impose his Bible on lay people; rather, he tapped into their own spiritual yearning for a direct and personal understanding of the Word of God.

Consider, for example, Rawlins White, an illiterate Cardiff fisherman, who sent his son to school during the reign of King Edward so that he could learn to read and write in English. The boy would read a portion of the Bible to his father each night after supper, and his father would commit what he heard to memory with such attention and accuracy that he could cite chapter and verse number. Another man, John Maundrel, purchased his own New Testament and carried it with him everywhere he went, even though he was illiterate. When he met anyone who could read, he would bring out his New Testament and implore them to read him a portion of "the Good Book," which he would duly memorize. Even more astounding is the testimony of Joan Waste, a blind woman from Derby who made her living sewing. She saved her meager earnings and bought herself a copy of the New Testament, which she had friends read aloud to her. It was reported that Joan could recite entire chapters of the Gospels by heart.

Like Wycliffe and Tyndale, these common men and women yearned to read and understand the Bible, and although it is almost unthinkable to us, each of them paid a terrible price for their devotion and fidelity. They were all arrested, tried and burned alive for the heresy of reading and possessing an English Bible.

In the end, if we are to honor their devotion and sacrifice, we must honor the Scriptures for which they died. The Bible is not like any other book. It is God's "true and lively Word" spoken to us and for us. The more intimately we come to know the Bible, the more emphatically it becomes OUR book. It becomes our frame of reference and defines our vision of what is possible. It shapes our hopes, our desires and yes, even our loves. This is possible because God's glory is indeed manifest throughout its pages. The Bible is the story of God interwoven with the story of us all, and it is the greatest story that can ever be told.

This is what John Wycliffe knew, and this is what William Tyndale, Rawlins White, John Maundrel and Joan Waste died for. When we read the Word of God, we encounter God as He has revealed Himself to be. To know God in this way empowers us to live in new ways. The larger the Bible looms in our imagination, the more skeptical we become of the Spirit of the Age and the Ruler of this World, and the more willing we become to live and die as Children of God. In this way, the Bible gifts us with spiritual vision. It pushes us to examine ourselves and our world anew. And it reminds us that the real gap, the real separation, that ought to concern us as followers of Jesus Christ is not the separation between culture and the life of the Church, but the separation between the life of the Church and the Word of God.

So, let us read. And as we give ourselves ever more faithfully to the words of Scripture, may the Word Himself dwell ever more abundantly in us.

Maccabees in the New Testament
Matthew Bryan

My last article presented several of Jesus' teachings from the Wisdom of Sirach and noted the fact that Matthew's gospel paid particular attention to those teachings. While Wisdom of Sirach had only a limited impact on the New Testament, the history of the Maccabees affected first century Judaism so strongly that our Protestant avoidance of 1st and 2nd Maccabees has enabled serious errors in some of our most central doctrines.

Like Sirach, 1st and 2nd Maccabees have been mislabeled as "apocrypha," a title originally reserved for heretical Gnostic writings;[1] but no apocryphal teachings arise in 1st or 2nd Maccabees. Even if one does not accept these books as Scripture, Martin Luther called them "profitable and good to read."[2] My hope is that this article will encourage many Christians to read these chronicles of resistance and victory, which strongly shaped Jewish culture at the time of our Lord's incarnation and the Writings which followed from His apostles.

Inspiration for Pharisees
A Pharisee is a "separatist." The title "Pharisee" occurs almost 100 times in the New Testament. According to the Jewish Encyclopedia, the word derives from the Aramaic "perishaya" and the Hebrew "perushim," meaning someone who *separates* himself from impure persons or things.[3] One man in particular inspired the "separation" of the Pharisees. His name was Mattathias Maccabeus.

Antiochus IV Epiphanes rose to power in the Greek Seleucid Empire in 175 B.C. 1st Maccabees 1:10 introduces Antiochus Epiphanes, then quickly turns its focus to the Jews of that time who rebelled against

---

[1] Athanasius, *Festal Letter 39*: "... nor is there in any place a mention of apocryphal writings. But they are an invention of heretics who ... may find occasion to lead astray the simple."
[2] Hills, Edward, "King James Version Defended" (Ankeny, IA: Christian Research Press, 1997) p. 98.
[3] See http://jewishencyclopedia.com/articles/12087-pharisees

God's law and covenant. They regretted their *separation* from the religions and cultures of other nations and therefore wanted to form a covenant with nations like Greece. In the New English Translation of the Septuagint, 1st Maccabees 1:11 and 1:15 read as follows:

> "In those days out of Israel came sons, transgressors of the law, and persuaded many, saying, 'Let us go and make a covenant with the nations around us, because from the time we **separated** ourselves from them many evils have found us.' ... and they fashioned foreskins for themselves and apostatized from the holy covenant and **joined** themselves to the nations and sold themselves to do evil." (emphases added)

In 168 B.C., Antiochus IV entered the temple in Jerusalem, massacring people and defiling the sanctuary. He demanded that the Judaeans become like the Greeks, a process known as "Hellenization." The ones who conformed to Greek culture and education were called "Hellenes,"[1] a word normally translated in our Bibles as "Greeks." King Antiochus decreed that all of Judaea should be Hellenized, "To the end they might forget the law, and change all the ordinances." (1st Mac 1:49 KJV)

In the Judaean town of Modin however, the elderly priest Mattathias refused bribes from the king's officers to make profane sacrifices. The King James Version of 1st Maccabees 2:21-26 records his "zeal for the law" as follows:

> "'God forbid that we should forsake the law and the ordinances. We will not hearken to the king's words, to go from our religion, either on the right hand, or the left.' Now when he had left speaking these words, there came one of the Jews in the sight of all to sacrifice on the altar which was at Modin, according to the king's commandment.
>
> "Which thing when Mattathias saw, he was inflamed with zeal, and his reins trembled, neither could he forbear to shew his anger according to judgment: wherefore he ran, and slew him upon the altar. Also the king's commissioner, who compelled men to sacrifice, he killed at that time, and the altar he pulled down. Thus dealt he zealously for the law of God like as Phinees did unto Zambri the son of Salom."

---

[1] See https://www.myjewishlearning.com/article/hellenism-judaism/

The events of 1st and 2nd Maccabees have been fictionalized in the excellent novel "My Glorious Brothers." In reality, Mattathias and his sons defeated the Greek armies, as prophesied in the book of Zachariah, and began a Jewish reign which is referred to as "the times of the separation" in the NETS of 2nd Maccabees 14:3 and 14:38. On his deathbed, Mattathias gives a rousing speech, which is so important that it inspired the Hebrews 11 "hall of faith." Running from 1st Maccabees 2:49 through 2:68, Mattathias' speech includes, "Now therefore, children, be zealous for the law..." and "Remember the works of our fathers..." and "Children, be brave, and be strong in the law, for by it you will be glorified." (NETS)

The New Testament word "Pharisees" is just a transliteration of the Greek "farisaion." If the word were actually translated, our New Testaments would read "Separatist" or "Separatists" nearly 100 times. These first-century Jewish Separatists originated during the Maccabean armed resistance to Greece and subsequent cultural resistance to Hellenization, whether by Greek forces or Roman forces.

Maccabean Salvation

The "glory" which Mattathias promised his sons was God's "salvation" from their enemies, which is *the* primary theme of salvation in the New Testament, not salvation from hell or from God's wrath, as is commonly thought in Protestantism. Jesus spoke about hell (directly or indirectly) in just 60 verses, 3% of our red-letter verses. Yet in the four Gospels alone, demons (including Satan) are specifically mentioned or quoted as speaking in 120 verses. This number does not include indirect references nor vague titles like "the enemy" or even the "evil one," as in the Sower parables.

On page after page, Jesus directly battles unclean spirits. When He frees people from demons, He speaks of Satan's kingdom and proclaims His own kingdom of heaven or "kingdom of God." He refers to Satan's kingdom as "this world" and "the world," setting Himself in opposition to it. Throughout the Gospels we hear of the battle between Light and darkness, as though the Maccabean battles had raged on without an end.

On his deathbed, Mattathias appointed his son Judas as the new commander. Judas continued spreading the message of zeal for the law, zeal for good works, and the expected *salvation* which God will give those who hold fast to His law. The KJV of 1st Maccabees 3:18-22 translates his words as follows:

"...it makes no difference before heaven to **save** by many or by a few. For the victory of battle standeth not in the multitude of an host; but strength cometh from heaven. They come against us in much pride and iniquity to destroy us, and our wives and children, and to spoil us: But we fight for our lives and our **laws**. Wherefore the Lord himself will overthrow them..." (emphases added)

When Judas Maccabeus prepares his troops before an army of enemies, he rallies them, saying, "Remember how our fathers were **saved** in the Red Sea when Pharao [sic] was pursuing them in force. And now let us cry out to heaven, if he will desire us and will remember the covenant of our fathers and will smash this company in front of us today. And all the nations will know that there is one who **redeems and saves** Israel."[1] (emphases added) At the close of that battle, the writer of 1st Maccabees declares, "And a great **salvation** came about in Israel on that day."[2] (emphasis added)

The Maccabean Revolution happened just 160 years before our Lord's incarnation. The Maccabean *salvation* lived on in first-century Jewish minds, and it followed from the lips and pens of Jesus and His apostles. In the Great Commission, hell and wrath get no mention, but the King of Kings' authority takes center stage. Later when Jesus commissioned Paul, He still did not offer a message about hell, but about His own authority and about *salvation from enemies*: "I am sending you to open their eyes, so that they may turn from darkness to light and from the power of Satan to God, that they may receive forgiveness of sins and a place among those who are sanctified by faith in me."[3]

We may recognize the implications of wrath and hell in the Great Commission or in Paul's commission, but the explicit and predominant theme throughout the New Testament is that of a war between two kingdoms and the escape of prisoners who "turn from darkness to light and from the power of Satan to God." We do not read 1st and 2nd Maccabees, therefore we overlook that theme and then offer the subtexts (wrath and hell) as the New Testament's primary theme. The Maccabees fought flesh and blood; our King and His apostles fought equally real enemies for the salvation of prisoners:

---

[1] See NETS 1st Maccabees 4:9-11.
[2] See NETS 1st Maccabees 4:25.
[3] See Acts 26:17-18 ESV.

"He has delivered us from the power of darkness and conveyed us into the kingdom of the Son of His love." (Col 1:13 NKJV)

"Put on the whole armor of God, that you may be able to stand against the wiles of the devil. For we do not wrestle with flesh and blood, but against principalities, against powers, against the rulers of the darkness of this age, against spiritual hosts of wickedness in the heavenly places." (Eph 6:11-12 NKJV)

Maccabean Zeal
When we overlook the histories of the Maccabees, we also misunderstand the context of some of the most important language in the New Testament—language which communicates Maccabean themes like salvation, works, Pharisees, zeal for the law, circumcision, and redemption.

Before our King's incarnation, Judaea and Rome had come together in peace through the efforts of a nephew of Judas Maccabeus named John. Two of John's grandsons fought one another in the Hasmonean Civil War, a war which the Roman Republic resolved by conquering Jerusalem in 63 B.C. and then demanding tribute.

The Roman Republic became the Roman Empire, and its power over Judaea had increased greatly by the time John the Baptist preached. The people of Judaea longed for the same salvation which Mattathias and his sons had accomplished. They believed in large part that separation (Pharisaism) was their means of salvation, in contrast with Hellenization. More simply stated, they believed that God would save the *zealous* separatists from their enemies.

Mattathias had called them to zeal for works of the law and zeal for the law itself, both of which showed their faith in God. The following excerpts are from the NETS of 1st Maccabees 2:50-68 (emphases added):
>"Now, children, be **zealous in the law**, and give your lives for the covenant of our fathers."
>"Remember **the works** of our fathers, which they did in their generations, and receive great glory and an everlasting name."
>"Was not Abraam found faithful in temptation, and it was accounted to him as righteousness?"
>"Ioseph in the time of his affliction **observed the commandment** ..."
>"Phinees our father, by becoming **zealous with zeal** ..."

"Elias, by becoming greatly **zealous for the law**, was taken up into heaven."

"Hananias, Azarias and Misael, because of their faith, were saved from fire."

"Children, be brave, and be **strong in the law**, for by it you will be glorified."

"And you shall draw to you all those who **observe the law** ..."

"Return what is due to the nations, and be attentive to the **ordinance of the law**."

Judas, son of Mattathias: "But we fight for our lives and our **laws**. Wherefore the Lord himself will overthrow them ..." (1st Mac 3:21-22 KJV emphasis added)

Jonathon, son of Mattathias wrote to Rome: "... we have the holy books of scripture in our hands to comfort us ... we have help from heaven ... we are delivered from our enemies, and our enemies are brought under foot." (1st Mac 12:9,15)

Simon, son of Mattathias: "Ye yourselves know what great things I, and my brethren, and my father's house, have done **for the laws** and the sanctuary ... Doubtless I will avenge my nation, and the sanctuary ..." (1st Mac 13:3,6 KJV emphasis added)

Eleazar the Scribe: "... manfully changing this life, I will shew myself such an one as mine age requireth, And leave a notable example to such as be young to die willingly and **courageously for the honourable and holy laws** ..." (2nd Mac 6:27-28 KJV emphasis added)

First of seven martyred brothers: "... we are ready to die, rather than to transgress the **laws** of our fathers." (2nd Mac 7:2 KJV emphasis added)

Seventh of seven martyred brothers: "... I will not obey the king's commandment: but I will obey the commandment of **the law** that was given unto our fathers by Moses. ... But I, as my brethren, offer up my body and life **for the laws** of our fathers..." (2nd Mac 7:30,37 KJV emphases added)

Testimony of Nicanor: "... the Jews had God to fight for them, and therefore they could not be hurt, because they **followed the laws** that he gave them. (2nd Mac 8:36 KJV emphasis added)

Regarding Judas Maccabeus: "And he resembled a lion in **his works** ... And he caused bitterness to many kings, and gladness to Iakob **by his works** ..." (1st Mac 3:4,7 NETS emphases added)

So likewise after the fashion of the Maccabean Separatists, the Apostle Paul wrote of himself, "a Hebrew of Hebrews; as to the law, a Pharisee; as to zeal, a persecutor of the church; as to righteousness under the law, blameless,"[1] As Mattathias and his followers described it, zeal and works came from faith. The Maccabees did not try to earn heaven by their works, but to live out their faith as Separatists who trust in God, rather than as Hellenes who forsake their faith in God.

By the first century, the Separatists (Pharisees) had perverted the zeal-and-works mindset of their Maccabean heritage into that of boasting. Yet zeal and works were not what we have misunderstood the New Testament to say; that is, works were not a method of earning heaven. Zeal and works were the Maccabean outcome of faith; a faith which resulted in divine "salvation" from enemies.

Circumcision in the Maccabees
Why in the world did the apostles talk so often about circumcision? After the Book of Joshua, circumcision and foreskins are mentioned just seven times in the Protestant Old Testament, aside from the use of the epithet "uncircumcised" for non-Jews. Three of the seven verses are about David's "bride price" for Saul's daughter Michel, leaving a paltry four verses on the topic across 33 books. Yet such genital surgery shows up a whopping 65 times in the words of the apostles.

Since the Protestant Old Testament prophets and historians almost completely omit the topic after the Israelites entered the Promised Land, we should ask how male genital surgery morphed into such a hot topic in the first century. If we open an Old Testament of one of the 2,000-year-old branches of Christianity, however, we get nine more passages, seven of which occur in 1st and 2nd Maccabees, both of which Martin Luther called "profitable" reading.

Wasting no time at all, circumcision shows up in the very first chapter of 1st Maccabees. A key aspect of Hellenization was the provision of gymnasiums where men competed naked. The KJV of verses 14 and 15 reads "Whereupon they built a place of exercise at Jerusalem

---

[1] See https://biblehub.com/philippians/3-5.htm.

according to the customs of the heathen: And made themselves uncircumcised ..."

You heard it right: "made themselves uncircumcised." Gymnasium competition was as important to Hellenized societies as bath houses were to Roman society. Therefore Judaeans who forsook the law would undergo epispasm or infibulation procedures, which Paul references in 1st Corinthians 7:18.

Twice I have visited a synagogue, and on neither occasion did anyone check to see if I had a foreskin. Yet circumcision was so important in 1st century Judaea, that even the apostle Paul felt it necessary to circumcise a Christian on one occasion,[1] because the events of 1st and 2nd Maccabees had left such a deep imprint on the Jewish culture of that era.

First-century Separatists (Pharisees) did not expect their missing foreskins to save them from Rome, much less get them into heaven. They had faith, however, that God would see their zealous separation, like that of the Maccabees, therefore He would *save* them from Roman rule, just like He had *saved* their ancestors from Greek rule. Uncircumcision and Separatism were polar opposites, one a sign of covenant with God and the other a sign of covenant with unbelievers: "And made themselves uncircumcised, and forsook the holy covenant, and joined themselves to the heathen ..." (1st Maccabees 1:15 KJV)

Works versus Grace
If it is true that New Testament "salvation" is primarily a Maccabean *liberation* from enemies, and if New Testament "works of the law" are acts of faith, including Pharisaism and circumcision (all being properly understood through the lens of the Maccabees), what then should we make of the works-versus-grace discussions? After all, Paul writes in such a way that grace and faith seem directly opposed to works.

In the history of the Maccabees, Jews were saved *by grace through works*. Since "grace" means divine generosity and "salvation" in that day meant divine liberation from Gentile rulership, first-century Jews who held a Separatist (Pharisaic) loyalty to their covenant with God would *by their faith*, do works which reflected God's law, believing by

---

[1] See https://www.biblehub.com/acts/16-3.htm.

faith that God in His generosity (grace) would save them from their enemies. In short, they believed they would be saved from Rome, by grace, through works of the law.

After King Jesus defeated the kingdom of this world, the Holy Spirit revealed the true battle to His apostles—apostles who lived in a post-Maccabean society where works, salvation, circumcision, and Separation from Gentiles all referred to the smaller-scale conflict of Gentile authority versus Jewish fidelity. The Maccabees needed to have faith in God's covenant in the face of grave temptation, in order to evoke God's grace to save them. Their faith in God's covenant resulted in works of the law, therefore grace and works were tied directly together.

In contrast, Christians simply believed that Jesus is the promised King of Psalm 2, which calls Him the "Christ" (meaning "Anointed") in verse 2, the King in verse 6, and God's Son in verse 7 who defeats the rulers of this world in verses 8 and following. Therefore unlike the Maccabean Revolt, works did not have to precede salvation from the apostles' enemies, because that battle had already been won. When people believed the apostles' testimony that Jesus is the victorious King, works followed; but salvation had already been won, therefore Paul could say, "For by grace you have been saved through faith ... not as a result of works..."

Conclusion

Maccabean salvation from enemies happened by God's grace through faith after works of the law by circumcised, zealous, Separatists. The Maccabean history markedly colors the New Testament, and our Protestant theology suffers from its omission from our reading. Here are a few additional Maccabean influences on the New Testament:
- The Feast of Hanukkah in John 10:22-36 comes from the events in 1st Maccabees 4:36-59 and 2nd Maccabees 10:1-8.
- Before Paul and James recounted Abraham's belief and God's having counted his belief as righteousness, the writer of the Maccabees also did so in his "Hall of Zeal."
- The Hebrews 11 "Hall of Faith" includes the mother from 2nd Maccabees 7:1-29 in Hebrews 11:35 which states, "Women received back their dead by resurrection. Some were tortured, refusing to accept release, so that they might rise again to a better life." (ESV) While many mothers lost their children in the Old Testament, none but she are recorded as seeing their

children tortured and refusing release so that they might rise again to a better life.
- 1st and 2nd Maccabees record the fulfillment of prophecies in Daniel 8:9-14 and Zechariah 9:13-17.
- Origen of Alexandria called 2nd Maccabees "holy Scripture" and taught the doctrine of creation *ex-nihilo*, based on the words of the same unnamed mother in 2nd Maccabees 7.[1]
- 1st and 2nd Maccabees were received as inspired Scripture by all four apostolic branches of Christianity long before the Protestant Reformation.

---

[1] Ante Nicene Fathers Volume IV, "Origen de Principiis," book II, chapter 1, paragraph 5.

Sola Scriptura's Relevance for the Modern Church
Alyssa Hall

In the fourteenth and fifteenth centuries, there arose a group of men and women that had become disillusioned by the excesses and misappropriations of the Roman Catholic church and, in a reactive movement, spawned the Reformation, and consequently, the Five Solas: *sola gratia, sola fide, sola scriptura, sola christus,* and *soli deo gloria*. While these five principles were never clearly grouped and articulated together by any one Reformer during that period of time, they have been devised in subsequent centuries by scholars to succinctly convey the core of most Reformation doctrines. Each of the *solas* bears weight for the church in America today, but one in particular, *sola scriptura*, seems to be one that is often left by the wayside, in favor of "cutting edge" psychological and scientific advances. Yet, I believe that if we return to this doctrine, we, like the Reformers, will become the salt and light that both the world, and the Western church need for us to be.

What does *sola scriptura* mean? Simply translated, it means "by Scripture alone." Of course, that concise phrase actually encompasses a whole ideology—the belief that God's Word alone, rather than the clergy, the Church, or any other human-made structure or framework, is the final authority for all forms of doctrine and practice. This principle is supported by 2 Timothy 3:16, which says "All scripture is given by inspiration of God, and is profitable for doctrine, for reproof, for correction, for instruction in righteousness."[1] (KJV) According to *sola scriptura*, God's Word alone, not the words or philosophies of man, is to be revered as the only inerrant authority.

Why did the Reformers deem it necessary to promote the principle of *sola scriptura* in their communication regarding the Reformed faith? In observing the state of the Catholic church from whence they had come out, these men saw that there had been such undue emphasis

---

[1] 2014. 2 Timothy 3:16 KJV.

placed upon church traditions as to usurp the authority of the Scriptures, to the detriment of the church and to the extreme elevation of mere human beings and their traditions. As John Calvin wrote, "But this is the difference between us and the papists. They think that the Church is the 'pillar of truth' (1 Tim. 3:15), just as if it controls the Word of God. On the other hand, we assert that the truth is possessed by the Church and handed down to others because it subjects itself reverently to the Word of God."[1] We may well understand that the Church does not rule the Scriptures; rather the Scriptures ought to rule the Church.

The reformers believed that each aspect of the life of the Church and the individual must be conformed to the will of God as revealed only in Holy Scripture. After all, Romans 3:10-18 clearly states, "As it is written, There is none righteous, no, not one: There is none that understandeth, there is none that seeketh after God. They are all gone out of the way, they are together become unprofitable; there is none that doeth good, no, not one. Their throat is an open sepulchre; with their tongues they have used deceit; the poison of asps is under their lips: Whose mouth is full of cursing and bitterness: Their feet are swift to shed blood: Destruction and misery are in their ways: And the way of peace have they not known: There is no fear of God before their eyes." (KJV)[2] If this is the wretched and helpless state of even the best specimen that humankind has to offer, then it is evident that we would do poorly to fashion our lives according to the word of man rather than the Word of God.

If we do not see Scripture alone as the final authority for the modern church, as other churches have in the past, we run the risk of committing transgression in a couple of different ways. First, we fall into the trap of exalting man's traditions, legalisms, or practices too highly, even to the point of idolatry. Jesus, speaking harshly to the Pharisees in Mark 7:6-8, said, "Well hath Esaias prophesied of you hypocrites, as it is written, This people honoureth me with their lips, but their heart is far from me. Howbeit in vain do they worship me, *Teaching For Doctrines The Commandments Of Men.* For laying aside the commandment of God, ye hold the tradition of men."[3] (KJV, emphasis added) Obviously, Jesus was displeased with the lack of

---

[1] 2003. The Title: "The Church" by John Calvin – The Highway. http://www.the-highway.com/titlechurch_Calvin.html.
[2] 2014. Romans 3:10-18 KJV.
[3] 2014. Mark 7:6-8 KJV.

respect and prominence that the Pharisees gave the Scriptures—the revelation of God to man—as they instead pridefully reverenced their own inventions and that of their fathers above God's Word. If we claim, as many rightfully do, that our Lord is the wellspring of all knowledge and wisdom, consider what hypocrites we make ourselves to be when we live by the traditions and inventions of men, which are pitiful when compared to the surpassing brightness of God, while pushing His own words to the back burner.

Secondly, if we do not keep the principle of Scripture alone always in the forefront of our minds, we leave the door wide open for false teaching to infiltrate both ourselves and the church. If we follow Paul, or Apollos, or Cephas, or anyone else other than Christ as He is revealed in the Scriptures, we will discover at some point, if we keep our eyes open and do not fall prey to delusion, that each of these are only men, prone to error, however well-intentioned they may be. Following men blindly, without the discerning power of the Bible, will certainly lead to sin. The Word of God praises the Bereans in Acts 17:11 saying, "These were more noble than those in Thessalonica, in that they received the word with all readiness of mind, and searched the scriptures daily, whether those things were so." (KJV)[1] Even when presented with truth, the Bereans beheld these new doctrines in light of Scripture and followed them willingly because they understood them to be the fulfilment of what they already knew to be true, as revealed in the Old Testament. They understood how easy it is for one to be overtaken by false teaching that comes as a wolf in sheep's clothing, as 2 Corinthians 11:14-15 says, "For Satan himself is transformed into an angel of light. Therefore it is no great thing if his ministers also be transformed as the ministers of righteousness." (KJV)[2] We would do well to follow the example of the Bereans in testing new ideas in light of the Scriptures, rather than merely accepting them at face value.

John Calvin said, "Now, in order that true religion may shine upon us, we ought to hold that it must take its beginning from the heavenly doctrine and that no one can get even the slightest taste of right and sound doctrine unless he be a pupil of Scripture."[3] Even though the

---

[1] 2014. Acts 17:11 KJV.
[2] 2014. 2 Corinthians 11:14-15 KJV.
[3] Calvin: *Institutes of the Christian Religion.* https://books.google.com/books?id=eABeezea4dwC&pg=PA72&lpg=PA72

"great cloud of witnesses"—the saints of the past and present spoken of in Hebrews 12— can be an excellent source of encouragement and wisdom for us, the elevation of their insights to those of the Word of God, or the study of them to the exclusion or neglect of the Scriptures is folly at best, and idolatry and false teaching at worst. Why should we cling so tightly to secondhand information, when the firsthand account is so readily available to us? We do not live in the time of the Reformation, when illiteracy was rampant and the only Bible authorized by the Church was the Latin Vulgate, something that most common people would never be able to read. It is understandable that the common person in those days would blindly follow human teachings. He had little choice, since the opportunity for learning to read either English or Latin, let alone having access to a Bible, was far out of reach. But, today, almost anyone who lives in a first world country has no excuse for not holding men's teachings and traditions accountable to the Word of God, seeing that we have the Bible so readily available to us in most bookstores and even on iPhone apps and that compulsory education laws mean that most of us are literate.

As Jesus said in Luke 12:48, "For unto whomsoever much is given, of him shall be much required."(KJV)[1] We have been given the privilege of having God's Word conveniently accessible to us and of possessing the ability to read it. May we not waste these things, but let us instead be diligent in using Scripture to "cast down imaginations, and every high thing that exalteth itself against the knowledge of God, and bring into captivity every thought to the obedience of Christ." (2 Corinthians 10:5, KJV)[2]

&dq=John+Calvin+true+religion+shine+upon+us&source=bl&ots=Xle6tz HV7u&sig=SvhQBOtTtHnm3J8lH6LLRomrxLw.
[1] 2014. Luke 12:48 KJV.
[2] 2014. 2 Corinthians 10:5 KJV.

Longings
Joshua Schendel

Or, Reflections on the Gospel of John in Response to Leonard Cohen

I hunger.
Bread fills me.
I hunger again.
I thirst.
Wine makes the heart glad.
My thirst is not quenched.
I question.
I have seen all done under the sun.
Truth eludes me.
I love
As the wonder of a man with a virgin.
Yet the unity is cracked.
I live,
Tasting, hearing, smelling, seeing, feeling all these mundane joys,
Yet I die.
Surely there is more
To being, to life;
Bread which satiates, drink which vivifies,
Truth that finds me.
Surely there is a marriage of unbroken communion.
Jesus says, I AM.

Faith Across Traditions

Tradition and Traditions

Even the most stringent of the *sola scriptura* crowd follow patterns when it comes to the practical side of faith. No church is an island, no believer alone in following Jesus. These essays dig into practicalities of liturgy, baptism, sacraments, church history, and corporate worship in ways that invite us to thoughtfully engage the traditions of the Great Tradition. Oh, and don't forget to read the first contribution in this section, which long reigned as the most popular article at *Conciliar Post*.

Essays

The Desert Fathers Play *Pokémon Go*, *Casberg*

Tradition Is the Answer to the Questions We've Forgotten We Have, *White*

Acts of Baptism, *Prahlow*

Mary, Mother of God, Mother of the Church, *Hyland*

Things I'd Rather Do on Sunday Morning Than Go to Church, *Casberg*

What John Calvin Taught Me About the Sacraments, *Schellhase*

Why Is Christian Liturgy So Repetitive, *Quick*

Three Things That Need to Change About Church, *White*

What's the Point of the Sermon, *Kim*

How Should We Choose the Church We Attend, *Aldhizer*

Faith Across Traditions

The Desert Fathers Play *Pokémon Go*
Chris Casberg

Two monks left their cell and appeared before Abba Anthony, who was praying. "Abba," said one of the monks, "My brother is in error, saying that Squirtle is the best starter when Charmander is clearly superior." The other replied, "Nay, it is my brother who errs, for Squirtle has the best evolution." Abba Anthony ceased praying and stood before the brethren. He pulled his own iPhone from within his robe and snapped it in half. "A house divided by itself cannot stand. Now, these starter Pokemon have become sin to you. Flee them three times." The two monks departed Abba Anthony's presence. When the starter Pokemon appeared on their phones, they fled three times as the Abba told them. The fourth time, a Pikachu appeared on their screens, and the brethren were amazed.

Amma Theodora had been in prayer for thirty nine days in her cell when a woman appeared with a child at her side. "My son is beset by demons, and I fear for his soul. What must I do to safeguard his salvation?" she asked. Amma Theodora said, "Tell me the manner of these demons." The mother produced a phone and placed it within the Amma's palm. She studied the phone and then said, "These are not demons but Ghost-type Pokemon. Your son should field some Dark-types, which are super effective against them. Also, you yourself must pray in solitude for forty days as our Lord did, for somehow you can't tell the difference between cartoon characters and actual, legit demons." With that, Amma Theodora knelt to pray, and then she floated away into the sky.

A band of robbers was guarding a Pokestop in a village near a cloister of brethren, preventing the people from refilling their stock of Pokeballs and potions. A pair of brethren traveled to the Pokestop and beseeched the robbers to leave, but the robbers beat them and took what food the monks had. The brothers sought out Abba Isidore, whom they found fishing a stream and putting both good fish and bad fish in a single basket. "Abba," said one, "Why are you taking both the good fish and bad fish?" The Abba pulled his line from the water and said, "That which is holy and sweet draws what is fair and foul alike, and all belong to the Lord." The brethren praised the Abba's wisdom, and they returned returned to the Pokestop and activated a Lure Module. This attracted so many Pokemon the robbers could not keep up, and they let the people come reap the harvest as well. Shamed by the generosity of the brethren, many of the robbers gave themselves to the Lord and took cells in the desert.

Concerning which Team Gym to join, Abba Simeon told this to the brethren: "One of them is called Team *Mystic*. This should be a no-brainer, guys."

Of Abba Macarius, Abba Peter had this to say: "One day Abba Macarius visited an anchorite who lived in a cave far outside of Alexandria. The anchorite was ill and could not walk. When asked what he required, the anchorite said, "I have the Word of the Lord as my bread, so I want for nothing." When asked again, the anchorite said, "I have tasted the cup of the Lord's salvation, and its sweetness gives me strength." When asked a third time, the anchorite said, "Abba, you are an important man, and I cannot waste your time. Send me one of the brethren who can walk my Pokemon eggs until they hatch." Abba Macarius took the anchorite's phone and himself walked through the desert until the eggs hatched, even though they were legendaries and took like forever. So humble was Abba Macarius, he said nothing, but the anchorite spread the word of his deed.

Amma Theodora came upon a group of sisters who were washing their clothes in the river while boasting of their Pokemon collections. The first sister boasted that in her self-denial, she had only collected twenty Pokemon. The second sister boasted she had only collected ten. The third boasted that she had collected zero Pokemon, and was thus the most spiritual collector of them all. "I store my Pokeballs in heaven, where neither moth nor rust destroy them," she cried. The sisters turned to Amma Theodora and asked how many Pokemon she had collected. "One hundred and fifty one, which is all of them," said the Amma. The sisters fell silent, and Amma Theodora taught them this: "When asceticism becomes prideful, it becomes sin, and the spiritual person must then abstain from abstaining to safeguard their salvation." With that, Amma Theodora knelt to pray, and then she floated away into the sky.

Two monks appeared before Abba Anthony as he prayed in his cell, asking whether it was best to evolve a low-level Pokemon or send it to Professor Willow for candy and pray a higher-level version would appear later. The Abba said, "What to the Scriptures say? 'Anyone who loves his life will lose it.' If you are afraid to send away your Pikachu, you are already dead inside, and evolving it to Raichu will mean nothing to you. Go to your cells and contemplate this." The brethren were amazed by his wisdom, and they returned to their cells to do as Abba Anthony commanded.

Twenty of the brethren came to Simeon the Elder as he prayed atop a pillar. Each held a scroll of parchment. "Abba," said one, "We have each written a hot-take on how *Pokemon Go* demonstrates what's wrong with Christianity and/or the culture at large. Shall we read them to you?" Simeon the Elder regarded them, and then he said, "Yes, but first you must each kneel and pray to the Lord that your words will be true." The brethren did as he commanded, and they all knelt and prayed. When they opened their eyes and looked at their scrolls, they were amazed! For the scrolls had turned into mirrors, and where they had written what was wrong with the world, there was only their own reflection. "Abba," said one of the monks, "That's a little on the nose, isn't it?" Simeon the Elder shrugged and resumed praying.

Faith Across Traditions

Tradition is the Answer to Questions We've Forgotten We Have
Barbara White

If you are a publicly confessing Christian for long enough you will likely encounter an interesting event: at some point a secular friend will ask for your prayers. It is often the same one who gets annoyed when you can't make brunch on Sunday morning, or who was obviously uncomfortable at your church wedding. Generally the request for prayer follows a moment of immediate need: a scary medical diagnosis, or a layoff with impending financial strain, or a child who is having particular difficulty in school or with friends. There are no atheists in a foxhole, and the human experience is one of finding yourself in and out of various foxholes.

For some people the request for prayer may be another way of saying "I am scared about this and I don't want to be alone." For others it might be "I don't know what to do, but need to do something." Whatever subconscious need it is expressing, everyone, even the most secular people, like to know that their religious friends are there. They like to know there are people who can hear these requests without rolling our eyes, people who will respond in good faith.

The same thing happens in communities and across cultures. The Western world spends very little time thinking about prayer. Politicians might mention it when they are in front of a constituency for whom prayer matters, but it isn't part of the regular warp and weft of our collective life. This may be because, as a whole, we are so safe and comfortable. We have our individual traumas, but we are safest and healthiest culture that has ever existed. We worry about rising food prices, but few Americans or other Westerners are really at risk of *starving* this year, the way people in developing countries are. We worry about rising crime, but we don't live with the daily violence and danger that our neighbors in Ukraine, Yemen, and Nigeria face every day. We do not feel we *need* to pray. The problems we have have other answers: legislation, education, organization.

Until, that is, something truly terrible happens to shake us our of our stupor. In those moments, prayer increases in popularity again. In the early days of the Russian invasion of Ukraine, I saw "Pray for Ukraine" signs pop up in yards of affluent neighborhoods. After the horrific murders in Buffalo and Uvalde, the predicted "Thoughts and prayers for the victims and their families" and more specific "Pray that Congress will pass gun-control legislation" "Pray for better mental health care" and "Lord have mercy on our broken society" prayers splashed across social media. When we feel helpless, when we know we need to do something but are powerless to know what it should be, our society turns again to prayer.

But even for those of use who are regular pray-ers, this creates a challenge: how do we speak to something that is unspeakable? What words are there to say that express the rage and grief of parents whose children were murdered, while the people paid to protect them stood aside? What words provide comfort to the women raped in Ukraine as an act of war? Have we, who have forgotten what real terror, danger, and impunity look like, also forgotten how to pray?

Maybe we have; but our tradition has not. One of the reasons I love being Anglican is that the memory of the Prayerbook extends further back than the last presidential election. Part of the wonder of worshiping with a liturgy that is more than 500 years old is that it holds the memories, anxieties, fear, and doubts of people who lived in times that were much more dangerous, divided, and hostile than ours. And so, when something unspeakable happens, our tradition still has something to say about it.

In the hours after the Russian invasion of Ukraine, when it seemed like world war and possibly nuclear war were imminent, I several members of my parish asked me if we could have a prayer service. They were full of grief and sorrow for the people of Ukraine, but they were also scared about what would happen next. It had been many years since anyone in my congregation had seen footage of tanks rolling into towns that looked just as developed and normal as the town we live in. There were no prayers I could write that would be as poignant or potent as the prayers of our forefathers. And so, on a Saturday morning, we gathered in our chapel. I asked them to open their prayerbooks, and we prayed The Great Litany togeher:

O God the Father, Creator of heaven and earth,
Have mercy upon us.

O God the Son, Redeemer of the world,
Have mercy upon us.

O God the Holy Spirit, Sanctifier of the faithful,
Have mercy upon us.

O holy, blessed, and glorious Trinity, one God,
Have mercy upon us.

Remember not, Lord Christ, our offenses, nor the offenses of our forefathers; neither reward us according to our sins. Spare us, good Lord, spare thy people, whom thou hast redeemed with thy most precious blood, and by thy mercy preserve us, for ever.
Spare us, good Lord.

From all evil and wickedness; from sin; from the crafts and assaults of the devil; and from everlasting damnation,
Good Lord, deliver us.

Students of Anglican liturgy, many of whom are drawn to this study in the first place because they love our Eucharistic Prayers, are surprised to learn that the Great Litany—which is used so rarely in churches these days— it is the very first piece of liturgy written in English. Archbishop Thomas Cranmer translated/wrote/edited it in 1544, when Masses across England were still said in Latin. It was first used in public worship during the reign of Henry VIII, just before the king's armies set sail to wage war with France. This means that for the majority of Christians in England, the first words of the liturgy that they ever heard *in a language they could understand* were these. As they came to church to pray for their sons and fathers preparing to fight King Henry's latest war, they would have heard and prayed:[1]

From lightning and tempest; from earthquake, fire, and flood; from plague, pestilence, and famine,
Good Lord, deliver us.

---

[1] I confess that I did not check the text of the current Great Litany (1979 Book of Common Prayer) against the text of the 1549 Book of Common Prayer, so I can't promise that this is *exactly* the same prayer that those English Christians prayed all those years ago. I am confident that they are similar enough in content and emphasis for my point to stand.

Faith Across Traditions

From all oppression, conspiracy, and rebellion; from violence, battle, and murder; and from dying suddenly and unprepared, *Good Lord, deliver us.*

By the mystery of thy holy Incarnation; by thy holy Nativity and submission to the Law; by thy Baptism, Fasting, and Temptation, *Good Lord, deliver us.*

By thine Agony and Bloody Sweat; by thy Cross and Passion; by thy precious Death and Burial; by thy glorious Resurrection and Ascension; and by the Coming of the Holy Ghost, *Good Lord, deliver us.*

In all time of our tribulation; in all time of our prosperity; in the hour of death, and in the day of judgment, *Good Lord, deliver us.*

And this is the prayer that, time and again, the Church of England and her offspring have turned to this prayer in times of war, famine, political unrest, and violence.[1] In the brutality of the American Civil War, churches in the north and South prayed it. As World War I raged, ultimately claiming the lives of more than 8 million Englishmen, they prayed it. During the Blitz, they prayed "Good Lord, deliver us." I strongly suspect, though I cannot verify, that African Anglicans prayed this prayed this prayer during periods of political violence, and during the Ebola and AIDS epidemics.

Moments of crisis call us to remember the finitude and contingency of the human condition, even for those of us who have the privilege of relative safety and comfort. They call us to suffer and mourn with those who share that condition. And they call us to remember that we are not the first ones to live through such a time as this. Tradition alone cannot end violence, hunger, and fear—only the Resurrection can do that. But it can give us a guide along the way. It gives us the voices of those who have gone before, and it gives us a way to join our voices with those who cry out to God for deliverance.

---

[1] Prior to the 1979 Book of Common Prayer, the Great Litany was said with much more frequency, at Morning and Evening Prayer and prior to Holy Communion, meaning that people were even more likely to have this beautiful text memorized and at their lips in times of distress.

That it may please thee to have mercy upon all mankind,
We beseech thee to hear us, good Lord.

That it may please thee to give us true repentance; to forgive us all our sins, negligences, and ignorances; and to endue us with the grace of thy Holy Spirit to amend our lives according to thy holy Word,
We beseech thee to hear us, good Lord.

That it may please thee to forgive our enemies, persecutors, and slanderers, and to turn their hearts,
We beseech thee to hear us, good Lord.

That it may please thee to strengthen such as do stand; to comfort and help the weak-hearted; to raise up those who fall; and finally to beat down Satan under our feet,
We beseech thee to hear us, good Lord.

Acts of Baptism
Jacob J. Prahlow

As anyone even somewhat familiar with Christianity knows, various Christian denominations have different, specific approaches to baptism—that all important rite involving water and the Holy Spirit. Depending on its theological commitments, a church may expect the person being baptized to be an adult (or, at least old enough to make a conscious decision to be baptized), to be fully immersed in water (rather than sprinkled or poured upon), to be triple immersed (rather than once), to have undergone rigorous catechesis prior to baptism, to manifest miraculous spiritual gifts (before or after), or to fulfill any number of other practices. It really depends on the church. I once spoke to someone who seemed to believe that the only *true* way to be baptized was to be triple immersed while wearing a white gown in the cool running water of the river near their church.

In principle, Christians taking Jesus' command to baptize seriously should be celebrated; in practice, however, our obsession with making sure that everyone is baptized *our way*—the *right way*—poses some problems.

Some Problems with *Right Way* Obsession
In the first place, there is the problem of rebaptism. Many people enter a new church having already been baptized. Or at least, under the impression that they were already baptized. That is, until someone convinces them their previous baptism was invalid and they should be baptized the *right way*. While there are probably some circumstances where a serious discussion about rebaptism may be permissible, making rebaptism commonplace seems to oppose the very unity that the Apostle Paul calls the Church to in Ephesians 4:1-6:
> I therefore, a prisoner for the Lord, urge you to walk in a manner worthy of the calling to which you have been called, with all humility and gentleness, with patience, bearing with one another in love, eager to maintain the unity of the Spirit in the bond of peace. There is one body and one Spirit—just as you were called to the one hope that belongs to your call— **one Lord, one faith, one baptism, one God and Father of**

all, who is over all and through all and in all. [Emphasis added]

Second, a focus on making sure that everyone has been baptized the *right way* potentially corrupts what baptism *is*. Romans 6:1-4 closely identifies the effects of baptism with the salvific work of Jesus' death and resurrection. Orthodox Christians of all denominations confess that salvation comes through this work of Jesus and is granted to humanity by God's grace. To then turn around and assume, as certain denominations do, that baptism must be undertaken in a highly specific manner undercuts that message of grace. It's like saying, "Yes, Jesus graciously offers you life, but *only* if you do the right (baptismal) works to get there."

Finally, a focus on making sure everyone has been baptized the *right way* tends to be utterly confusing for congregants. This is particularly true for those who are new to faith, on the fringes of belief, or in the process of changing churches. In some contexts, the emphasis on being baptized the *right way* can even lead people to question their relationship with God—or to doubt someone else's relationship with God. Beyond the differences in how different denominations baptize, such confusion can lead people to question the value of baptism itself.

Right Way versus *Big Tent*

Although nothing apart from the Second Coming is likely to get Christians on the same page when it comes to baptismal practice, I think there is an approach to baptism that is scriptural *and* can help cut through some of the problems fostered by a *right way* approach to baptism. I call this perspective the *big tent* approach to Christian baptism.

The *big tent* approach to baptism recognizes the internal diversity of baptismal practices recorded within scripture and recognizes as valid differing contemporary baptismal practices when they conform to the diversity of these scriptural models. This approach fits best in a *big tent* approach to Christianity more generally; but it is also tenable in ecclesiastical contexts that work with the diversity of contemporary Christian instruction and practice.[1] Indeed, many denominations

---

[1] For instance, the increasingly common practice by many denominations to recognize the seminary degrees, communion practices, or theological perspectives of other denominations.

already practice this kind of *big tent* thinking when it comes to baptism.

Acts of Baptism
The book of Acts serves as the best example of the *big tent* approach. Luke records about ten distinct narratives of baptism in Acts[1] and, although there are clear theological parameters governing these baptisms, no two are precisely alike. Consider that:
- Some baptisms occur "in the name of Jesus Christ" (8.5-13; 10.44-48; 19.1-5), others appear to be "in the name of the Father, the Son, and the Holy Spirit" (8.36-38), and still others are silent on the matter of "in whom" people are baptized.
- At least one baptism narrative is preceded by repentance of sin (2.37-41), another seems to make confession of faith central (8.36-38), another baptismal narrative is preceded by speaking tongues (10.44-48), and still others focus on the importance of belief (8.5-13; 16.13-15; 16.27-34).
- Some water baptisms precede the baptism of the Holy Spirit (19.1-5), other times the Holy Spirit is poured out before water (9.17-19; 10.44-48), and many times water baptism is not explicitly connected to the baptism of the Spirit.
- Finally, some passages record individual baptisms (8.36-38) while others use household language (10.44-48; 16.13-15; 16.27-34; 18.5-8) that, if nothing else, set the stage for infant baptism.

Clearly Acts records significant diversity of baptismal practice in the early church. Why then are contemporary Christians so committed to picking-and-choosing a handful of these examples (or other New Testament references to baptism) and interpreting them as the *right way* to baptize? A *big tent* approach better reflects the diversity of practice within the New Testament itself—as well as Christ's prayer for unity among His followers.

---

[1] Depending on how you subdivide narratives.

Conclusion

The New Testament consistently portrays baptism as an essential[1] part of what it means to follow Jesus—as a matter of obedience to the command of Jesus (Matt. 28.18-20), as a sign of entrance into God's new covenantal family (Gal. 3.27; Col. 2.12; 1 Cor. 12.13), and as a seemingly salvific act of God's grace (1 Pet. 3.21; see also Mark 16.16). What the New Testament does *not* portray as essential is the precise method of baptism; to the contrary, a variety of specific practices seem to be affirmed. Accordingly, Christians should baptize new believers in a manner consistent with New Testament models and recognize as valid baptisms by other Christians that fit these *big tent* parameters.

God's work through baptism is a gracious gift, one we should continue to celebrate, practice, and reflect upon. In the spirit of Christian unity, however, we should adopt a *big tent* approach to recognizing the validity of baptism at the hands of others. For scripture itself suggests that we make our acts of baptism a little less about us and a little more about the God who is at work in His people.

---

[1] Here, of course, we must draw the distinction between *essential* and *required*. If we take Jesus' words to the thief on the cross seriously, then we cannot expect that no one who has not been baptized belongs to the family of God. Still, exceptional theology should not undermine normative theology. Accordingly, it's appropriate to confirm the long-standing practice that every person who is able who follows Jesus should be baptized.

Mary, Mother of God, Mother of the Church
Daniel Hyland

Given that yesterday the Church celebrated the memorial of the Most Holy Name of the Blessed Virgin Mary, I thought that this week instead of my usual poem I would share a prayer, a traditional litany in honor of her beautiful Name.

As I prepared this piece, I couldn't help thinking that much of the prayer's language will be unfamiliar to my Protestant brothers and sisters. It might even be troubling for you to see with what high regard the Church views Our Mother, and with what love she is praised. I would like to offer you some thoughts on this.

October 13th of this year brings us to the 100th anniversary of Mary's final appearance at Fatima, Portugal (if you are unfamiliar, please read about the events at Fatima. They are among the most important in modern history.) At the month's end, October 31st will mark the 500th anniversary of the Protestant Reformation's formal beginning. There are no coincidences—I would say "in God's eyes," but the plain truth is that what we see "in God's eyes" is simply reality. He exists; His Providence governs all; everything is planned, nothing is accidental. Not even this little parallel between the 13th and the 31st of October, 2017, one number the inversion of the other.

100 years and 500 years—although Mary herself and Marian devotion predate Martin Luther by over 1,500 years; and Mary's role as the Mother of God has been held in the Divine Will, fixed and immutable, from eternity. But there is nevertheless something of a David and Goliath here, in the sense that on one hand you have five centuries backing the general Protestant distaste for Our Lady, which I myself shared in for a time; and on the other, a mere centenary highlighting Our Lady's mission of love for all the world, and first of all for her children.

It isn't for nothing that the Church calls Protestants "our separated brethren," for they are also the children of Mary, as are all "who keep the commandments of God and bear testimony to Jesus" (Revelation 12:17). Yet these children of hers most often refrain from honoring her, become uncomfortable at the mention of her name, and view her with a distrust that on a purely natural level must arouse sympathy and sadness in the heart of any mother.

At best, Protestants distance themselves from Mary out of fear that devotion to her implies a disregard or disdain for her Son, Whom they love and seek to honor. The love is real, but the fear is more immediate, I think. Fear of trespassing against a sacred boundary between God and His creatures mixed in with simple fear of the unfamiliar. We do not know Our Mother as we should.

While I can't put forward a sustained apologetic here, I will say that the answer to this fear is the love of Mary. I mean this in the sense of our love for Mary, because she is Our Mother and Christ's; but more deeply in the sense of Mary's love for us, because we are her children. Her Son is the Head, we are the Body, and Mary is Mother of the whole Christ. Jesus Himself affirms this from the Cross, only moments before His death, when words cost Him most:
> When Jesus saw His mother, and the disciple whom He loved standing near, He said to His mother: "Woman, behold your son!" Then He said to the disciple, "Behold, your mother!" (John 19:26-27)

In the most abandoned moments of our affection, my wife and I fall into a pattern of praise that finds nothing too small to love, nothing insignificant in the other: "I love the way you laugh when you're nervous. I love your teeth. I love the smell of your hair. I love the way you forgive. I love your eye for beauty. I love it when you paint Amelia's nails. I love you, I love you"–and so it goes, dissolving into small, unmeasured kisses given without regard to time or number, landing where they may.

In the same way, a litany is a profusion of love. It is born of the desire to go on: What else can I say? What more can I give you? What else can I find in you to love? If you pray it aloud, you will find that it takes some time. But as you enter into the praises with love, with genuine interest, even with a holy and generous desire to understand those who can say these things seriously, you will find that the time is forgotten, and the love is remembered.

To answer this call of Jesus, to behold Mary, I think this beautiful Litany of the Holy Name of Mary will be helpful. In fixing ourselves on her Holy Name, we find that she fixes us fast on the Name of Jesus.

Hers is the soul that magnifies, increases, makes great within us, the Name above all names. She never tires of saying to us, "Do whatever He tells you" (John 2:5). She never ceases to form in those who turn to her the likeness of her Son–the first to love the Holy Name of Mary.

Litany of the Holy Name of Mary
V. Lord, have mercy.
R. LORD, HAVE MERCY.
Christ, have mercy.
CHRIST, HAVE MERCY.
Lord, have mercy.
LORD, HAVE MERCY.
Son of Mary, hear us.
SON OF MARY, GRACIOUSLY HEAR US.
Heavenly Father, of Whom Mary is the Daughter,
HAVE MERCY ON US.
Eternal Word, of Whom Mary is the Mother,
HAVE MERCY ON US.
Holy Spirit, of Whom Mary is the Spouse,
HAVE MERCY ON US.
Divine Trinity, of Whom Mary is the Handmaid,
HAVE MERCY ON US.
Mary, Mother of the Living God, PRAY FOR US.
Mary, daughter of the Light Eternal, PRAY FOR US.
Mary, our light, ETC.
Mary, our sister,
Mary, flower of Jesse,
Mary, issue of kings,
Mary, chief work of God,
Mary, the beloved of God,
Mary, Immaculate Virgin,
Mary, all fair,
Mary, light in darkness,
Mary, our sure rest,
Mary, house of God,
Mary, sanctuary of the Lord,
Mary, altar of the Divinity,
Mary, Virgin Mother,
Mary, embracing thy Infant God,
Mary, reposing with Eternal Wisdom,
Mary, ocean of bitterness,
Mary, Star of the Sea,
Mary, suffering with thine only Son,

Mary, pierced with a sword of sorrow,
Mary, torn with a cruel wound,
Mary, sorrowful even to death,
Mary, bereft of all consolation,
Mary, submissive to the law of God,
Mary, standing by the Cross of Jesus,
Mary, Our Lady,
Mary, Our Queen,
Mary, Queen of glory,
Mary, glory of the Church Triumphant,
Mary, Blessed Queen,
Mary, advocate of the Church Militant,
Mary, Queen of Mercy,
Mary, consoler of the Church Suffering,
Mary, exalted above the Angels,
Mary, crowned with twelve stars,
Mary, fair as the moon,
Mary, bright as the sun,
Mary, distinguished above all,
Mary, seated at the right hand of Jesus,
Mary, our hope,
Mary, our sweetness,
Mary, glory of Jerusalem,
Mary, joy of Israel,
Mary, honor of our people,
Mary, Our Lady of the Immaculate Conception,
Mary, Our Lady of the Assumption,
Mary, Our Lady of Loreto,
Mary, Our Lady of Lourdes,
Mary, Our Lady of Fatima,
Mary, Our Lady of Czestochowa,
Mary, Our Lady of the Miraculous Medal,
Mary, Our Lady of Mount Carmel,
Mary, Our Lady of the Angels,
Mary, Our Lady of Dolors,
Mary, Our Lady of Mercy,
Mary, Our Lady of the Rosary,
Mary, Our Lady of Victory,
Mary, Our Lady of La Trappe,
Mary, Our Lady of Divine Providence,
Lamb of God, Who takest away the sins of the world,
SPARE US, O LORD JESUS.
Lamb of God, Who takest away the sins of the world,

GRACIOUSLY HEAR US, O LORD JESUS.
Lamb of God, Who takest away the sins of the world,
HAVE MERCY ON US, O LORD JESUS.
Son of Mary, hear us.
SON OF MARY, GRACIOUSLY HEAR US.

V. I will declare thy name unto my brethren.
R. I WILL PRAISE THEE IN THE ASSEMBLY OF THE FAITHFUL.
LET US PRAY.
O Almighty God, Who beholdest Thy servants earnestly desirous of placing themselves under the shadow of the name and protection of the Most Holy Virgin Mary, vouchsafe, we beseech Thee, that by her charitable intercession, we may be delivered from all evil on earth, and may arrive at everlasting joys in Heaven, through Jesus Christ Our Lord. R. AMEN.

Things I'd Rather Do on Sunday Morning Than Go to Church
Chris Casberg

The following, as the title of the article slyly implies, is a list of things I'd rather do on a Sunday morning than go to church. I am being only partly facetious with these.

- **Make a fancy breakfast**. I've taken a liking to the art of cooking these past couple years, and weekend mornings are an exceptional time to practice the craft. Duck confit rolled into crepes; poached eggs over arugula and toast, smothered in bearnaise; sourdough pancakes with a side of thick bacon; omelettes built with with whatever leftover meats and vegetables that did not make it into the week's entrees. . .the list goes ever on. Sadly, Sunday services cut into the time (hours, really) needed to make such extravagant dishes, leaving Saturday with the sole morning out of seven in which to make a fancy breakfast. That is a crime.
- **Head to Sunday brunch**. Sunday brunch is another food-related festivity upon which attending church impinges. Sure, one could always go *after* church, but we all know by then the French toast will be rubbery and all the shrimp will be gone, leaving only a small pool of partially melted ice cubes and discarded shrimp tails in the platter. Further, and this is doubly so for brunch in the American South, the later one gets to brunch, the greater the mob becomes. When I lived in Georgia, I quickly learned that eating out mid-to-late Sunday morning was a practical impossibility; parking lots were bursting at the seams with hungry parishioners just out of service, and the line at the hostess's podium stretched for veritable miles.
- **Sleep**. Okay, this one really isn't me at all. Mornings are the most beautiful part of the day, filled with sleepy silence and golden morning rays. It'd be a shame to waste them in bed—or nodding off in a pew.
- **Finish *The Witcher 3***. This is a videogame that came out early 2015, and as it is a long and dark experience, I've yet to even make it halfway through some fifteen months later. It's

won a great many awards from the game industry, and I can absolutely see why. The time spent handing out bulletins and holding open doors when I'm on usher duty at church, could instead go a long way in solving digital murders and hunting digital monsters, not to mention saving the digital world.

- **Childproof my house**. My infant daughter somehow learned to stand on her feet in the last few weeks. I don't know who taught her how to do this—and I will have a harsh word with them whenever I sniff them out. Rather than deposit her in the kids' nursery for a wasteful hour every Sunday, where she "socializes" with other infants (whatever that means), that time could instead be spent identifying objects which she could not avoid the devilish temptation to gulp down. I could also spend that time nailing bookshelves to the wall. She has a frightful proclivity for attacking books and I don't know if it's mere childlike curiosity or a dark authoritarian streak.
- **Read the Bible**. Really, why drag all the tedious work of religion into one's spirituality? Is it really not enough that I occasionally leaf through that dusty old book and say my prayers once in awhile? After all, it's about my personal relationship with God, and that's nobody else's business, is it? I've been saved and that should be good enough. I find it all a little undemocratic—even un-American—that there are people who'd think to tell me how to practice my faith. Rather than listen to a thirty-five minute sermon I'm doomed to forget all about as soon as the benediction is finished, I could read Matthew for just *five* minutes and then forget all about it as soon as my coffee is finished. All of the religion in a fraction of the time! Now that's American.
- **Listen to Spotify**. Forsooth, why sing the dusty old hymns and counterfeit pop songs we call worship songs when you can get the Rolling Stones and Kendrick Lamar on your phone? What's more, I could be *doing things* while singing these tunes, rather than standing still and waiting for the guy on the tech team who's running the slides of lyrics to find the words to the chorus again. The odd insistence of Sunday service that we become still and rest for a moment also seems un-American.
- **Catch up on trendy ideas**. Yes, I know, Christianity has some smart people: Augustine, Anselm, and Aquinas. Luther and Calvin. Chesterton, Lewis, and Tolkien. Schaeffer. However, they are all quite old and thoroughly dead, and this makes their philosophies irrelevant to today's audiences who

go through ideas like my daughter goes through onesies. We've been teaching the Bible for coming up on two thousand years in our Christian gatherings. All of it is quickly becoming passe, though—if it's not already out of date. Plus, if you go to a few church services, you've been to them all. Christ crucified and all that. We've heard it all before. Why not watch a few TED talks on Youtube instead? One needn't even change out of their pajamas or go engage in a bunch of awkward small talk with strangers seen only once a week.

Fishing, practicing with my bow, grocery shopping before the post-church rush, house cleaning —there's no end to the things that I could do in the hour-and-a-half to two hours we put in every Sunday morning. Yet somehow, week after week, month after month, I find myself in the pews, gazing upward at the rough-hewn cross, made for our church by a talented local woodworker, singing the same litany of songs over and over again—and doing so gladly.

There is something to church that cannot be found elsewhere, although someday it will be found everywhere. All the pleasures and duties and chores that seem so important outside the church gate will always pale in comparison once inside. These things become like shadows or echoes once we enter the sanctuary. Indeed, church is the opposite of the Allegory of the Cave; it is *within* that we come face with reality, and when we step into the dark of the chapel, we see the world as it truly is. Your local church is an image of the world as God intends it to be. It is both an outpost of Heaven and a blueprint for Earth.

This is why I go to church when there are so many more attractive things to do. It's to experience something real, something lasting—like the sharing of Communion, a meal that binds all believers across time and space to Christ, or the gathering of brothers and sisters with whom we will share God's kingdom. It's to glimpse into a future eternity and to be joined to all those who come to glimpse the same thing. Yes, I could stay home and make a fancy breakfast—but that would be to miss the Supper of the Lamb.

What John Calvin Taught Me About the Sacraments
Peter Schellhase

I became a Calvinist in my teens. Before this, my religious understanding had been stunted by my family's involvement in a cult-like parachurch group. Reacting to toxic fundamentalism, I found new life in the rich soil of Calvinistic theology. Yet, after almost ten years, I was still a "teenage" Calvinist. Much like Jeff Reid, I had read many modern, derivative theological works in the Reformed vein, but nothing by the great Protestant theologian himself.

Browsing the University of Virginia bookstore one day, I discovered a nice little volume of selections from Calvin's writings introduced by Marilynne Robinson, a favorite writer of mine. This seemed like the perfect way to actually become introduced to the man himself.

My church experience, and most of what I had read of theology up to that point, was of the reformed Baptist genre. Baptists deviate somewhat from the magisterial Reformation in their views of the sacraments and the Church. Wayne Grudem gives a moderate version of the reformed Baptist position when he claims that "participation" in the body of Christ means "a sharing in the benefits of Christ's body and blood given for us"[1] and that God rewards with "spiritual blessing" those who partake in the Lord's Supper in obedience to his Scriptural command. Grudem's take on baptism is the same. However, many Baptist churches take a still more distant view of the grace communicated through the sacraments, up to the point of an effective divorce of the ritual from the grace it supposedly conveys. (The "real absence," as Trevin Wax quips.)

My understanding of other reformed perspectives, such as Presbyterianism, was that they regarded baptism of infants as a sign of entering a visible covenant with the Church. What I did not realize was that the founder of Calvinism maintained an opinion closer to

---

[1] Grudem, Wayne, *Systematic Theology* (Grand Rapids, Michigan: Zondervan, 2000) 955.

what I understood as the catholic view: in short, that the visible signs of water, bread, and wine not only symbolize a reality separate from themselves, but are used by God to make the grace of that reality present in the life of the Church.

In "A Short Treatise on the Lord's Supper" (written in 1541), Calvin approaches the subject from the perspective of human weakness. If it were possible for us to apprehend Christ through the teaching of the gospel alone, Calvin reflects, we might not need these other ordinances. But, "seeing we are so foolish that we cannot receive him with true confidence of heart when he is presented by simple teaching and preaching," Calvin explains, "the Father, not at all disdaining to condescend in this matter to our infirmity, has desired to attach to his word a visible sign by which he represents the substance of his promises to confirm and fortify us and to deliver us from all doubt and uncertainty."[1]

But if the sacraments are an accommodation to our weakness, shouldn't Christians eventually cease to require them as we grow in faith and knowledge of Christ? Calvin envisions no such possibility in this life. To him, our present state is such that we must gratefully submit to this dispensation without pride. "It is indeed true," he writes, "that this same grace is offered us by the gospel; yet as in the Supper we have a more ample certainty and fuller enjoyment, it is with good reason that we recognize such a fruit [of grace] as coming from it."[2]

Calvin's sacramentology stops short of affirming the "real presence" of Christ in the elements. But neither does he affirm that it is the faith of the participant, or their corporate enactment, which makes the sacraments an effective means of grace. The active part belongs to God.

> "Now, if it be asked nevertheless whether the bread is the body of Christ and the wine His blood, we should reply that the bread and wine are visible signs which represent to us the body and the blood; but that the name and title of body and blood is attributed to them, because they are as instruments by which the Lord Jesus Christ distributes them [his body and

---

[1] Calvin, John, *John Calvin: Selections from His Writings*, Elsie Ann McKee, trans., Emile Griffin, ed., (HarperSanFrancisco, 2006.) 57–58.
[2] Ibid., 59.

> blood] to us. . . . It is a spiritual mystery which cannot be seen by the eye or comprehended by human understanding. It is therefore symbolized by visible signs, as our infirmity requires, but in such a way that it is not a bare figure, but joined to its reality and substance. It is therefore with good reason that the bread is called body, since not only does it represent it to us, but also presents it to us."[1]

Calvin thus rejects the idea that the Lord's Supper should be seen as a mere memorial or symbolic representation of the Lord's death and resurrection, since God, through the bread and wine, communicates to us the very substance of these eternal realities. There is at most a very slight difference between this understanding and the Lutheran or even the Roman Catholic understanding of the sacrament, as it has been articulated by someone such as Pope Benedict XVI. I realized that Calvin is far more catholic in this respect than most protestants. For me, reading Calvin was an important step in the spiritual journey which led me that year to join the Anglican church. In the same treatise, Calvin warns of the danger of approaching the Lord's Supper while holding hatred against a fellow believer. As I sought to enter into sacramental fellowship, I had the opportunity to deal with a sinful hatred I had developed toward certain people who had offended me and my friends. For teaching me how important it is to walk in forgiveness, and freeing me to truly recognize the body of Christ, I'm deeply grateful to John Calvin.

---

[1] Ibid.

Why Is Christian Liturgy So Repetitive
Jacob Quick

Christian liturgy involves cycles of repetition. We have recurring liturgical calendars, weekly gatherings of worship, the Eucharist, and the recitation of important prayers. The repetitive nature of Christian worship is, in my experience, one of its greatest strengths. It is through such liturgical repetition that we engage in disciplined spiritual formation, remind ourselves of the gospel, and actively engage in historic practices of the Church.

But what is happening when we engage in these repetitive liturgical practices? While that question admits of more than one answer, I've found that the philosophy of Jacques Derrida offers some compelling insight into the transformative power of Christian liturgy.

Repetition and Change
Repetition plays an important role in Derrida's philosophy, especially with regard to one of his most important themes: iterability. In order to get a grasp on iterability, it's helpful to explore Derrida's commentary on language. According to Derrida, a word can only properly function if it can be repeated: "Love" is a legitimate word precisely because it can be used in countless instances and in different contexts. To use another example, if I could not place my name on different documents at different times, then it would cease to be my name, since part of the function of a name is that I can use it to refer to myself, or others can use it to refer to me, in a theoretically infinite number of scenarios.

Derrida highlights one of the more paradoxical implications of repetition: it requires change. While many assume that repetition involves different instantiations of an identical, stable sign, it actually denotes multiple instantiations of a dynamic sign that is constantly in flux. After all, if you're able to use the same word in multiple contexts, then that word must be able to adapt to each new context in which it is used. To build on our earlier example, imagine a couple who is celebrating their 50th wedding anniversary. Throughout their relationship, they have told each other "I love you" countless times. With each iteration of that phrase, it takes on a new meaning, as the

"I" and "you" have changed, and the nature of their love has altered. Saying "I love you" to someone who just agreed to marry you is different from saying "I love you" to your spouse of 40 years whom you have just nursed back to health. Yet, at the same time, there is a continuity of meaning that persists through each utterance.

Now, once you consider how many people have uttered "I love you" in different relationships, for different reasons, and to different ends, etc., you can start to picture the dynamic nature of repetition.

So repetition involves a paradox: a sign can only remain the same in different iterations so long as it is able to change with each iteration. Repeating the same word is, at the same time, uttering something new. And it is precisely this paradox that Derrida references with the term "iterability."

It's important to keep in mind, however, that Derrida does not insist that each repetition of a word brings about an *entirely* different word. Rather, he's pointing out that, while a word may never mean the exact same thing twice, it also doesn't mean an entirely different thing altogether. Language is elastic and dynamic. It can adapt and bend to each new situation, all the while neither becoming entirely new nor remaining absolutely identical. So repetition, for Derrida, operates between the poles of identical recurrence and absolute novelty.

Liturgical Repetition
So what does all of this have to do with liturgy? Derrida's philosophy highlights the dynamic and transformative power of liturgical repetition. When we recite ancient prayers, follow liturgical calendars, and celebrate the Eucharist, we join the saints in praising God and conforming ourselves to Christ's image. At the same time, we are participating in fresh expressions of these ancient traditions, exploring their surplus of meaning. For millennia, across countless contexts, people of different nations, tribes, and tongues have proclaimed the love of Christ. And with each proclamation, the mosaic of Christ's body grows in its beautiful complexity and boundless diversity.

Christian liturgy is not about repeating abstract propositions, but affirming the truth of the gospel with our whole being. As a result, Christian liturgy requires a sacred repetition which calls us to embody Christ anew in each moment, all the while participating in the same tradition of our forebears. Such is the compelling paradox of Christian liturgy.

Faith Across Traditions

Three Things That Need to Change about Church
Barbara White

My husband and I went through a phase where we spent too much time watching Kitchen Nightmares, the reality show where celebrity chef Gordon Ramsey tries to turn around failing restaurants. In one episode, Gordon asks the owner of a sad and shrinking diner, "What do you think is the biggest problem with your restaurant?" "No customers" the owner replies. When he pressed her about why the restaurant didn't have more customers she said "Because they aren't here. They just need to come."

I've written previously about the lack of "customers" in churches in America—the so-called "Nones" who report having no religious affiliation. I and many Christians think this is a troubling trend. I have no fears about the church "going away" or "becoming irrelevant," because the church is a teleological certainty. I do worry, however about what a culture unmoored from traditional religion will wreck, and about the future of those people who have no community to which to turn in times of crisis. Within the church, much is made of the fact that the people who are still religiously affiliated are more faithful than ever. People have quit coming to church out of obligation, but the people who come voluntarily are in it for the long haul. This, to be sure, is a good thing; I want vibrant churches full of true believers.

But this is no excuse for abdicating our responsibility to evangelism and mission. Study after study has shown that Americans are more addicted, more lonely, and more depressed than ever. The birth rate is lower and the divorce rate higher than in years past. The human being, it turns out, was not meant to be "unaffiliated." We have a responsibility to make disciples of Jesus Christ as citizens of His Kingdom, and we must provide comfort to the suffering. To do both of these, we need to reach out to this lonely generation.

This leads to the next question: how exactly are churches supposed to reach this elusive group? In my time as a member and a minister in a mainline protestant denomination, I've heard and seen several tactics discussed and deployed. The decline in average Sunday attendance is not a new problem. I remember grownups discussing it extensively in the 90s when I was still a child playing in the pews. All of them have been pushed with the implication that the Church must modernize her inherited tradition if she is going to "attract" the skeptical and weary grandchildren of the Baby Boomers.

The driving impulse behind much of this culture shift within the Church seems to be "meeting people where they are." Millennials and Gen-Z report caring about social justice, so ministers show up to protests and rallies. They prioritize health, fitness, and quasi-eastern spirituality, so we host "Yoga in the Cathedral" and call Whole30 a Lenten discipline. They're engaged on social media, we rush to open church social media platforms. COVID restrictions on worship led to a flurry of excitement over new "online" churches. And, perhaps worst of all, we meet them in the middle of their characteristic doubt and skepticism, with web banners that say "You don't have to change who you are" and "A safe place to explore your faith" and where Jesus Christ is hardly mentioned, for fear of triggering an avalanche of baggage.

While "meeting them where they are" may seem like an innovative strategy, all of these are Christendom tactics in new clothes. Each of these assumes that if the church could just increase her visibility and show the Nones how relevant she is—including that we've done away with stuffy worship and outdated doctrine–then they will come running. "We care about the things you care about" we cry "Come care about them with us!" Like the sad restaurant owner, we assume that the problem is no customers. If they just knew how good the food was here, they'd be here already.

And, while I don't love the tactics, I do think there is a nugget of truth in the impulse: we are going to need to meet the Nones where they are, by recognizing that "where they are" is a post-Christian world. As Christendom continues to shrink, all ministry is going to have to be missional ministry. And so, in the spirit of being part of the solution instead of just complaining about the problem, I'd like to offer three thing that church ministering in a post-Christian world should consider doing differently.

Boldness in Doctrine
My time in both post-Christian California and a progressive mainline seminary taught me that "doctrine" and "dogmatics" are considered dirty words among those who want to be skeptic friendly. Doctrine is seen as divisive, as a top-down approach to determining who is in and who is out. If we spend too much time pushing doctrine, it is argued, we will exclude those who have questions and doubts.

But is that true? Are young Americans so intellectual uncurious that they will reject all firmly held beliefs just because they are firmly held? Wishy-washy Christianity seems much more likely to be off-putting to a generation whose entire ethos centers on rejecting the phoniness in advertising, politics, and media.

I don't think the Nones are put off by conviction in and of itself. I think they are put off by the assumption that the things we are convicted about preclude the things they are convicted about. And this may, at times, be true. The Christian tradition is not without boundaries. Our tradition places restrictions on things that the rest of culture treats as unimportant: who you have sex with, what you spend your money on, and how you spend your time. But changing Christian mores or pretending these restrictions don't exist is not the answer. The challenge is to compassionately, pastorally, and confidently hold this line in the face of a culture that tells us we're crazy. We have to show people that the freedom offered in Christ is infinitely better than the freedom to make arbitrary choices offered by the dominant culture.

Prioritize Catechesis
I believe that it is a mistake to assume that the Nones have tested Christianity and found it wanting. I doubt that many of my friends who have no religious affiliation could tell you concisely what it is they don't believe. The time has come for ministers to stop assuming that people—even the ones already in the pews—have a good understanding of what the Gospel is and what the Christian faith teaches. At the height of Christendom, much of the Christian story could be absorbed by osmosis; scriptural motifs and Christian doctrines were in pop-culture and everyday encounters. But our culture has moved on, and it is up to us to carry the torch. Our preachers and pastors must be prepared to be teachers and apologists for the Christian faith.

This isn't a call to exhort people or to transmit facts about faith into their brains but to do our homework—to learn what we believe and to learn to teach it bravely, gently, and well. We can't help the unaffiliated see how their story is swept up into the story of the Gospel unless we are rock solid on what that story is. We should be prepared to have well-informed answers to questions about what our faith teaches, why we believe what we believe, and why we worship as we do. This brings me to my final point.

Recover Ritual
There may be good arguments against the use of vestments, incense, chanting, kneeling, and making the sign of the cross, but the fact that these gestures seem alienating or foreign is not one of them. Recently my husband showed me the Yelp page of a yoga studio in the town we used to live. What was most striking about this studio was how ritualistic it appeared. This was no run-of-the-mill fitness studio. There were brightly colored silk cushions, prayer beads, and incense burners. There were mandalas, sound bowls, and tapestry hung on the wall. And, in the Yelp photos at least, the place was packed. These young men and women—many of whom were likely not regular churchgoers—weren't put off by the fact that the studio seemed different, or even unapproachable.

I am not advocating for using more ritual worship just because it might attract the unchurched, and I am certainly not advocating for incorporating quasi-eastern spirituality in the Christian churches. But I am suggesting that we don't need to be afraid of ritual. We need to be prepared to explain why we do what we do. That ritual is more than "just a symbol," and that there is something else going on.

Many of our rituals predate Christendom, which means they are ripe for recovery in a post-Christian context. This was, in essence, the entire gamble of the Liturgical Renewal movement. We face different challenges than our pre-Christendom ancestors: an ancient pagan is not the same as a modern secularist. And yet, there may still be something there. If church looks like anywhere else you could be on a Sunday morning, why would you be there?

Ritual, symbol, and mystery tap into the deep parts of the human heart—even those hearts that are atrophied by too much social media and 24-hour news cycles. What if instead of making church more user-friendly, we invited the unchurched to take a gamble on the unknown, by inviting them into a space that looks, sounds, and smells different than any other place they have ever been. Ritual and mystery might not be the otherizing and isolating forces we assume. They might just be the key that could begin to unlock the Nones closed hearts; the beginning of a crack through which the light of Christ can begin to shine. What if ritual and mystery weren't the isolating and otherizing forces we sometimes assume but are the gateway to an open heart?

Faith Across Traditions

What's the Point of the Sermon?
Chad Kim

Too often when I enter the pew on a Sunday morning, I dread the coming sermon. Like many raised in Evangelical circles, the singing and musical part of the service seems the most natural. It is easy in our modern culture to connect emotionally and spiritually to music, perhaps too easy. Yet I know that after 20 minutes or so of beautiful hymns, I will have to endure 30 to 45 minutes of a person speaking to me about things that I have studied my entire life. I wrote about this in a previous piece. The driving question behind all of this writing is this: what am I looking for when I sit and listen to a sermon?

The previous piece gave no positive answers, but rather background and setup. I hope in this piece to start answering that question: what the point is of a sermon. Too often, I find myself sidetracked by questions about whether or not the pastor is entertaining, funny, eloquent, serious, or other adjectives that I think describe a good speaker. In the internet age, I can download a podcast or watch a video of some of the best speakers in the world in an instant. It has made me wonder about the value of suffering through a much weaker speech. Why subject myself, week-in and week-out, to someone who not only has responsibilities to speak every Sunday, but also has to care for the needs of an entire congregation? Wouldn't it be easier if churches just decided to outsource preaching to the best speakers and let the pastors do other necessary work? Why should pastors try to do the impossible and match the most captivating and winsome personalities the internet has to offer?

This is a consummately 21st century mindset. We are given more options for toothpaste than my grandfather could ever conceive. We walk into the grocery store and every single aisle is overflowing with options all competing for our attention. If the Church is not careful, we will fall prey to the same mentality. We will ask our pastors and preachers to cater to our every whim and when he or she does not meet the exacting standard of every particular taste, we will walk out. What if there was a different way to think about the act of preaching?

I submit that the Church's proclamation of the Word of God has a different aim and intention. When the pastor stands before the congregation, their goal cannot be to satisfy every single preference of every single person sitting in the pew. They cannot compete with the multitude of options available for iTunes download in an instant. What follows is a theological exploration of why the Church must continue to preach. It will also hopefully offer a few points of encouragement for the next time I, or the reader, finds themselves captive to a preacher that might not fit all their qualifications of a perfect speaker.

Karl Barth, a 20th century Swiss-German theologian, says "The Church stands or falls by this function which is enjoined upon her."[1] That "function" is the Proclamation of the Word of God. With this sobering statement in mind, the next three pieces will hope to contribute to the Church's sustained commitment to the local preaching of the Word of God. I will look at all three forms of the Word of God because the sermon is just one part of a Trinitarian structure. Barth says:

> The revealed Word of God we know only from the Scripture adopted by Church proclamation, or from Church proclamation based on Scripture.
> The written Word of God we know only through revelation which makes proclamation possible, or through the proclamation made possible by revelation.
> The proclaimed Word of God we know only by knowing the revelation attested through Scripture, or by knowing the Scripture which attests revelation.
> There is only one analogy to this doctrine of the Word of God.... the doctrine of the three-in-oneness of God.[2]

The first piece will deal with the actual preaching of the Word of God. The second will explore the medium of the preaching of the Word of God, the Scripture. The third will deal with what all of this is based on, the only true Word of God revealed in the person of Jesus Christ. These three are intimately linked, so if it seems like I am missing something in what follows, it is only because it will be covered next. In the final installment, I will look at the reason anyone preaches or listens: the Word made flesh, Jesus Christ.

---

[1] Karl Barth, *Church Dogmatics (CD)* I/1, 91.
[2] *CD* I/1, 136.

I draw most of what follows from my favorite Church Father, St. Augustine. Augustine was a gifted North African preacher from the 4th and 5th century A.D., who wrote a manual for preachers and preached for 30 years in a small North African town on the edge of the Roman Empire. He is the only person from the first five centuries of the Church who has left to history much by way of instruction regarding early Christian proclamations of the faith. His manual was the first of its kind in the ancient world, written in two parts over the course of his adult life. He wrote some of it when he began his life as a preacher, and some of it after having preached for 30 years, every Sunday, twice a day, and on special days throughout the week. It is believed that Augustine preached as many as 4,000 sermons in his lifetime. Augustine has inspired preachers throughout Christian history, especially in his work *On Teaching Christianity*, which became *the* medieval manual for preachers. The other great preacher from the same time period, John Chrysostom, left us no such manual, just copious amounts of sermons that he delivered to his people in the Greek East, admonishing them to serve the poor and remember Christ's sacrifice.

Ever the Trinitarian, much like Barth above, St. Augustine mentions three essential elements of the preaching moment in a sermon from A.D. 410 on the plagues of Egypt. He writes:

> So in the name of our Lord I have undertaken to explain [the plagues] as best I can, with his grace to help me and the devout attention [pia intentione] of your hearts to support me. Those [congregants] who made the suggestion know what they suggested...the exegesis I serve to you as your minister [literally *servant*] will provide nourishment for them. I am sure that [God] will help me, if not for my sake then certainly for yours, to say what is right to say and useful to hear, so that we may be found worthy to walk together on the way of his truth and hasten homeward together.[1]

This one dense quote gives us much to think about when considering what takes place in the proclamation of the Church, and what we should be listening for as congregants.

First of all, Augustine calls on the grace of God to help him. It should be little surprise that this "Doctor of Grace" does not want to lean only on his own abilities. In a manual on preaching he writes that "the

---

[1] Augustine, *Sermon* 9.2.

speaker who is awash with the kind of eloquence that is not wise is particularly dangerous because audiences actually enjoy listening to such a person on matters of no value to them, and reckon that somebody who is heard to speak eloquently must also be speaking the truth."[1] Sometimes a speaker can lead us astray if they are merely gifted, given to much *ethos* and *pathos* and no *Logos*.[2] Even someone as eloquent and profound as Augustine knew that he could not deliver his messages but for the grace of God. Just because someone is a gifted speaker does not make them a preacher of wisdom. These preachers might have charming words and winsome personalities that bring people to hear them, based on outlandish promises that can never be fulfilled. Their words sound good, but their content is empty. But it's not only prosperity-gospel eloquence that deceives those not paying attention. If you preach love and tolerance without an awareness of the God who embodies that for us, and teaches us the content, the *Logos,* of love, but does not convey the deeper truths of the Word of God made flesh in the revelation of Jesus Christ, this too is a misused eloquence. Many preachers will stand before large audiences with good intentions, but still fail to proclaim the enduring truth of the Word made flesh.

Second, Augustine mentions the "devout intention" of the hearers that support him. Throughout his corpus of sermons, Augustine in several places encourages his listeners to be prayerful in their listening to the sermon. He desires that they come into church eager to hear what the Word of God will speak to them. Sometimes this can be quite difficult if our only measure of a good sermon is how eloquent the speaker is and whether or not the preacher's words match our own notions about what they should be saying, or how they should be saying it. If we stand in judgment over the preacher, we cannot be humbly listening for God speaking to us. God has chosen to use preaching as one means of speaking to his people. As Luther writes, following Augustine's many metaphors of preaching, "Now I and any man who speaketh Christ's Word may freely boast that his mouth is Christ's mouth. I am certain that my word is not mine but

---

[1] Augustine, *De Doctrina Christiana*, or *On Teaching Christianity*, (DDC) 4.17.
[2] For those unfamiliar, the three classical elements of a good speech are pathos, persuasion and the emotional element, ethos, the well chosen words and format, and finally the logos, the rational or logical form of the argument. Jesus Christ, is also called the Logos, translated most often as the "Word" of God.

Christ's word, therefore my mouth must also be His whose Word it speaketh."[1] When we sit in a sermon, we are listening for Christ's mouth to speak to us. This requires us to let go of our own arrogance and stop assuming that we know best about the right way to deliver a sermon. One other aspect of humility that has taken much of my life to learn is that not necessarily every sermon is meant for me. God asks that I be present, but also be prayerful for the pastor and the community to hear what they need from God, even if that message is not meant for me.

Third, the preacher herself matters. Notice the very end of the above quote, "we may be found worthy to walk together on the way of his truth and hasten homeward together." Augustine, in the person of the preacher, walks with his congregation towards home, in the way of truth. The preacher has to be deemed worthy herself to lead the congregation. Augustine says in his manual on preaching that the preacher must read the Scriptures constantly and be continually in prayer to prepare the sermon. Barth writes, "it is further a decisive test of our humility towards God that we learned to render obedience to His Word not as one spoken directly from heaven, but just as it meet us, in the mouth of a *homunico quispiam ex pulvere emersus* [a diminutive nobody who has emerged from the dust] (translation mine) who is in no relation better than ourselves."[2] We learn humility by not choosing to look elsewhere for someone who might say something we wish to hear, and by not simply eschewing the discipline of going to church to "look for God in nature." Our first instinct should be to listen to how God may be using our preacher. We submit to the preacher in trust that the person God has chosen to speak from the pulpit brings us the Word, meant for us. That is not say that we should continue to submit to someone whose heart has strayed from the Lord; they too are to submit to the Word whom they proclaim, and that is what Augustine means in this third part of the triad. The preacher true will entrust herself to the God who we wait for to speak through the preacher.

On final interesting note is that Augustine regards the point of the proclamation as orienting both preacher and congregant to the true meaning of life: their path homeward. The home of the Christian is not found on this earth. Our daily lives at work, in school, or wherever we spend our days might distract us from the journey that we are on.

---

[1] *CD* I.1107.
[2] *CD* I/1 108, the Latin coming from Calvin's *Institutes* IV I,5.

Without the continual reminder of the sermon, we might forget to orient our lives to God. The sermon helps us see how all parts of our lives are aimed at our Creator and our sustainer. This helps us to make meaning out of the daily activities that can seem overbearing, stressful, or pointless. With the proper orientation, we learn through the Proclamation of the Church to find meaning in our lives through the resurrected Word of God.

In Augustine's work on the Trinity, he writes that "the Holy Spirit is the love that exists between the Father and the Son."[1] Through the power of the presence of the Spirit—the *Holy Breath* is an equally valid translation—if a preacher seeks the Word whom he is meant to proclaim, the Holy Spirit is present among all in love. Preacher, Congregant, and God are all present in a trinitarian relationship at the point of proclamation—as Jesus even says in the Gospel of Matthew, "where two or three are gathered in my name, there am I with them." Augustine is so aware of the lives of the community to whom he preaches that he knows when people are in mourning because of the loss of loved ones or the fears of barbarian invasion. His sermons evidence a man uniquely in tune with the concerns of his hearers. This is the power of a preacher proclaiming the Word of God to a people present to him. This does not happen at some remove, whether through online teaching or radio and television broadcasts. he preacher in those cases cannot know who specifically he or she is speaking to. How can they know if the people understand what is being said? How can they know if they communicate well what God moves them to speak if the preacher cannot see the congregation? Where is the love that exists between proclaimer, hearer, and the Word?

If there is one thing that I hope to come out in the next several pieces it is the place of love in the proclamation of the Church. As Augustine writes, "For if understanding brings delights in its purest recesses, it should also be a delight to us to have an understanding of the manner in which *charity*...witnesses that it has sought nothing from those to whom it has descended except their everlasting salvation."[2]

"Caritas" means the unconditional love of Christ, and it is the root of the word "charity." That word is not commonly used in the way it was

---

[1] Augustine, *On the Trinity* XV.17.24.
[2] Augustine, *De Catechandzis Rudibus*, or *On Catechizing the Uninstructed*, DCR 12.

originally defined, but it should connote the abiding love of Christ, the Word made flesh, which dwells in the lover and the loved alike, the person giving to another and the person receiving from another. This very thing happens in the moment of proclamation of the Church. The guiding principle of what actually happens is that the love of God for His people is proclaimed for all to hear. Augustine says this love seeks nothing from them but their salvation: their wholeness, their wellbeing, and of course their deliverance from their own sinful natures. Understanding, learning, knowledge, these are fine things...but they are nothing without *Caritas*. This *Caritas* exists in a Trinitarian fashion between God, Preacher, and Congregation, made known in the Word, Jesus Christ. This is the proclamation of the Church.

Faith Across Traditions

How Should We Choose the Church We Attend

George Aldhizer

When a Christian moves into a new town or city, typically one of the first things one does is look for a church. This situation commonly requires attending a number of different churches on Sunday mornings to see if the particular church fits in some way with predetermined criteria for how a church ought to be. Does the preaching proclaim the gospel? How is the music? How friendly are the people? What are the demographics of the church? How is the church involved in the community? What is the history of the denomination or non-denomination?

Given that I am moving to a new city later this year and will have to go through this process of finding a different church home, and given that I am not tied to a particular denomination at this point in time, I thought that I would use this space to examine the criteria of choosing a church. As an upfront admission, this article will read less like a well-thought-out thesis, and more like less-than-coherent question asking. As I've explained before in other articles, my experience here at Conciliar Post has probably been more disorienting than orienting, an experience best explained by the old adage, "The more you know, the more you know you don't know."

First, for the person who isn't tied to a denomination whatsoever, an impulse that seems increasingly prevalent among American Christians these days, is it problematic to use the criteria mentioned above to choose a church? Certainly, it seems like churches should encourage teaching that is grounded in scripture, music/liturgy that is both worshipful and artistic, and friendly interactions between church members. It seems to make sense that when visiting a church for potential membership that one ought to see these markers as important. After all, every Sunday for the next number of years will be spent hearing these sermons, worshiping with this style of music, and gathering with these sorts of people. Though, there is certainly the danger that consumerism seeps into our church shopping, creating the need for a perfect product or never deciding on a product at all, rather than binding ourselves to an imperfect and sinful body. On the flipside, it seems equally dangerous to have no criteria whatsoever.

Second, for those that are denominationally focused, though not absolutely committed to a particular denomination (a camp I would place myself in), how much weight should be placed in sticking with that particular denomination one has historically focused on? As someone who has spent his college years bound to the Presbyterian Church in America (PCA), what does that mean for myself weighing the possibilities of attending other Reformed bodies, or of going "high-church" to Anglicanism? It seems that this adds more criteria and specificities to the base-line of word and sacrament mentioned above. Questions that I will wrestle with such as, How liturgical is the Church? How did the denomination historically distinguish itself from other Christians, and are the reasons for which the church split from other churches intellectually satisfying?

Third, for those that are comfortable binding themselves to a particular Christian tradition (perhaps the majority of writers on this website), these sorts of questions of word, sacrament, and community are still pertinent. Certainly, when multiple churches of a particular denomination or tradition exist within the area, one will have to choose which church body is the best fit. Though, when only a single church of that denomination exists in the area, it seems that these questions are still pertinent. What if one has chosen that a particular denomination is the true one (I'm thinking particularly of the Catholics and Orthodox of this blog), and yet the congregation in one's area cares little for the gospel, the poor, or evangelism. What if the "ancient church" exists in a building within the city limits, the true sacraments are administered, and yet that church does not have a heart, mind, strength, and soul for the Lord? Recent *Pew Research* data show Catholics and Orthodox to be among the least involved Christians in their local churches, much lower than evangelical Protestants (and, to our collective shame, even lower than Mormons and Jehovah's Witnesses). I point this out not to disparage these two traditions, certainly this point could apply to any congregation, but to ask whether this consideration overrides others. Might there be pragmatic criteria for one's spiritual well-being that override the intellectual, Conciliar Post-y questions of historical rootedness, sacramental and liturgical fidelity, and scriptural corroboration?

Empty Hands
Johanna Byrkett

I want to hold my worth in my hands;
to trace my accomplishments
in gilded letters on spine and cover;
to smell them in ink and paper.

But my desire is a dream awakened,
and all I can trace are tears
of shame, that I have nothing
to hold out in offering but empty hands.

Empty hands—not clenched fists,
angry, or grasping at given gifts;
Empty hands, ready to hold another's,
to serve, to open and receive.

To receive trust—a hand placed
in mine by a friend or a child;
to receive that broken bread,
spoken over, speaking over me: "You belong."

To belong, to be welcomed,
is not something I can close my hand
around—my palm is empty
on this pilgrimage, ready to give.

I cannot hold my worth in my hand,
but I can hold His most precious Body;
hold the hand of one in His Body;
be a hand in His Body—empty. . .

Sin and Salvation

If Scripture and its interpretation takes the gold for the most popular *Conciliar Post* topic, this section takes the silver. How does salvation work? What has Christ done for us and for our salvation? From what are we rescued? And what does this interplay mean for everyday faith? The essays in this section delve into these questions and more as they explore sin and salvation.

Essays

The Natural Desire to See God, *Winter*

The Pandemic and the Wrath of God, *Fletcher*

It Is Not a Sin to Wear a Facemask, *Townsend*

On Original Sin and Racism, *Cline*

The Atonement of Irenaeus, *Bryan*

Dare We Hope for the Salvation of All, *Winter*

The Problem of Predestination, *Aldhizer*

Is Christian Existentialism Unbiblical, *Tillman*

The Natural Desire to See God
Benjamin Winter

The human person—with his openness to truth and beauty, his sense of moral goodness, his freedom and the voice of his conscience, his longings for the infinite and for happiness—questions himself about God's existence. In all this he discerns signs of his spiritual soul. The soul, the "seed of eternity we bear in ourselves, irreducible to the merely material," can have its origin only in God (CCC 33).

Such says the Catechism of the Catholic Church. Do you agree? The purpose of this article is to help you determine (or at minimum, help you *consider*) your position on humankind and the natural desire to see God. To achieve that end, I will recount the high points of a debate I witnessed between two venerable scholars: David Bentley Hart and Lawrence Feingold.

First, a bit of confessional and topical background. David Bentley Hart is Eastern Orthodox; Larry Feingold is Catholic. Their debate centered on the theological reception of Henri de Lubac (1896—1991), a Jesuit who spoke out against any rigid dichotomy between "natural" and "supernatural" realities.[1] De Lubac was part of the *Nouvelle Théologie*, a school of thinkers who aimed to break free from the rigid version of Thomistic theology known as manualism. The manualist tradition upheld a strict separation between natural and supernatural orders of being. In this system, it becomes possible for grace to be viewed as a "super-added" gift that has nothing to do with natural existence. Grace comes in, as it were, *only from the outside*. De Lubac attempted to correct this error.

Both of our speakers admire de Lubac's work, while nonetheless interpreting his legacy differently. For Hart, de Lubac was absolutely right to assert that rational consciousness—at its base—must be an orientation toward the vision of God. For Feingold, this statement is

---

[1] A recent Conciliar Post article by Joseph Green does an excellent job arguing against a stringently "two-tiered" Christianity: https://conciliarpost.com/christian-traditions/eastern-orthodox/cosmic-communion-the-role-of-creation-in-our-journey-with-christ-part-2/.

also "correct," but must be accompanied by certain theological and anthropological qualifications. Both Hart and Feingold believe that the destiny of humankind is to see God; our end and fulfillment is found in God alone. So the real question of their debate is not *whether* the desire for God exists in humanity,[1] but *how* this desire interacts with the constitution, abilities, and end(s) of the human person.

I have done my best to concisely present the views of these authors in a form that remains true to my transcribed notes from the lecture. If anything is "lost in translation" or misconstrued, please attribute it solely to my error. I encourage you to examine the publications of both participants for further clarification.

Debate Summary: Question 1 of 3

Moderator: How do you understand the legacy of De Lubac?

Feingold: He ignited a debate that had been going on for seven centuries. It began with St. Thomas Aquinas, who held that perfect happiness is the fulfillment of all our natural desires. The desire to see God is the highest natural desire, yet it is a natural desire that nothing natural can satisfy. Aquinas draws from St. Paul (1 Cor 2:9) to show that the vision of God's face is above all natural desire and above our innate inclinations. He does not, however, resolve the tension between natural desire and its "super-natural" fulfillment in God. Later on, theological divisions emerge between various interpretations of the natural/supernatural question.

Hart: De Lubac's first intuition was that the terms "natural" and "supernatural" are too tidy. Though convenient, they distort the revelation of God in Christ and in Creation. Although there is no way to get a satisfactory answer from Aquinas on this question,[2] I believe that de Lubac reinvigorated Aquinas by reading him as an inheritor of Patristic tradition.

---

[1] If you would like to discuss reasons why this desire might not exist, feel free to bring them up in the comments, below. I would be happy to write a response to any question, as well. Or, you could always use the "Ask" page to receive a response from our staff!

[2] For example, the Thomistic tradition allows for unbaptized babies to enter a place where they do not lack what they did not desire, namely, the beatific vision. Hence, a separation between natural and supernatural orders. But in the *Summa Contra Gentiles*, natural desire is portrayed more as a way-station than as an end in itself.

Debate Summary: Question 2 of 3

Moderator: Humanity's natural desire for God is often described with reference to the *intellectual capacities* of the human person, who engages in an ongoing search for Meaning, Truth, and Goodness. [See the Catechism quotation in the opening of this article.] Can *rational consciousness* be anything other than a natural desire for God?

Hart: No. Consciousness is, of its nature, intention. It is a necessarily-ecstatic movement toward an end in nature, but an end in nature to which it can be related only because, primordially, it is related to Truth as such. It's not just the case that our desire for God is elicited by worldly desires. "I see a teacup, and start wondering about God." Rather, it's the case that I see the tea cup itself, and *I cannot do this if I do not have already an insatiable desire for Truth itself as a Transcendental*. Rational consciousness is what allows us to see the world within the embrace of a primordial intuition that it can never come to rest with the finite. We find nothing in the world desirable simply in itself.

Feingold: Actually I agree with that. We have a natural inclination, as rational beings, for the Transcendental.[1] We could go further, and say that this is the quest of all culture. In fact, I think one of De Lubac's contributions is pointing to the radical nature of this desire as the "motor" of culture.

Hart: So, the issue is really the way this question is posed in debates, which tend to be more polemical than probative. In these debates, the desire for God "full stop" is counter-posed to natural desire, which merely elicits, by experience, this fervent desire for God. I believe that the embrace of supernatural desire is what makes natural, rational experience a possibility. How deep is this supernatural desire embedded in the human person?

Feingold: To answer that question, I need to make a fourfold distinction about desire:
    1) Proportionate Desire is the human desire to know causes and essences. We gain knowledge of the universe by

---

[1] This desire is manifested in Platonic philosophy (see, for example, the *Symposium*). When Justin Martyr talks about his conversion to Christianity, it wasn't until he met the Platonist that he realized the philosopher's true quest.

interacting with created things. Hence, the (natural) human desire to know is *proportionate* to our created condition.[1]

2) Elicited Desire is a desire of the intellectual faculty to know things in their essence. Drawn forth by knowledge and experience, this desire involves the search for Beauty and Truth. Elicited desire goes beyond proportionate desire because it seeks answers *outside of observable creation*, and points toward a "mountaintop" or "mystical" awareness of God as the Uncaused First Cause, or as Beauty beyond my own capacities of understanding. Additionally, God gives us Revelation and Sanctifying Grace. These two gifts change or "add to" the natural desire for God.

3) Revelation. When God reveals himself, we receive a beautiful encounter with what we naturally desire—to see the face of Beauty. The message of the Gospel is that there's a meeting between my natural desire and God's desire. Revelation changes that natural desire and gives it a foundation, allowing us to hope for it in the firmest way. We now *know* that this natural desire can be fully realized.

4) Sanctifying Grace. Another element is added to natural desire through sacraments. Here, I receive a share of participation in God's nature, and therefore a mysterious proportionality with God's own end. I now realize that this end (the beatific vision) is somehow related to me proportionally. I realize that I *do* have an innate desire for God's own end. Even though we both agree that this desire was present in the beginning, I am stating that it is realized in me, *in a new way*, by grace. Grace is what shows me that I have something proportionate (rather than infinitely disproportionate) to God.

Hart: Could there be a reality in which your actual intellect experiences no elicited desire, and does not concretely desire God as God?

Feingold: Yes.[2]

---

[1] This is explained further, below.
[2] See Pius XII, in *Humani Generis* 26: "Others destroy the gratuity of the supernatural order, since God, they say, cannot create intellectual beings without ordering and calling them to the beatific vision."

Hart: That is a logical impossibility; it's like a square circle. Even the ability to recognize the very concept of causality already occurs within an intentionality of consciousness and desire that is irreducibly oriented toward the vision of God. In an *ex nihilo* universe, beings are created specifically for union with God. Within this framework, rational consciousness is a way to recognize that any created cause is not yet final. Rational consciousness leads us to the One Final Cause. It is, of its nature, a participation in the knowledge of God, and can be nothing other than the movement of created being toward the full disclosure of Being. If all this is so, are we really bound to the notion of proportionality in the created world?

Hart: We live in a reality where rational beings are called out of nothingness into union with God as the very *ground* of their existence. They can't give themselves being, desire, or consciousness. It's not even logically possible for rational consciousness to be satisfied with a natural end. This is why I push back against the "supernatural and natural" language. My side grants that the *fulfillment* (by grace) of our desire for God is supernatural and therefore exceeds the natural capacity. But the desire itself was already supernatural.

Debate Summary: Question 3 of 3

Moderator: One of the hot-button issues here is the idea of "pure nature." Comments?

Hart: This notion of pure nature didn't cause modernity, but is it complicit in the history of secularization? Through "pure nature," it became possible to think of revelation as erupting into history from above. Revelation becomes reduced to the facts of Scripture and salvation history, and there is a vast incontinuity between social order and the greatness of God. De Lubac felt that the entire notion of a "supernatural realm" received part of the pathology of modernity. He wanted our reality to be absolutely saturated in a notion of the Incarnate Logos, he wanted every moment to be open to the infinite. Hence, he saw a troubling consequence in separating the sphere of sanctifying grace (the true end of nature) from a "nature" that could be sufficient unto itself without being worried about Christ. Then, Christ becomes the revelation of a purely gracious super-addition to nature. He makes it intelligible perhaps in a new way, but is not required to make it intelligible all the way down.

Feingold: This is a good example of how it is important to frame a debate rightly. I think the question of "pure nature" is simply not the right question. Instead of asking, "Could God create human, rational nature without calling it to a supernatural end?", we should ask a more fundamental question: "Does it make sense to speak about an innate end of humanity in coordination with a supernatural end?" What my side is saying is that this human nature I have is a reality. In addition to this nature, I perceive sanctifying grace. But this human nature that's in me, does it contain an innate or *connatural* end that's proportionate to *it*? Aristotle and Plato asked this question, and answered in the affirmative. Aquinas says that the ancients got this one right. The innate end of human nature is contemplating God through the mirror of creation. So the natural end is God, but the way of contemplating God naturally is through things made. Is that a *perfect* end for man? No, it leaves a natural desire (that of seeing Beauty fully) unsatisfied. Hence, this contemplation is in some sense immeasurably imperfect, *but not for that reason nothing*.

Hart: We usually hear that the paradox is an irreducibly natural desire for an irreducibly supernatural end. But if you say that an innate desire is *unfulfilled*, are you really talking about an end that satisfies at all? If the prior orientation of consciousness toward God is what makes the desirability of natural ends possible, then any degree of satisfaction with natural ends is so imperfect that it could never be understood as any kind of fulfillment of human nature. Back to the question of pure nature: I'm willing to retain the category of pure nature under the form of an impossible possibility. I would say this: I think of pure nature as I think of pure nothingness. I don't see a "dialectic" with pure nothingness, it is that which is always already-overcome in the act of creation. Prime matter doesn't have an existence of itself outside of creation. The very first moment of creation is an act of unmerited grace. When we introduce "here's a proper stopping point, but then the second gift has to be super-added" this is coherent within a certain Aristotelian framework, but I don't think it's coherent in a framework of conscious desire necessary for faith in an Incarnate God. When God becomes human, what is revealed? That End is the only possible End for all created nature, for all rational nature.

Feingold: So, Aquinas teaches a twofold gratuitousness of grace: 1) God didn't have to make me out of nothing; and 2) We have been assigned a supernatural end, which is proper only to God. That end is to see God as He sees himself and to Love God as He Loves himself. And that end can't be proper to any created nature.

Hart: Why not? Do we need a concrete nature in order to make grace truly gratuitous? If you didn't believe that human nature is destined to conform to the logos, then no. But we do believe this...

Implications: Part 1 of 2
Question: What are the implications of this difference between us?

Feingold: The twofold gratuitousness of grace is a key teaching for Catholics in the school of Aquinas. We need the twofold distinction to preserve the revealed and "gifted" sense of grace. This matches the Christological paradigm, where we have a distinction of two natures without separation. But the distinction remains something crucial. So in the Christian, a distinction between two sorts of gratuitousness must be preserved.

Hart: Of course, in Christology we are not talking about a union between "natural and supernatural" but between divine and human. Christ is the only perfect human precisely because he is also God. What is revealed in Christ is not a super-addition to the human, but a recognition of humanity's fulfillment. It is dangerous to see the revelation of God in Christ as incidental to the structure of created being. In becoming human, God did not undergo a metempsychosis. There is no conflict between divine and human natures from the beginning. Human nature is already an instance of participation in the divine nature. Everyone [or, at least Catholics and Orthodox] is willing to grant that there are innate ends. It's about the degree to which you posit a final satisfaction of those ends for a rational nature, and the degree to which rational nature could "be" a desire for those ends alone.

Feingold: Aquinas might add that even if one were to only have had natural ends accessible, there would still be a desire to go Beyond those ends. This desire would not preclude eternal resting, although it would preclude the *perfect* eternal resting.

Implications: Part 2 of 2
Question: How could we have fallen from a state of sinlessness?

Hart: East and West are different in this regard. Thomism verges on the Promethean vision. You need a deceiver, a winsomely beautiful snake. The human intellect, in the East, is more understood in terms of progression toward wisdom, toward Sophia. Evil is ignorance. Our first parents knew not what they did, but the truth will make you free. The Greek [Orthodox] position is that everything is being drawn back to its true course. It's all *one gift*; deification. Does this ultimately lead toward universalism? Yes, it does. But see Maximus the Confessor on the Gnomic will (and hence the experience of heaven as an experience of Hell).

Closing Thoughts (i.e. "tipping my hand")

I hope this exchange has challenged you to think in new ways about the inherent relationship (or the inherently-possible relationship!) between humankind and God. I also hope it will stimulate some lively discussion. Nonetheless, don't we want to know who won? To be honest, I believe Hart took the day. He consistently highlighted the potential problems with Feingold's view, while Feingold was unable to do so, with respect to Hart, on the same level. But this does not mean I think Feingold's position was *wrong*.

Feingold could have pressed Hart further on the potential danger of reducing all rational things to God, or of upholding "no conflict between divine and human natures from the beginning." Rigidly insisting upon this position denies the reality of the human will's ability to resist God, which is a Scriptural truth. For example, I encountered the following illuminating text among the readings for Tuesday of the Fifth Week of Lent:

> Jesus said to the Pharisees: "I am going away and you will look for me, but you will die in your sin. Where I am going you cannot come." So the Jews said, "He is not going to kill himself, is he, because he said, 'Where I am going you cannot come'?" He said to them, "You belong to what is below, I belong to what is above. You belong to this world, but I do not belong to this world. That is why I told you that you will die in your sins. For if you do not believe that I AM, you will die in your sins."

Sounds a bit like a natural / supernatural distinction! Clearly, Christ distinguishes between "this world" and "the world to come." Hart's views, of course, do not contradict our Lord in this matter. Hart's perspective is simply that *of* the coming world. It is eschatological. When we understand Christ's speech about the I AM, we enter into a new awareness of Truth. This awareness begets new understanding, helping us realize that we cannot truly see anything without the desire to see God, or that God is continually drawing all things back to God's self. But these propositions cannot be "true" or "known" to a non-Christian, to someone who is like the Jews in the passage quoted above. In this way, I think Feingold's vision actually accounts more-fully for the daily experience of the universe that we all share, as human beings. There is no inherent untruth within the natural/supernatural distinction, at least not as Feingold explains it.

Postscript
Especially as someone who once identified more with the world than with Christ, I find that it's a hard sell to uphold the Reality of monism in a dualistically-divisible universe. But thank God for the Trinity, which always shows us that there is a third option, namely, taking up both "one" and "two" in mystical dialog, a dialog wherein both reveal pieces of the Truth to our minds "through a glass, darkly..."

The Pandemic and the Wrath of God
Sam Fletcher

In dark moments, I have sometimes wondered whether, when disaster struck, I might lose my faith. Perhaps my God of unbounded kindness would fall away in the face of crisis—shown to be phantom conjured up by an over-hopeful imagination—sand leave me alone in the universe. Yet as it has turned out, the real danger was of this God morphing into a god of wrath, his face twisting into stern, unfamiliar expressions. In this midst of a pandemic, I do not fear losing God, but I am learning what it is to feel the fear OF God.

Before the virus, the language of plague and deadly pestilence belonged to the world of the Leviathan, of burning sulphur falling from the sky, of the Nile turning to blood. Now, for all the great leaps forward in medicine and technology, we find ourselves in that world again, afraid of the miasma that fills our supermarkets. Meanwhile, a plague of locusts afflicts East Africa and South Asia, and an outbreak of African swine fever has killed 40% of the pigs in China. In Britain, children place rainbows in their windows: 'When the bow is in the clouds, I will see it and remember the everlasting covenant between God and every living creature of all flesh that is on the earth,' said the Lord. Yet still the waters rise.

To blame natural crises on the wrath of God has often seemed, in the modern age, to be the preserve of fundamentalist charlatans. The televangelist launches a tirade against gays, or abortion, or feminism, for having caused the earthquake, and the only serious theological question is whether we should consider this response demonic or merely idiotic. Yet in recent years, the Christian left has also flirted with the language of divine retribution with regard to the climate crisis: the conjunction of rising seas, famines, and wildfires with the scientific consensus that these are caused by humanity's rapacious disregard for God's creation has made a theology of wrath irresistible. Some have swiftly re-applied to the present health crisis the language designed for the climate catastrophe. Liberation theologian Leonardo Boff, for example, has called the coronavirus 'a reprisal of Gaia for the offences that we continuously inflict on her.'

The notion that pandemics are a consequence of God's anger recurs throughout the Christian tradition, with a consensus that the proper response to pestilence is repentance and penance, so that God may relent. It comes to its most graphic manifestation in the reaction to the Black Death, which saw fanatical bands of flagellants roam through towns lashing their bleeding backs to atone for the sins of the world. A more typical, less gruesome, expression of penitence is encapsulated in a prayer to be used '*In The Time Of Any Common Plague Or Sickness*' from the *Book Of Common Prayer*:

> O Almighty God, who in thy wrath didst send a plague upon thine own people in the wilderness, for their obstinate rebellion against Moses and Aaron; and also, in the time of king David, didst slay with the plague of pestilence threescore and ten thousand, and yet remembering thy mercy didst save the rest: Have pity upon us miserable sinners, who now are visited with great sickness and mortality; that like as thou didst then accept of an atonement, and didst command the destroying Angel to cease from punishing, so it may now please thee to withdraw from us this plague and grievous sickness; through Jesus Christ our Lord. Amen.

Cranmer recalls the fact that we worship the same Almighty God who sent plagues on his people in the times of Moses and David. If we are to acknowledge some common identity between our God and the God of the Israelites—the only alternative being Marcionism—we must reckon with these stories.

Old Testament plague and disaster accounts function, in part, as theodicy. The Hebrew Bible was composed and compiled across a history of intense suffering for the Israelites: war, exile, and no doubt many disasters, famines and plagues. How, in view of this suffering, could they substantiate their claim that they were the chosen people of a loving and mighty God? One response—one so primal that theists have always reached for it instinctively—is that suffering is a punishment for sin. Exile and war and pestilence are divine retribution for idolatry, the neglect of the poor, or rebellion against the commandments of God. God is loving but also just, and suffering is explicable in these terms. By telling stories which closely associate natural disaster with identifiable sin—the destruction of Sodom as a response to the brazen sexual violence of every man in the city—we make sense of the catastrophes humanity faces. Such sense-making is a basic aspect of human religiosity.

Yet there is also a second strand in the Hebrew Bible, which sees painfully well the inadequacy of such a theodicy. This voice speaks in the Book of Job, in Psalm 73:1-14, and in Ecclesiastes 7:15:
> In this meaningless life of mine I have seen both of these:
> the righteous perishing in their righteousness,
> and the wicked living long in their wickedness.

In such moments, we are confronted with the truth that suffering is very often senseless. Jesus' preaching in Luke 13:1-9 sits well in this tradition:
> Those eighteen who were killed when the tower of Siloam fell on them—do you think that they were worse offenders than all the others living in Jerusalem? No, I tell you; but unless you repent, you will all perish just as they did.

Jesus rejects the assumption that suffering is explicable in terms of the sinfulness of the sufferer. All are in mortal need of repentance, but he firmly denies any necessary connection between the level of a person's sinfulness and the suffering they face. Of course we know this—we know holy, kind, amazing people afflicted with the virus—but, so strong is the religious propensity towards sense-making, we should remind ourselves of it often.

It can be profoundly important to face up to the meaninglessness and randomness of evil. David Bentley Hart writes:
> There is no more liberating knowledge given us by the gospel—and none in which we should find more comfort—than the knowledge that suffering and death, considered in themselves, have no ultimate meaning at all.

This acknowledgment is a refusal to indulge the religious instinct to make sense of suffering, and especially to make sense of it by attributing it to divine wrath. Good Friday elicits this refusal: Jesus is without sin, and is brutally executed. Before we attempt to make sense of this death—piling on doctrines until we can call the thing 'good'—we must acknowledge is utter senselessness.

All I have suggested so far I already held before the pandemic broke out. I still hold to it, as tightly as I can. Yet the virus has stirred in me an impulse to say something else, something perhaps more dangerous. I want to stand valiantly against the heresy of making sense out of suffering, to rail against the gods of vengeance as idols and demons. Yet when I read of God flooding the earth, sending plagues on the Egyptians, smiting rebellious Israelites, it strikes a freshly familiar note. Those stories feel frighteningly real at the moment. The words of the Book of Common Prayer—*have pity upon us miserable sinners, who now are visited with great sickness and mortality*—feel resonant today. I feel moved to pray not that I might recognise the senselessness of suffering, but that God might have mercy and relent. What if God, seeing our worship of Mammon, our reckless disregard for his creation, our cynical and inhumane governments, has seen fit to bring the whole thing down? What if God, in his wrath, has decided to crash the economy, ground the aeroplanes to a halt, let every social and political norm dissolve, and push the reset button?

To think in these terms is to think of God as a god. This is exactly how gods behave: they are angered by humanity's behaviour, and so inflict great disasters upon us, which will cease if we appease them. The god of the ancient Israelites is most certainly no exception here, and there is no reason he should be. The Bible, by virtue of its divine inspiration, is the most deeply human book ever written. And one of humanity's most inescapable instincts is to believe in gods: gods who demand appeasement and sacrifice, who reward the good and punish the evil, who send down famines and thunderbolts and pandemics. We cannot neatly assign this instinct to our sinful nature, since it appears—via the words of the Psalmist—on the lips of our Lord: 'my god, my god, why have you forsaken me?'. It is perhaps notable that 'my god' here is not Abba or Yahweh but Eloi, from El, the generic Semitic word for 'god'. It is used frequently to refer to Yahweh, but also to any other Ancient Near Eastern deity. When Jesus speaks here, he echoes humanity's cries to all our gods, those inscrutable cosmic rulers from whom we demand answers but so rarely get them. He is asking the question we always ask in times of anguish. Why are you doing this to me? What could I have possibly done to deserve this? Jesus takes no solace in 'the knowledge that suffering and death, considered in themselves, have no ultimate meaning at all', but seeks—in vain—for an explanation. He, like all human beings, is religious, and so cannot relinquish the excruciating instinct to search for meaning in our pain.

With Christ we cry out in bafflement to our god: Why have you sent this pandemic upon us? Why, supposing this plague is some kind of judgment on our social order, should it be that shop workers, homeless people, and refugees suffer most? Why have you forsaken them? Perhaps there is also a place within this muddle for that other primal response to divine wrath: repentance. It is, it bears repeating again, fundamentally anti-Christian to suggest that those who are ill in any way deserve this. Still, we have sinned. Because it is a respiratory disease, the virus' threat to life is increased in areas of greater air pollution, where our abuse of creation has made our cities less inhabitable. *Lord, Have Mercy.* The present plague of locusts in East Africa and South Asia is likely linked to climate change. *Christ, Have Mercy.* The horror in our hospitals has been aggravated by a systemic underfunding and devaluing of our healthcare system. *Lord, Have Mercy.* In Luke 13:1-9, Christ denies a relationship between an individual's suffering and their sin, but in the same breath calls all of us to repent, lest we should perish.

So I turn to my god, torn between penitence and baffled indignation, and beg for deliverance. In doing so, I do what human beings have always done when faced with a pandemic. Yet the Gospel opens up something new. 'Our Lord is above all gods' because our God has been crucified. He knows the anguish of senseless suffering. He has felt the wrath of our god from *our* side. Therefore, on the cross, the logic of the relation between god and creature upon which all sacrificial religion depends is totally subverted. The atonement is made, but it is God himself who provides the lamb. Here is a sacrifice to end all sacrifice, so that—our sins forever forgiven—'there is no longer any offering for sin.' The spectre of the vengeful, bloodthirsty god dissolves, revealing a triune God of boundless grace. A new relationship between humanity and God bursts forth from the empty tomb. 'There is therefore now no condemnation for those who are in Christ Jesus.'

Nevertheless, this side of the eschaton, I am not sure that humanity—and least of all the Church—will ever leave behind the god of wrath. Nor, necessarily, should we. Instead, we are caught in the oscillation between mere theism and Christianity, between retribution and grace. This dialectic is close to the heart of the Gospel, and forms the foundation of the sacrament of reconciliation. Over and over again, we fall into sin, experience God's furious anger, come before him in penitence, and receive his forgiveness, and in all this God never changes in the least. All the movement is on our side, in the changing expressions we project onto the face of Christ, in being brought once again to the foot of the cross and the mouth of the empty tomb.

Ultimately, the juxtaposition between the god of wrath and the God of Jesus Christ must fall away. The God we cry to in confusion and rage, who we come before in penitence and beg for deliverance, is the same God who—as the human being Jesus of Nazareth—was tortured and died at Calvary, who 'has borne our infirmities and carried our diseases.' In the early sixteenth century Matthias Grünewald painted the Isenheim Altarpiece, which depicts the crucified Christ afflicted with the sores of a victim of plague. Today, he is struck with fever on the cross, and struggles for breath as the inflammation in his lungs worsens.

'There is none like you among the gods, O Lord, nor are there any works like yours.'

It Is Not a Sin to Wear a Facemask
Luke Townsend

Anyone perusing social media these days will be well aware that the latest politicized controversy dividing American society is about wearing facemasks during the COVID-19 pandemic. One cannot make a simple trip to the grocery store without becoming bogged in a morass of invisible social pressure, judgment, and labels regarding whether one decides to don a face covering or not. Christians and Christian Churches are divided, largely along political lines, as to the compulsoriness of facemasks. A recent article published by America Magazine, describes the mask issue as dividing faithful Christians, because, "some see mask use — or not — as a partisan issue or a political statement, with political conservatives less likely to mask than political liberals." Evincing this division, some Catholic dioceses, like St. Louis, require facemasks for mass attendance, while others, like Milwaukee, only recommend masks, presumably out of respect for personal freedom and decision-making. Arguments for wearing facemasks by Christian authors and theologians thus far have tended to make the case that wearing a facemask should be seen as a form of charity for one's neighbor, or as a sign of respect for authority and care for the weak among our society, i.e. as a *voluntary* action that goes above and beyond what is strictly required. I think Christians and the Church need to go further in taking a moral stand on this issue. I argue that freely refusing to wear a facemask is a sin. Period.

The Catechism of the Catholic Church, in agreement with the majority of the Christian Tradition, defines sin as follows: "Sin is an offense against reason, truth, and right conscience; it is failure in genuine love for God and neighbor caused by a perverse attachment to certain goods. It wounds the nature of man and injures human solidarity. It has been defined as 'an utterance, a deed, or a desire contrary to the eternal law.'" The final phrase quoted in the definition, as is footnoted in the Catechism, comes from St. Augustine and is interpreted largely through the lens of Thomistic natural law theology. (Thomas Aquinas draws upon the same Augustinian phrase for his definition of sin in the *Summa Theologiae*.) I suggest we take a moment to draw from this resource in order to understand what the Church means by sin, and then apply it to our current context.

What St. Thomas teaches, roughly, is that a sin is doing something bad. More specifically, a sin is doing anything other than what would be chosen by a perfect, loving, all-knowing, all-powerful being that never makes any mistakes. Hence, a sin is freely doing anything contrary to the will of God. Sin is making a bad decision; it is choosing the bad action over the good action; or, it is choosing a lesser good over a greater good. Thomas fully understands the practical difficulty of his definition. Humans are not perfect, all-knowing, or all-powerful. Humans do not know the will of God with infallible accuracy. In fact, humans are pretty darn good at mistaking their own will and their own self-interest in any given situation, for the will of God. Hence, Thomas, in his typical style, makes some distinctions. He says that there exists a single, true, absolute, objective right and wrong thing to do in every particular situation. He calls this the eternal law, and he teaches that it exists perfectly only in the mind of God. Humans do not always know the absolute right and wrong thing to do in every situation because they do not have, but have to interpret, the mind of God. From our limited perspective, the moral world appears usually as a muddy grey, rather than a clear black and white.

What humans do have access to, first and foremost, is something Thomas calls the natural law. Humans are not all-knowing, but they are a little knowing. We do not know everything, but we can use our minds to know some things. Thus, there are some instances in which humans can use their reason to reliably figure out what is good and what is bad. For instance, the vast majority of humans and cultures throughout history have agreed that murder, rape, cruelty, stealing, etc. are bad, or sinful, actions and that almsgiving, telling the truth, caring for other people, doing an honest day's work, etc. are good actions. We do not need God specially to tell us right from wrong in these instances. The ability to reason, which is given to humans by God, can tell us these things.

There are other things, though, that our reason cannot tell us. No human and no society has ever figured out on its own that God wants us to love every other creature, even our worst enemies, like they are our own brothers, sisters, or children. A perfect, loving, all-powerful, all-knowing being, like God, would certainly treat everyone with the same respect, dignity, and value as everyone else, regardless of merits, but our fallen finite human reason fails us; it leads us to view true selflessness as madness, rather than as the one thing needed

(Luke 10:42). We think we are entirely justified to love our friends and hate our enemies (Matthew 5:43). To correct this fault, St. Thomas thinks that God gave humans some extra help in addition to the obvious, agreed-upon, natural law. Thomas called this extra law the divine, or revealed, law, which includes the whole of Scripture, Tradition, and Church teaching. For Thomas, God had to spell out to us that we should love our enemies, because our own reason (after the fall) was too weak to get us there.

Now, let us return to the Catholic Tradition's definition of sin. The Church teaches that a sin is any offense against truth and reason — either our own reason, which we have access to, or God's reason, which we have access to only insofar as God has revealed it to us and we have understood it. Sin is transgressing either the natural or divine law. The question at hand regarding wearing facemasks during a pandemic is thus: Does freely and knowingly refusing to wear a facemask violate either the natural law or the divine law? Does failing to wear a facemask during a pandemic go against either right human reason or God's revealed higher reason of love? I argue that it does, that it in fact goes against both, and thus that refusing to wear a facemask in our current context is a sin.

Human reason, often expressed in scientific findings, unquestionably dictates that wearing a facemask during a respiratory-based pandemic is good. I will demonstrate this at two levels. First, even basic animalistic self-interested human reason would affirm the following: Dying is bad. A lot of people dying is really bad. Catching a disease that might kill you is bad. Giving a disease to other people that might kill them is bad. If you can even potentially avoid dying and killing people, you should. Facemasks potentially prevent people from dying during a respiratory pandemic. Therefore, wearing a facemask is good.

Second, at a more complicated societal level, human reason no less dictates the following: Convenience is good. Being comfortable, physically, socially, and in one's normal routines, are good. Maintaining personal freedom is good. Avoiding economic shutdown and disruption is good. On the other hand, avoiding sickness is also good. Avoiding dying is good. Avoiding a lot of people dying is good. Avoiding a significant risk of a lot of people dying is good. Some goods, unfortunately, are mutually exclusive. Sometimes, to get one good, like a pizza, one has to give up another good, like $10. Not all goods are equal. Thus, giving up a less valuable good in order to get a more valuable good is good. The good of not dying outweighs most other goods. The common good outweighs most private or individual goods. *Accordingly, if one can advance the common good and avoid mass death, but it comes at the cost of private comfort, personal freedom, or individual political ideology, one should.* Facemasks advance the common good by helping to avoid mass death, potentially at the cost of one's comfort, personal freedom, or political ideology. Therefore, wearing a facemask is worthwhile and is good. Freely and knowingly acting against the good that right human reason compels all to affirm is none other than rejecting the good and choosing the bad. To do so is to break the natural law and, in the Christian tradition, to sin.

As Thomas Aquinas knew, however, human reason is weak, short sighted, and easily confused. Sometimes, faulty human reason leads well-intentioned people to disagree upon or even act against right and true reason, which is God's reason and God's will. Sometimes, as the Catechism states, faulty human reason leads persons to fail to love God and neighbor, due to a "perverse attachment to certain [lesser] goods." Sometimes, perhaps oftentimes, faulty human reason leads people to act against the love of neighbor, or even against their own self-interest. It leads people to choose a greasy hamburger rather than a healthy salad, fully knowing that eating one is good and eating the other is bad. It leads people, selfishly and absurdly, to offend reason and violate the natural law by choosing personal comfort over the common good. And sometimes, it leads people into valuing one's worldview, one's political beliefs, or the delusion that one knows everything and has been right all along, more highly than one values life itself. For exactly these times, Thomas taught, God gave humans some extra help in the form of the divine, revealed, law.

For Thomas, divine revelation, which is chiefly expressed in Scripture, expands upon, amplifies, and clarifies the conclusions of human reason, as grace perfects nature. Looking to Scripture for guidance in the facemask debate, one finds exactly such confirmation and clarification. Scripture often depicts sin as the absurd choice of lesser goods over higher goods; and, it frequently warns against choosing death over life. Adam and Eve, for instance, literally chose death, suffering, toil, and Hell over a life of joy, peace, and paradise (Genesis 3). They did so not because they wanted to die, but because they found death preferable to feeling weak, uncomfortable, ignorant, or wrong. They more highly valued the delusion of their own omnipotence and omniscience than they valued the actuality of a life of dependence and giftedness. They flouted reason and reality itself because their faulty human reason lead them to conclude that, in the words of Milton, it might be better to reign in Hell than serve in Heaven. Such a choice is the exemplar of sin. It is, more precisely, the original sin.

Absurd human choices against right reason echo throughout the divine law in Scripture. God set the ancient Israelites free from the Egyptian empire, but they cried out to return to slavery rather than wander the wilderness in freedom (Numbers 14:4). They made the absurd decision that they would rather die than be free (Exodus 16:3). In Deuteronomy, God calls the faithful to choose life over death, by following God's commandments, precisely identifying that the problem with people is that they absurdly choose death and disobedience over life and righteousness. The text states, *"I call heaven and earth to witness against you today that I have set before you life and death, blessings and curses. choose life so that you and your descendants may live!"* (Deuteronomy 30:19). In the time of the prophets, Isaiah similarly laments people's absurdity. God acted in Isaiah's day to satisfy people's needs with true water and true bread, with wine and milk that have no price. Yet, absurdly, the people refused what good sense would counsel. To which, Isaiah cries, *"Why do you spend your money for that which is not bread, and your labor for that which does not satisfy?"* (Isaiah 55:2). The early followers of Christ, no less, saw people making the same absurd choices. Christ came into the world to save people from their sins. He spent his life freely serving others and doing nothing but speaking the truth. God became incarnate in Christ purely to bless us and reveal the depth of God's love. Our response was the absurdity of the cross. Our response was to reject and murder God incarnate for expressing infinite love. Hence, John writes, *"And this is the judgment, that the light has come into the world, and people loved darkness rather than light because their deeds were evil."* (John 3:19).

The divinely revealed law in Scripture, therefore, leads those who will listen to be on the lookout for perverse human absurdity that violates right reason. Scripture warns us to repent of this sin before it is too late. As is evident from even a cursory glance at our society, people today are no less evil, no less absurd, and no less tragically misguided than the people confronted by Moses, the prophets, Christ, and the early Church. People today are still choosing their own deaths and delusions of self-righteousness over repentance, salvation, the common good, and their own life. Christians, therefore, with the extra help of divine revelation to guide their reason, should make no mistake. Choices like refusing to wear a facemask during a pandemic in order to defiantly proclaim one's political allegiance at the cost of human lives, are none other than absurd choices of death over life. Choices like stubbornly reopening schools, Churches, professional sports, and businesses as a means of willing our society back to normalcy because one has counted the costs and more highly values profit and economic health than one values people and personal health, are exactly absurd choices of death over life. Such choices blatantly work against the common good; they thus violate reason, the natural law, the divine law, and the eternal law. Such choices wound humans, injure human solidarity, and are a failure of genuine love of God and neighbor. Such choices have always been called by their true name in the Christian Tradition. Such choices are sin. Period.

On Original Sin and Racism
Timon Cline

A great thing about writing for *Conciliar Post*: any time I'm unsure of what to write about, all I have to do is read recent posts from my fellow contributors and without fail a) a writing topic is sparked by one of their pieces, or b) I find something I disagree with and decide to respond. Both are welcome sights. This time, it's the latter and directed at AJ Maynard (my resident competition in facial hair).
In his recent article, "Reclaiming Original Sin in the Face of White Supremacy," AJ argues,
> [N]ow is the time for every white Christian to consider, perhaps counterfactually, not *if* we are racist, but rather *how* we are racist.
> Just as one may identify oneself as a sinner without being able to explicitly identify [with] every personal sin and its impact, white Christians must accept the likelihood that our collective worldview and individual behaviors are the inevitable byproducts of overt, racial sin.

AJ's premise, the "not *if* but *how*," is now common parlance, courtesy of Robin DiAngelo, and requires certain ideological commitments to become tenable (more on that in a bit). AJ is correct, of course, that sin is not just the sum of discrete actions, but a moral status before God resultant from the departure from his law and idolatrous worship. In distinctly modern terms, sin is an *identity*. But as Jody Byrkett rightly reminded me when reviewing this article, for those of us who are in union with Christ, we *are* sinners no longer. Though we sin we *are* saints before God.

What is specious at best is the suggestion that the necessary and inescapable result, in every person, of this debased moral status is the *particular* sin of racism. In support of this premise AJ repurposes the doctrines of original sin and total depravity in service of his claim. He sees a contradiction in the fact that Christians willingly admit their fallen, sinful nature but are generally unwilling to acknowledge their racism.

> [M]any white Christians, despite being unable to always identify their sin, freely identify as sinners. However, I have yet to encounter white Christians who—despite the racist history of the American Church, and the likelihood of possessing implicit, anti-black bias—freely identify as racist. This raises the question, "Why is it easy for a white Christian to identify as a sinner, but not as a racist?" Is our reality truly one in which white Christians see themselves as susceptible to the impact of Original Sin to the point of radical corruption, but remain immune to the impact of hundreds of years of white supremacy? Is it not possible that you and I—despite our intention, and perhaps without our complete awareness—possess inherently racist beliefs?

Here AJ equivocates between racism as a sin in particular and the root cause, the hereditary principle that yields corrupt, disordered inclinations of sin generally. The first sin of our parents—whether properly defined as pride, as Catholics would have it, or unbelief, as Protestants see it—infects all their descendants but manifests in diverse ways. However, in AJ's mind, original sin necessitates that sinners commit the sin of racism. AJ then reiterates his basic claim: Institutional racism is the world we live in; it is our Original Sin. You and I may not personally believe black individuals are, by nature, inferior to white individuals. But we nonetheless live within, and benefit from, a system built and maintained by people who did. Because of this, every white Christian should now consider not *if*, but rather *how* we are racist.

But, following this logic, what is to stop us from doing this with any other sin? Indeed, scholars of critical race theory would say that white supremacy (which has been redefined) is marked not only by racist policies and institutions but a history of genocide, rape, and plunder. Is rape or plunder or murder original sin?

As an aside, it would be more consistent with AJ's line of reasoning to say that white supremacy is the original sin. White supremacy, of course, is now synonymous with the domination of whites via hegemonic power. To say that America was founded on white supremacy is to say that it was built by white men, for white men, to privilege white men over and against non-whites. Racism is simply the natural outgrowth of this design. The racialized society we live in today is merely the result of the dominant class seeking to preserve their dominance by "othering" everyone else. This "othering" is then implanted in societal institutions, structures, and culture. At least that's what the "experts" say.

But if we follow this progression, the concept of "original sin" would lose all meaning, becoming mere shorthand for whatever sin is in focus. Even "white supremacy," assuming adoption of the updated definition, doesn't take us far enough back. The theological work done by "original sin" would be eroded.

Further, the pervasiveness of sin in all humans does not—at least no theologian of note would hold—require that *every* sin is, in fact, committed by *every* sinner. And the doctrinal of total depravity is caricatured when it stands for *complete* depravity. Rather, total depravity's reference is to scope, not depth.

And although our nature is fallen, our faculties diluted, and our desires disordered, moral cognizance and the basic natural endowments of the intellectual faculties remain. Otherwise, moral culpability would be eroded. Further, not every intention or resultant action is depraved, nor is every demonstrably depraved action as depraved as it could be.

The Christian belief in original sin and total depravity are theological doctrines drawn from divine revelation. All have sinned and fallen short of the glory of God and his moral law promulgated through the prophets and the writings of Scripture. Christian fealty to Scripture as the *norma normata* requires that they accept such an explicit presupposition about humanity.

AJ's claim that racism should also be categorized as original sin (at least in a modern Western context) leans heavily on a particular understanding of socialization, that is to say, not on biblical revelation. This distinction does not summarily defeat AJ's claim, but merely situates it upon unsure footing, at least from a Christian perspective. Doctrines drawn from Scripture, systematized, integrated, and enshrined in tradition cannot be frequently *contextualized*, as they say, without risking constant instability.

AJ seems to suggest that the sin of racism is inescapable because whites have been conditioned by a white supremacist, racialized society. Even if, as individuals, we do not harbor racist bias, AJ contends that, as beneficiaries of a society constructed by whites, for whites, we are necessarily racist. These conclusions are in line with much of the ideology, drawn from critical race theory (CRT), that grips our national discourse on racism; indeed, they are impossible to hold without the assumptions and commitments of CRT.

Theorists like Robin DiAngelo, for instance, define racism in terms of systemic complicity, that is, the failure or refusal to buck the system, so to speak (the system being inherently and irreconcilably racist). One is racist if they benefit from the system. Even those who have embarked on the perpetual journey of divesting themselves from whiteness remain, per DiAngelo's own admission, decidedly racist. She calls herself racist—in her words, just as racist as Donald Trump. Though she positions herself on her imaginary racist spectrum on the pole of divestment from whiteness, she holds that she will never fully arrive, as it were. Like Ibram X. Kendi, for DiAngelo, there is no such thing as non-racist; there is only racist and antiracist, and the latter does not entail, for a white person, total relinquishment of racism (they are merely actively combating racism, which is to say, themselves).

In any case, for critical race theorists (DiAngelo's discipline is critical whiteness studies), racism is defined almost totally in systemic terms. That is why the question of not *if* but *how* one is racist exists—it is the inevitable result, they think, of existing in a racialized society constructed by white Europeans. As AJ said, "Institutional racism is the world we live in." It is, as Nikole Hannah-Jones would have it, the essence and distinguishing mark of American society on every level.

Systems of domination, and social location therein, is all. Not only does the dominant class (the white, heteronormative, cisgender, patriarchy) benefit materially and otherwise from the power dynamics wrapped up in the system, but their norms, beliefs, and even aesthetic tastes are determined by the cultural or ideological hegemony. They think racist thoughts because they exist in a racist system, and said "racist" thoughts are, more or less, any thoughts that affirm the status quo as objective, normal, or inevitable. Because the status quo suits the members of the dominant class, said members willingly or otherwise ignore the systems of domination they inhabit and from which they benefit. They are not critically conscious, they are not "woke" to reality.

Recognition and repudiation of the status quo is the only path towards divestment of whiteness—whiteness being that which garners social capital in an allegedly white supremacist system—and leveraging their white privilege to pursue "equity" for the oppressed. But even then, so long as one benefits from the status quo, they are still racist. The sin of racism *is* the existence of systemic racism. The sin is imputed to individuals according to their relationship to the system, pervasive and, in a sense, alive.

The question Christians should be asking themselves is whether such a standard of culpability, i.e. guilt by social location within Western society, conforms to reason, experience, and revelation. First, a preliminary question and analogy is needed to illustrate the reality of structural or systemic sin.

Abortion is a perfect example of systemic manifestation of sin, one that no conservative evangelical would deny. Our laws and healthcare system codify and support abortion regularly (as we saw in the Stare Decisis gymnastics of the Chief Justice, who feebly appealed to Edmund Burke as justification, in *June Medical*). The prospect of *Roe* being overturned becomes less likely by the day. The sin of abortion increasingly pervades societal norms—teens TikTok their trips to abortion clinics for giggles and 'likes'—and expectations. Institutions like the media, entertainment industry, and education system uphold and perpetuate said "norms" intentionally and consistently.

And yet, it is acknowledged that though the sin of abortion is enabled and supported structurally and socially, individual actors are obviously required for the particular sin to be committed. The precedent of *Roe* and *Planned Parenthood v. Casey* and their progeny may be unjust in principle, and therefore sinful, but they are not the sin itself; they are not abortion. The relevant precedent merely affirms and enables the sin performed—indeed, abortion and especially support of its practice is increasingly becoming performative, a sort of celebrated public ritual— by individuals.

Doubtless, law (given its pedagogical and normative role), and certainly entertainment and education, affect public consciousness. But, again, they are not themselves the sin (even if celebration and affirmation of sin are themselves sinful, such secondary sin must still be attributed to persons, not inanimate, unmanned systems). Rather, abortion is the act of murdering unborn (or, maybe, *born*) infant persons.

The action requires individuals, and specifically individual volition for it to be performed, for the sin to exist at all. Culpability is diminished as soon as 1) a person's volition is diminished, or 2) a person's agency is diluted.

All the precedent in the world would not matter if everyone simply refused to act in accordance therewith. One of the common liberal arguments in favor of abortion is that even if it is not legalized people would still do it. Best to make it "safe and rare." Like marijuana, best to regulate it. These arguments implicitly acknowledge the necessity of individual actors to give life to abortion (no pun intended). The entire premise of the *Roe* et al. is the privacy and agency of women; reserving their right over their own bodies—"pro-choice." Self-determination of mothers is the rallying cry.

Right or wrong, abortion policy is in service of protecting human choice [except that of the unborn human] to the utmost. It is the manifestation of radical autonomy built into the sociopolitical theory of liberalism. By its own logic, abortion as policy could not have *not* happened. The cruel irony of abortion doctrine (a confused and confusing thing, by all accounts) is that to fully realize radical self-determination over and against all natural (or otherwise) constraints, the self-determination, agency, and humanity of others must be subverted, viz., not only that of fathers, but of the most vulnerable members of our society, children.

But I digress. Abortion doctrine is a battle for supreme autonomy played out in the courts, one in which the living have run roughshod over the not yet born, contra the convictions of the dead (however shortsightedly the court might try to frame "history" and "tradition"). Arguably, the brand of originalism championed by Bork and Scalia does not permit *Roe*. But in a better, more robust originalism now slowly coming into vogue, there is no question of its invalidity. Abortion violates the natural law in the first instance, was literally unprecedented until 1973, and further frustrates the chief interest of the state, the common good (of the WHOLE person and WHOLE society).

Returning to the point at hand, abortion is an act that, despite all the institutional precedent and propaganda justifying and enabling said act, requires volitional individuals. There can be no abortion without abortionists. There are systemic reverberations of the thing, but they are not the thing itself. No one would agree that any woman that lives in a society wherein abortion is systemically propped up is, by potentially or actually benefitting therefrom, complicit in the system and therefore guilty of abortion herself until every last abortion clinic is closed and any reference to *Roe* scratched from the record books.

Neither do conservative Christians—those who detest the legalization of abortion—believe the whole system of law, healthcare, entertainment, and education is defunct simply because it has a history of permitting the murder of unborn, defenseless children. Abortion doctrine is a bug, not a feature, of constitutional jurisprudence.

As presented by critical race theorists, racism conceptually differs. It requires no racists (in the traditional sense) but will inevitably produce them. It is rather an invisible, toxic, oppressive force that stalks the land and is baked into every facet of the system—American institutions are "stamped from the beginning"—the "beginning" being 1619, not 1776.

Law, a "Eurocentric enterprise," in particular is a leading proliferator of racism. It is indeterminate, inherently political, and a tool of oppression. Along these lines, Jack Balkin characterizes law—not a particular law, but generally—as an apology for, or legitimizer of, power. In the Gramscian conception of law, championed by Kimberlé Crenshaw and others, it is a key element of the hegemony, one which blinds people to their oppression via a veneer of procedural consistency and fairness, thereby stifling their utopian imaginations and preserving the control of the dominant class.

All of this regarding abortion is at odds with the characterization of systemic racism today. Per theorists of critical social justice, there needn't be racists for there to be racism because racism has been almost totally identified with structural inequity (equity being, more or less, equality of outcome, controlling for historic injustices).

The evidence for structural racism is disparities which are taken (on faith) to be per se evidence of racism. Any unfavorable outcome is racist regardless of intent, motive, or purpose of the policy charged as the culprit. As is often said, impact is more important than intent. A policy with a justifiable impetus could nevertheless be deemed racist if disparities along racial lines in any way result (the original purpose or intent behind the policy is then backfilled as racist).

Racism would exist without any individual actors harboring racist prejudice (although that is assumed, too). The system has a life of its own for critical race theorists. The sin of racism, insofar as it is considered on an individual level, is marked by mere (perceived) complicity in the system—i.e. not being actively against it, not problematizing and deconstructing it, not leveraging all available resources to combat it.

We can recognize the potentiality of sin's representation or manifestation at the systemic level, but we can never dismiss the necessity of individual sinners to make the system tick. As I have said, if the conviction that abortion is monstrous, by some act of special Providence, swept the nation, *Roe* would become irrelevant. The structural outgrowths of the practice would not, on their own, continue to perform abortions.

That is to say, and as others have said, the reality of systemic sin should be heartily affirmed by Christians, but not without qualification. What should be affirmed is that sinners produce individual sinful actions and, given that humans construct institutions, norms, and other civil mechanisms, it should be expected that the ramifications of individual sin will be apparent at a structural level. What should not be affirmed is systemic sin in the sense that it is peddled by the proponents of critical social justice, a conception that removes individual accountability and inserts ubiquitous, collective, inescapable guilt from which no repentance can be made, apart from revolutionary measures.

Most importantly, as Albert Mohler recently pointed out at *Public Discourse*, solutions to systemic manifestations of sin of any kind must be tailored to the true cause of the same. The importation of sin into human structures (or anything else constructed by creatures) is incontrovertible. However, it is *individuals* that are sinful, not structures as such.

This means that no structural overhaul, no revolution, no eradication of biblical Christianity will secure lasting justice and peace…We are called to do everything within our power to expunge sin from the structures of our society…At the same time, we cannot accept that the structural manifestations of sin are the heart of the problem. No, the heart of the problem is found in the sinfulness of the individual human heart.

No doubt the "just preach the Gospel" crowd borders on hyperbole and, without desiring to be too heavy-handed, hypocrisy. The manifestation of sin at a high, societal level should be combatted because we know that, left unchecked, it will perpetuate, excuse, and exacerbate individual sin. This is especially true in law. Licentious laws are no laws at all (which is not to suggest that all matters of morality should be legislated or litigated).

This long excursus on systemic sin returns us to AJ's claims about culpability via systemic racism. Whether systemic racism exists, and to what extent, is a matter for real, considered debate (not one clouded by pseudo-Marxist gobbledygook). And there's real evidence that systemic problems *do* exist. In addition to the abortion example given above, pornography—which is not only legally permitted but props up other evils like human trafficking and abuse—would be another systemic manifestation of sin. The point of this article is also not to deny the presence of sexist and racist prejudices in powerful people, nor that said prejudices do not affect civil institutions. Most of all, it is not to deny the history of real, brutal, systemically-expressed racism throughout human history.

However, what must be asserted at the outset of any such discussion is that individual culpability unto racism cannot be defined by one's social location *vis a vis* the hegemony, and neither is the existence of systemic racism the analog to the doctrine of original sin, a doctrine which differs from racism as to scope and particularity. Lastly, my contention is that sociopolitical structures may perpetuate or exacerbate a problem but they cannot *independently* create or animate the problem.

As I said last month, regarding David Justice's recent writing, I genuinely appreciate the discussion starters from other *CP*'ers, and welcome further conversation on the difficult and pressing topic of race dynamics in American society.

The Atonement of Irenaeus
Matthew Bryan

Imagine if one of the twelve disciples of Jesus had personally discipled a man whose pupil had written a short book for us, a book that explains the barest essentials of the apostles' teaching. What a treasure it would be if we found such a book! In 1904, a priest of the Oriental Orthodox Church of Armenia uncovered exactly such a book, the *Demonstration of the Preaching of the Apostles*. Its author, Bishop Irenaeus of Lugdunum (modern Lyons, France) had learned under Bishop Polycarp of Smyrna, a disciple of the Apostle John. Irenaeus wrote this short book of roughly fifty pages to his beloved friend Marcianus. Just one generation removed from the Apostle John, Irenaeus gifted Marcianus (and us) with an early "manual of essentials" so that Marcianus (and we) could learn "in a short space all the members of the body of truth."[1] This book by Irenaeus surprised me in three ways:

- By quoting almost exclusively from the Old Testament Scriptures rather than from the Apostles.
- By framing most of his topics through the overarching theme of authority, beginning with that of God, then moving consecutively through the authority Adam, then Satan, and finally Jesus.
- By resolving the problem of sin, not through justice or a substitutionary death, but through the transformation of humanity. It is this surprise which I present for consideration today, the resolution of the problem sin according to Irenaeus.

Three Irenaeic Problems

Just a few sentences into *Demonstration*, Irenaeus encouraged his beloved Marcianus to stay on the "one way" which leads to the kingdom of heaven. Then he warned him, "Other ways bring down to death, separating man from God." At the outset, Irenaeus was concerned not about the torments of hell, but of death's chief power: "separating man from God." He then framed the purpose of the

---

[1] For all references, see Irenaeus, *The Demonstration of the Apostolic Preaching*, (The MacMillen Co, New York, 1920). More recent translations of *Demonstration* include that of John Behr and that of Iain McKenzie.

incarnation of Jesus, not for justice nor for satisfying divine wrath, but, "in order to abolish death and show forth life and produce a community of union between God and man."

A little further on, Irenaeus recounted the fall of humanity at Eden. Surprisingly, he laid the blame for humanity's fall at the feet of Satan rather than Adam: "But man was a child, not yet having his understanding perfected; wherefore also he was easily led astray by the deceiver." When describing Satan's persuasion, Irenaeus credited him with the transformation of humanity, saying he "made man sinful." So Irenaeus added a second problem for Jesus to solve. Not only was humanity separated from God, but humanity had also been transformed from innocence into sinfulness.

Finally, Irenaeus wrote about human bondage. He said God appointed humanity to rule over all the earth, even over the angels and the archangel Satan who Irenaeus said dwelled here. Yet after summarizing the Old Testament, Irenaeus said that Satan had enslaved *us instead:* "in the original formation of Adam all of us were tied and bound up with death . . . death reigned over the flesh . . . flesh which sin had ruled and dominated . . ." The pupil of the Apostle John's disciple presented three human problems: separation, transformation, and bondage. He did not emphasize God's wrath, nor damnation, nor justice, nor any debt owed toward God.

Irenaeic Incarnation
As noted above, Irenaeus first framed the incarnation of our Lord for the purpose of "establishing a community of union between God and man." Having laid out the problems of our transformation into sin and bondage to Satan, he then returned to that first thought in chapter 31: "So then He united man with God, and established a community of union between God and man . . ."

The word "atonement" has become heavy-laden with theology over the years, but it simply means "unity" or "reconciliation." The Oxford English Dictionary defines atonement as, "The condition of being at one with others." We might expect Irenaeus to tell us that Jesus atoned us unto God by suffering His wrath in our place, but he made no such claim. For Irenaeus, atonement occurred through Jesus' becoming "the last Adam," and through our being "born again."

In the West, we tend to consider the incarnation as simply the preparation for suffering. We view Christmas primarily as equipping

Jesus to experience human suffering by giving Him a human body. In contrast, Irenaeus claimed the apostles presented the incarnation as the equivalent of Adam's work:

- **Jesus summed up humanity:** "God took dust of the earth and formed the man, the beginning of mankind. So then the Lord, summing up afresh this man, took the same dispensation of entry into flesh, being born from the Virgin by the Will and the Wisdom of God; that He also should show forth the likeness of Adam's entry into flesh and there should be that which was written in the beginning: man after the image and likeness of God."
- **Jesus counteracted Adam:** "And just as through a disobedient virgin, man was stricken down and fell into death; so through the Virgin who was obedient to the Word of God, man was reanimated and received life."
- **Jesus swallowed death:** "For it was necessary that Adam should be summed up in Christ, that mortality might be swallowed up and overwhelmed by immortality."
- **Jesus killed rebellion:** "And the trespass which came by the tree was undone by the tree of obedience, when, hearkening unto God, the Son of man was nailed to the tree; thereby putting away the knowledge of evil and bringing in and establishing the knowledge of good: now evil it is to disobey God . . ."
- **Obeying destroyed disobeying:** "So then by the obedience wherewith He obeyed even unto death, hanging on the tree, He put away the old disobedience which was wrought in the tree."
- **Jesus formed a better humanity:** "He manifested the resurrection, Himself becoming the first begotten of the dead, and in Himself raising up man that was fallen, lifting him up far above the heaven to the right hand of the glory of the Father."

According to the pupil of John's disciple, the apostles preached an atonement quite foreign to many modern Christians. Irenaeus did not learn from the apostles that Jesus satisfied God's wrath, nor that he had satisfied our legal penalties which divine justice had required. The pupil of John's disciple said that the apostles taught our Lord's atonement as the summing up of humanity in the last Adam and the reversal of Adam's rebellion. Jesus swallowed Adamic rebellion and destroyed it, raising up an obedient form of humanity, in the image and likeness of God. Thus it was written to the Hebrews, "Inasmuch then as the children have partaken of flesh and blood, He Himself likewise shared in the same, that through death He might destroy him who had the power of death, that is, the devil, and release those who through fear of death were all their lifetime subject to bondage" (Heb 2:14-15 NKJV).

Entering The Atonement

We would ask Irenaeus then, how someone can benefit from the atonement of the Lord Jesus. He taught us that there are two forms of humanity, the fallen lineage of Adam and the risen lineage of Jesus. How then, does one manage to move from the old to the new, from dead humanity to living humanity? Irenaeus would reply that we enter the living humanity in the same way we entered dead humanity, by being born:

- "And that this baptism is the seal of eternal life, and is the new birth unto God, that we should no longer be the sons of mortal men, but of the eternal and perpetual God."
- "And for this reason the baptism of our regeneration proceeds through these three points: God the Father bestowing on us regeneration through His Son by the Holy Spirit."

Result Of Atonement

Irenaeus filled most of his little book for Marcianus with Old Testament prophecies of Jesus (including some from the books of Baruch and Sirach), but he ended with the claim that the second birth renders us completely new persons:

- "those inflict no hurt at all who in the former time were, through their rapacity, like wild beasts in manners and disposition."
- "Coming together in one name, they have acquired righteous habits by the grace of God, changing their wild and untamed nature."
- ". . . so great is the transformation which faith in Christ the Son of God effects for those who believe on Him."
- "Behold, with the Father we speak, and in His presence we stand, being children in malice, and grown strong in all righteousness and soberness."
- "For no longer shall the Law say, "Do not commit adultery," to him who has no desire at all for another's wife; and "Thou shalt not kill," to him who has put away from himself all anger and enmity; and "Thou shalt not covet thy neighbor's field or ox or ass," to those who have no care at all for earthly things..."

This atonement will sound strange to many modern ears, but all Christians taught it in similar terms as Irenaeus until the 12th century. Today, Eastern Orthodoxy, Oriental Orthodoxy, and the Assyrian Church of the East still present the atonement in this way. It is often called "Christus Victor" by those who are more accustomed to a justice-and-wrath view of atonement. Paul thoroughly explained our atonement in Romans 5:12-21, climaxing in verse nineteen: "For as through the disobedience of the one man, the many were constituted sinners: so also through the obedience of the One, shall the many be constituted righteous" (YLT).

Finally, what we believe about atonement strongly shapes how we live our lives. Did Jesus only get me off of the hook from my punishment, or did he utterly transform me? If I believe that He rescued me from punishment, then I might find righteous living optional since unrighteousness no longer bears consequences. If I try to reflect righteous living, then my motive will be gratitude rather than absolute necessity.

If atonement actually transforms us though, then my unrighteous deeds will rightly cause me to question whether I have truly been atoned. I must necessarily forsake unrighteousness or realize that I am not in fact atoned to God. If I believe that atonement completely transformed me, then I do not try to reflect righteous living since such is the natural outcome of atonement. Rather, I must ask the scriptures and Christian traditions how it is that I am hindering the Holy Spirit from displaying the righteousness which is now natural to me. This latter question I have found best answered thus far by the Eastern Orthodox tradition. For those interested in an outsider's investigation of Eastern Orthodox spirituality, I recommend *The Spirituality of the Christian East* by Roman Catholic Cardinal Tomas Spidlik.

Faith Across Traditions

Dare We Hope for the Salvation of All?
Benjamin Winter

1 Timothy 2:1–4: "*I urge that supplications, prayers, intercessions, and thanksgivings should be made for everyone, for kings and all who are in high positions, so that we may lead a quiet and peaceable life in all godliness and dignity. This is right and is acceptable in the sight of God our Saviour, who desires everyone to be saved and to come to the knowledge of the truth.*"

2 Peter 3:8–9: "*But do not ignore this one fact, beloved, that with the Lord one day is like a thousand years, and a thousand years are like one day. The Lord is not slow about his promise, as some think of slowness, but is patient with you, not wanting any to perish, but all to come to repentance.*"

These two beautiful passages ground my thoughts in this article, the purpose of which is to argue (from a Catholic perspective[1]) that Christians can, and indeed should, hope for the salvation of all humanity.[2] I will begin by discussing one of Christ's sayings that evokes eternal damnation. Then, I will provide my exegesis of the two passages quoted above. Finally, I will make some general comments on hell and the teaching of the Catholic Church.

Example of Christ's Words
Hans Urs Von Balthasar's book *Dare We Hope that All Men be Saved* continues to guide my thinking on this matter in general, and particularly on the subject of hell as depicted in the Bible. Balthasar proposes that Biblical descriptions of hell should be read primarily as personal warnings against the potential consequences of unrepentant sin. In Matthew's Gospel, Jesus reminds his followers that when we

---

[1] But a perspective heavily formed by the East—from the Greek (and Syriac) Fathers to modern teachers of Orthodoxy like David Bentley Hart, who spoke to me about God getting what God wants (see paragraph 2, below).

[2] Note that I am not saying we are in a position to know with certainty whether this will happen, and that I am not addressing the separate (but related) question of whether all created things—including the devil—will eventually return to God.

help the hungry and thirsty, the strangers, and those needing care, we do these things to Him.[1] Those who fail to act in this way are commanded to "depart from [Christ] into the eternal fire prepared for the devil and his angels."[2] Reflecting on this central passage, Balthasar comes to understand that its purpose is to bring about a change of mind (*metanoia*) in the reader. In this change of mind that is also a change of heart, "my seemingly small omissions take on such weight that I no longer have any time at all for glancing left and right in order to see how others are faring."[3] When a person falls at the feet of Christ in broken repentance, he can no longer "contrive his own escape from damnation through a purely individualistic conception of salvation ... [and] abandon everyone else to the grinding wheels of hell."[4] Only by listening to Christ's warnings with humility can believers become convinced that the love we so desperately need is, in fact, so much greater than our sin. This love—by its very nature—must extend to fill the entire universe![5] As Balthasar resoundingly affirms, "The conviction that 'I am the least of all' leads to the sudden awareness of my own precarious existential condition: the threat of eternal perdition is addressed, indeed, to me!"[6] In another text, *Love Alone is Credible*, Balthasar clearly summarizes the Christology behind his views on the personal character of hell. Emphasizing the importance of Holy Saturday, he states that in "the God-forsakenness of the Crucified One," human beings "see what we have been redeemed and saved from: the definitive loss of God, a loss we could never have spared ourselves [of] through any of our own efforts outside of grace."[7] Hence, Scripture passages talking about eternal torment are misused when applied to people other than ourselves, or when taken as primarily ontological (rather than primarily moral or exhortative) statements.

---

[1] Matt 25:31-46.
[2] Matt 25:41.
[3] Balthasar, *Dare We Hope*, 90.
[4] Hans Urs Von Balthasar, *Love Alone is Credible*, trans. D. C. Schindler (San Francisco: Ignatius, 2004), 97.
[5] See Romans 8:31-32, 38-39: "What then are we to say about these things? If God is for us, who is against us?He who did not withhold his own Son, but gave him up for all of us, will he not with him also give us everything else? ... For I am convinced that neither death, nor life, nor angels, nor rulers, nor things present, nor things to come, nor powers, nor height, nor depth, nor anything else in all creation, will be able to separate us from the love of God in Christ Jesus our Lord."
[6] Balthasar, *A Short Discourse on Hell*, 248-49.
[7] Balthasar, *Love Alone is Credible*, 93.

Exegesis

In the 1 Timothy passage (above), the historical leaders in "high positions" were hardly ever amenable to Christianity. In fact, most of them advocated emperor worship. These people were clearly not "on track for heaven." And yet, Jesus commands us to love our enemies—to pray for those that hate us. If we are to pray for "everyone," it follows that we should pray for those who have passed out of this world and into the next.[1] Hence the Catholic Catechism #1058 states: "The Church prays that no one should be lost: 'Lord, let me never be parted from you.' If it is true that no one can save himself, it is also true that God 'desires all men to be saved' (1 Tim 2:4), and that for him 'all things are possible.' (Mt 19:26)"

---

[1] The modern view of what happens directly after death is very different from views held in the past. In the early and medieval periods, practices like prayer to the saints and prayer for the dead arose because of attitudes people held concerning what happens after death. This is a very difficult subject to talk about today, since reflections on what happens to the soul (the part of us that is not tied to the body, the part that "survives" our death here in this world) has really faded away in most Protestant circles. For example, when I was trying to explain to a relative why Catholics ask saints to pray for us, she looked at me and said: "Ben, those people can't pray for you...they're dead." I replied, "No, they are alive in Christ!" Life does not end at death, and a person does not cease to be who they are when they die. Here it may be helpful to recall that the Catholic Church, drawing from both tradition and Scripture, distinguishes between *a particular judgment* (which happens to each soul at the moment of death) and *the final judgment* (which happens to all people when Christ returns). Without this separation between the two judgments, which was held in common throughout the early and medieval periods, there would never be practices such as prayer to saints or even prayer for the souls of the dead. Protestants tend to conflate the particular and the final judgment, typically using Hebrews 9:26–28 ("once to die and then the judgment," but here the context speaks of Christ primarily—clearly the author is not writing to describe what happens after death. Even if he were, the passage could easily describe the particular judgment) and 1 Corinthians 15:52 ("blink of an eye," but this describes the final judgment, since it speaks of the dead being raised from the earth, and of other final judgment events like us regaining our bodies). I think it is possible to argue from Scripture for a separation between particular and final judgments. A great example that cannot be explained in the Protestant paradigm is the story of Lazarus the beggar (Lk 16:19–31). For more on this topic, see the Catholic Catechism. I may write a separate article at some point about these doctrines, but for now I merely give this info to expand on my point about prayer "in this world and the next."

Consider the following line of reasoning in light of both Scripture passages quoted above: If God desires something, then that something must be good. If God desires something good, it seems very hard for me, as a human, to say that God *can't* have what God wants! God isn't like a child (or even an adult human), who often wants something that is not truly good. What God wants (or what God "wills") is only thwarted by the freedom God has granted to rational creatures.[1] For example, we know from the Scriptures of an angelic fall, in which some creatures used their freedom to turn against God. Because these beings are outside of time, their choice was single and final. The good angels, then, did not turn away from God. They used their freedom correctly.[2] But as humans, we live in time (unlike angels) and we make mistakes *continually*. The way we desire things cannot really be compared to the "wants" or "wills" of God, or even of angels. What is stopping God from fulfilling God's desire that all be saved is human interference, human "headbutting" against God's

---

[1] It makes no sense to say that God's sovereignty, God's "supreme power or authority," can somehow contradict what God wants. God is not a sadist. God does not WANT to damn people. It always happens because humans turn away from God. And this is evidenced throughout the Bible (except perhaps in the difficult case of Saul, the only truly tragic hero in Scripture). We all do it to some extent, but we are wrong to imagine a bifurcated universe with God on one end and hell on the other—the dualistic universe this image seems to suggest. In reality, God is all that there is. If unconvinced, read Pseudo-Dionysius, *Divine Names*, Chapter 4.

[2] As the book of James reminds us, God's law is a "law of liberty" (Jas 2:12).

will.[1] If we are too insistent about the power of this disobedience, it would seem as if we are placing the human will to rebel on par with God's loving will to curb or redirect that rebellion. The situation wherein a person is continually rebelling forever and ever against God's desire is theoretically possible (again, given human freedom), but highly implausible. Hence my stance on the issue is that we are in no position to go about saying that God can't get what God wants. In fact, it makes more sense to align our "wants" to God's "wants," and pray that all be saved.

The Catholic Church Today

In his General Audience of 28 July 1999, Saint John Paul II stressed that hell is "the state of those who definitively reject the Father's mercy, even at the last moment of their life." Likewise, CCC 1033 teaches that "to die in mortal sin without repenting and accepting God's merciful love means remaining separated from him for ever by our own free choice. This state of definitive self-exclusion from communion with God and the blessed is called hell." Rather than a place, hell is simply what is experienced by those who condemn themselves, by rejecting God, to separation from God. See footnote 11, below, for arguments against a dualistic universe with heaven on one side and hell on another. Yet despite this line of reasoning ("state not a place"), the Catholic Catechism nonetheless also teaches the following:

> The Church affirms the existence of hell and its eternity. Immediately after death the souls of those who die in a state

---

[1] Unless you want to create a third variable (such as "nature" or "circumstances") somehow not under God's control which separately influences man; or, unless you want to say that God can will some not to be saved, which directly contradicts the two passages that begin this article. "To think that my choice can go up against God's choice in a mano a mano way is to shrink God down to a creature. If I have to choose between me and God, then I haven't understood God rightly. Judas is the focal point for this mystery: freedom and responsibility are part and parcel to what it means to be a human being. This image is helpful: God is like a lure beckoning us into the future, and we're walking toward God, and God is walking backward, laying out possibilities for us. We make a choice, then God says 'OK, let me lay out these choices for you here.' Those possibilities are offered, in a sense, as gifts. There are many choices, and it's not equivalent to a person being 'stringed along.' Those who seek ultimate human autonomy would say 'This is not real freedom, because the possibilities are limited.' But this is just a way to imagine what it would look like from our perspective, in time. God is eternal—everything is now for God."

of mortal sin descend into hell, where they suffer the punishments of hell, 'eternal fire.' The chief punishment of hell is eternal separation from God, in whom alone man can possess the life and happiness for which he was created and for which he longs.[1]

If a person dies in a state of mortal sin (i.e., rejecting God, sinning against the Holy Spirit), condemnation to hell follows. Furthermore, Christians traditionally did not pray for the souls of those dead who denied Christ. These facts, however, should not stop us from praying that 1) before death that person repented,[2] and that 2) God's mercy will prevail, in a general sense.

In John 12:32, Jesus says that his sacrifice on the cross will "draw all people to himself." The cross was a universe-changing event. Because of Christ's all-sufficient sacrifice, because of God's overflowing love that provides the offer of salvation to all, it is possible to pray that all will be saved. Indeed, it is an exercise in loving even our worst of enemies to pray for their salvation.

Concluding Remarks
Christ's command, "do not judge, or you too will be judged" (Matt 7:1) applies, methinks, to us when we are tempted to use those passages in Scripture about eternal punishment against other people. Returning to Von Balthasar, we should really be looking to ourselves. We are the ones who need to repent! So in humility, let us turn to the Lord. In humility, let us consider others better than ourselves. In humility, let us dare to hope that God will save all people—not naively, in the sense of a "blanket" of universal salvation thrown over the recalcitrant—but in the sense that all will eventually come *to their senses* and stop placing obstacles in the way of God's love.

---

[1] CCC 1035.
[2] Which is always possible, especially since biological death is tricky to define, and no one really knows what journeys we may go on during those last few seconds of brain activity.

The Problem of Predestination: Reformed and Catholic Theology in Dialogue
George Aldhizer

> *"For he chose us in him before the creation of the world to be holy and blameless in his sight. In love he predestined us for adoption to sonship through Jesus Christ, in accordance with his pleasure and will—to the praise of his glorious grace, which he has freely given us in the One he loves. In him we have redemption through his blood, the forgiveness of sins, in accordance with the riches of God's grace." Ephesians 1:4-7*

What beautiful good news. God, before all of creation, has decided to give grace and the status of adopted son to me, chief of sinners. Though I am not "holy and blameless," God's righteous son Jesus surely is, and I have been predestined to be united with his riches. What a glorious gospel Christians share.

I write this introductory paragraph of worship because there is an awful misconception that Calvinists and Reformed theology are about "predestination," whereas other Christians are about "free will." Battle lines are drawn and weapons are forged in a war that largely misrepresents the other side's position (see Catholics massacre some Calvinists in the above image of the St. Bartholomew's Day Massacre, I'm only being tongue-in-cheek of course). In what follows, I hope to faithfully elucidate where the real war is and should be waged, for both believe in some form of predestination and free will. Further, I will argue that what many non-Calvinists believe as the problem of the Calvinist understanding of predestination, namely that God arbitrarily elects a chosen people for no reason and leaves the rest for damnation, is a burden that is actually shouldered by both sides of the debate. To do this, I will be utilizing the 1992 *Catechism Of The Catholic Church* and the 17th century Reformed confessional document Canons of Dort.

The *Catechism of The Catholic Church*[1] reads in the scriptures a God who wills the salvation of every individual human being, God in Christ "tak[ing] the initiative of universal redeeming love."[2] The *Catechism* cites in evidence 2 Peter 3:9, in which God does not want "any to perish, but all to come to repentance." God thus wills that each would freely respond to his drawing, as "all mankind" is "called by God's grace to salvation."[3] Probably the most direct statement concerning predestination within the *Catechism* is found within statement 600, "To God, all moments of time are present in their immediacy. When therefore he establishes his eternal plan of "predestination", he includes in it each person's free response to his grace."[4]

Predestination, within this plan, is thus conditional upon the faith of the individual. God in eternity looks down the halls of history, knowing that a certain person will exhibit saving faith in response to God's universal redeeming love, and incorporates that person into the elect, the predestined. This understanding of a predestination predicated on foreseen faith has the priest to recite this Eucharistic prayer, "Father, accept this offering from your whole family. Grant us

---

[1] Readers need note that I am using the Catholic Catechism of 1992 as the representative for Catholic doctrine. I intentionally use the *"Catechism"* rather than "Catholic doctrine" or "Catholics believe" because of the following. In a conversation with my Catholic editor, I learned that Molina's view of predestination, alongside of Thomas Aquinas's view of predestination and the view that predestination is a mystery, is one among three acceptable doctrinal positions for faithful Catholics to take. Aquinas, fascinatingly, in my reading of him, contradicts the *Catechism* on this point of predestination, in favor of a more Reformed understanding. Following Augustine, Aquinas believes that God draws some and not others, allowing for God to display both his mercy and justice upon sinners. This seems to contradict the tenor of the *Catechism*, that favors a universal-drawing and equal-grace-giving God to each individual human being. The *Catechism*, in my reading, is not impartial among three different opportunities for faithful Catholics to believe concerning predestination, but decidedly promotes the Molinist view.
Read "Reply to Objection 3" within Article 5, http://www.newadvent.org/summa/1023.html.
[2] Catholic Church, "Jesus Died Crucified," *CCC*, 602.
[3] Catholic Church, "The Church Is One, Holy, Catholic, and Apostolic," *CCC*, 836.
[4] Catholic Church, "Jesus Died Crucified," *CCC*, 600.

your peace in this life, save us from final damnation, and *count us among those you have chosen."* (my emphasis)[1]

Contrary to the *Catechism's* understanding of conditional predestination based on foreseen faith, the Reformed understanding of predestination is unconditional, not predicated on anything God sees (faith or otherwise) in the creature. Also contrary to the *Catechism's* reading of the scriptures that understands God to long for the salvation of every individual, the Reformed understand God to *effectually will* the salvation of the elect. Based upon readings of Ephesians 2, in which humanity is declared "dead" in our sins, in order to freely respond to God's grace, we must be "made alive" in Christ. Freedom, then, is only found when God's spirit releases one from enslavement to sin, *bringing* one from death to life. Further, the Reformed do not view the faith of a Christian as incorporating one into the predestined (see "count us among those you have chosen" above). Rather, the faith of a Christian is a result of God's having predestined them. The Reformed place heavy emphasis on Romans 8:30 which reads, "Those whom he predestined, he also called; and those whom he called, he also justified; and those whom he justified, he also glorified." The Canons of Dort summarize this Reformed logic:

> "Before the foundation of the world, by sheer grace, according to the free good pleasure of his will, God chose in Christ to salvation a definite number of particular people out of the entire human race, which had fallen by its own fault from its original innocence into sin and ruin. Those chosen were neither better nor more deserving than the others, but lay with them in the common misery. God did this in Christ, whom he also appointed from eternity to be the mediator, the head of all those chosen, and the foundation of their salvation."[2]

In response to the idea of predestination predicated on foreseen faith, explained above within the *Catechism Of The Catholic Church*, the Canons of Dort criticize,

> "This same election took place, not on the basis of foreseen faith, of the obedience of faith, of holiness, or of any other good quality and disposition, as though it were based on a prerequisite cause or condition in the person to be chosen, but

---

[1] Ibid., 620.
[2] "Canons of Dort," *Christian Reformed Church*, Divine Election and Reprobation, Article 7.

rather for the purpose of faith, of the obedience of faith, of holiness, and so on. Accordingly, election is the source of every saving good. Faith, holiness, and the other saving gifts, and at last eternal life itself, flow forth from election as its fruits and effects. As the apostle says, "He chose us" (not because we were, but) "so that we should be holy and blameless before him in love" (Eph. 1:4)."[1]

Rather than making this article an argument of exegesis as to which document has the scriptures right concerning predestination (personally, I find Romans 8:30, among other passages and arguments, very persuasive in favor of the Reformed view), I want to clear up a common misconception concerning the Reformed view of predestination. This misconception runs something like this, "The Reformed view of predestination is arbitrary. In this view, God elects some and not others and therefore God would have to be unjust for sending the non-elect to hell and the elect to heaven. The true God is not arbitrary, therefore the Reformed understanding of predestination is wrong." In the following, I want to argue that the *Catechism's* (and other Protestant) views of predestination predicated on foreseen faith fall into this same criticism of arbitrariness.

Again, just to reiterate: the *Catechism's* view of predestination understands that God, prior to creating the world, looked down the halls of history, as it were, to see those humans that would freely choose saving faith. Those humans are therefore incorporated into God's plan of predestination. Faith, on this view, is a free decision of the human being in response to God's initial drawing by his grace. Now, let's assume two basic propositions that shouldn't be very controversial across Christian traditions. First, some people in this world, as a result of their sin and rejection of their creator, will be separated from God in hell. That is, salvation is not universal. Second, God could've created a world other than this world. That is, God is free to create various colors, animals, elements, laws of physics, and human beings as he pleases.

Stay with me. Within the *Catechism's* view, 1) God predestines people based on their foreseen faith, 2) some humans that are created are eternally separated from God, and 3) God could've created a different world other than this one. Sixteenth century Jesuit theologian Luis de

---

[1] Ibid., Divine Election and Reprobation, Article 9.

Molina argued, utilizing these presuppositions, that God knows what would be the case if God were to place human beings in different circumstances than they have been placed.[1] God utilizes what molinist philosopher William Lane Craig describes as "counterfactuals of creaturely freedom," in order to place human beings into circumstances in which they, on their own free will, will respond to God's saving grace.[2] In this understanding of divine foreknowledge, God creates a world in which X person exhibits saving faith as a result of his own free decision, and Y person does not respond to God's extended arm of grace. Molina then recognizes, if God were to create a different world, then different people could be saved or damned. Person X could be given different parents, exposure to persuasive humanist literature, an early death, and on and on, such that he would be damned. Person Y, on the other hand, could be born in other circumstances to bring her to faith. Thus, it seems to me, if we grant the three propositions laid out earlier, 1) God predestines based on foreseen faith, 2) Universal salvation is not true, and 3) God could've created a different world than this one, then those who follow the *Catechism* ought to agree with Molina that God predestines persons to salvation or damnation as a result of the circumstances God places them in.

Now, if this is true, then the criticism of Calvinists that God arbitrarily elects some to salvation and leaves others to damnation is true of both sides of the debate. Catholics (and it seems to me, all, if not most non-Calvinist Christians)[3] are not immune to this critique, for God could have created the world in circumstances that predestine X person to foreseen faith or to foreseen eternal separation. God, within both understandings of predestination, falls into the same critique of arbitrariness in his predestination of individuals. Thus, this argument of arbitrariness is not a good argument against the Reformed view of predestination.

---

[1] "Middle Knowledge," *Internet Encyclopedia Of Philosophy*, http://www.iep.utm.edu/middlekn/.
[2] William Lane Craig, "God Directs All Things On Behalf of a Molinist View of Providence," In *Four Views On Divine Providence*, (Grand Rapids: Zondervan, 2011).
[3] The only Christians immune, it seems to me, would be Open Theists, who deny that God knows the future with certainty. This, in my view, would undermine any belief in predestination.

Some may say this debate is useless, that I am splitting useless theological hairs. To the contrary, this analysis should pull all believers into worship of the God who has chosen to bestow the riches of his grace upon us, his predestined elect. Though I was dead in my sin and undeserving of grace, God has called me into fellowship with the Trinity and union with his Son. Though God could've created a world in which sin reigned until death swallowed us whole, Christ has swallowed up death in his resurrection, reigning victorious for those who trust in him.

Is Christian Existentialism Unbiblical?
Micah Tillman

One of our readers has posed the following question: "is the movement called Christian existentialism biblical or unbiblical? Can a true Christian also be an existentialist, or does the bible prohibit it?"

This is a great question, if I do say so myself. Don't worry if you don't know what existentialism is. I'll explain as we go along. To begin, let's talk about our feelings.

What It's Like to Be an Existentialist

The core emotion or mood for existentialists is angst (often translated "anxiety" or "anguish"). The primary task of an existentialist is to figure angst out. This involves exploring what it is, why everyone has it, why some people claim they DON'T have it, and what we should do about it.

In exploring these issues, existentialists often come to the following general conclusion. Humans experience angst because we have a fundamental need for meaning—a need for our lives and world to make sense and have purpose. However, meaning, sense, and purpose seem to be missing, so our need goes unmet.[1]

Existentialists then try to figure out how we got into our angst-inducing predicament. They often trace angst back to the fact that being free is a huge responsibility. Even if a god handed us life's meaning on a silver platter, for example, we would still be responsible for whether we chose to accept or reject it. We cannot push off responsibility for how we live onto anyone or anything else. And that's a lot of weight to bear.[2]

---

[1] This is essentially how Albert Camus describes what he calls "the absurd" in his *The Myth Of Sisyphus And Other Essays*, trans. Justin O'Brien (New York: Vintage International, 1991).
[2] I'm thinking in this paragraph particularly of Søren Kierkegaard and Jean-Paul Sartre.

What, then, should we do about the angst we experience? Once again, existentialists usually conclude that we should take responsibility. We have options, and thus are responsible for how we respond. Will we make meaning, since we cannot find it in the world?[1] Will we accept our culture's prefabricated meanings?[2] Will we conclude that life is only *apparently* meaningless, and look again for the meanings we missed?[3] Will we choose a source of meaning that transcends the apparently-meaningless world?[4]

Existentialists believe that none of these options are forced upon us. How we deal with our angst is a choice we each have to make. Often, however, existentialists argue that one of these choices is authentic, while the others are inauthentic.[5] One way of responding to our situation is faithful to the truth—to how we and the world really are—while the others are evidence of denial and self-deception.

What's Wrong with Existentialism?

The question I am supposed to answer is whether or not existentialism is excluded by scripture for Christians. This implies that there might be reasons for suspecting that existentialism is opposed to biblical Christianity. What might those reasons be?

Perhaps the most obvious is existentialism's association with atheism. Jean-Paul Sartre gave existentialism its name and argued that existentialism is a logical consequence of atheism. Without God as a ground or source, we are left in a kind of limbo. Everything—including what it means to be human—is left up to us. The non-

---

[1] The option preferred by one of my professors in grad school.
[2] The option that Martin Heidegger explicitly and extensively rejected as fleeing into "the They [DAS MAN]" (*Being And Time*, trans. John Macquarrie and Edward Robinson [San Francisco: HarperSanFrancisco, 1962]).
[3] The option that Viktor Frankl explicitly and extensively argued for in *Man's Search For Meaning*, rev. and updated (New York: Washington Square Press, 1985).
[4] The option that I believe Kierkegaard argued for, that Paul Tillich might have preferred (I do not know Tillich's work well enough), and which I prefer.
[5] Here, I am particularly thinking of Heidegger, Sartre, and Camus.

existence of God is where angst comes from, and thus atheism is where existentialism begins, according to Sartre.[1]

Another potential problem with existentialism is its association with moral nihilism or relativism. There are two reasons for this. The first is the fact that Friedrich Nietzsche is widely regarded as one of the original existentialists, and most people believe he was a nihilist.[2] The second is the fact that thinkers like Sartre believed that morality was meaningless without God. Therefore, existentialism seems to involve the claims that there is no such thing as right and wrong, or that what's right and wrong is up to you.

A third potential problem with existentialism is that people might be suspicious of famous Christian existentialists. Søren Kierkegaard, for example is a father of existentialism. Yet he was a singular character, and singular characters can be difficult to classify. Furthermore, theologians like Paul Tillich and Rudolf Bultmann get treated as part of the Christian existentialist movement, but I hear people have doubts about their orthodoxy.[3]

So, if existentialism is an atheistic, nihilistic movement attractive to unorthodox Christians, it would make sense to wonder whether existentialism and biblical Christianity are compatible. I think they are. But to explain why, I need to walk us through a little history.

Where the Term "Existentialism" Comes From

The term "existentialism" comes from Jean-Paul Sartre and is supposed to distinguish his philosophy from a group of philosophies we might call "essentialist." According to essentialists, everything has an essence. A thing has an essence because (a) it is a particular kind of thing, and (b) things of that kind have certain properties and requirements. A human's essence, for example, is "human nature." Because each of us has this essence, we each have certain properties like being able to think rationally, having a body, having emotions, and so on. And because each of us has the human essence, we each

---

[1] See Sartre's "Existentialism Is a Humanism," in Walter Kaufman, ed., *Existentialism From Dostoevsky To Sartre*, rev. and exp. (New York: Plume, 1975), 345–69.

[2] He wasn't. He was the "prophet of nihilism." That is, his job was to warn Europeans that if they didn't seriously rethink their worldviews, they would all end up as nihilists.

[3] I don't know either well enough to comment.

have certain requirements. We have to eat. We need to love and be loved. We ought to behave rationally.

So, essentialists believe that how humans exist, and how they ought to exist, follows from what humans are. All humans have the same essence, and so they are required to live their lives in a distinctively human manner. The requirements are physical, logical, and moral.

In contrast, Sartre took Martin Heidegger to have shown that, "existence precedes essence"[1] for humans. This means that humans only come to have a settled nature or character because of how they have chosen to live. You exist first. While existing, you make choices and undertake actions. These choices and actions define you. They create your habits. They give you your character. It is through existing, therefore, that you become a particular kind of person. It is through existing that you develop an essence.[2]

Existentialism as a Broader Movement

"Existentialism" applies first and foremost to the philosophy of Sartre. But he thought of his work as developing the philosophy of Heidegger. And Heidegger, like Sartre, was heavily influenced by Kierkegaard, with Nietzsche and Dostoevsky mixed in.

The term "existentialism," therefore, has come to apply to the entire movement that includes Sartre, Heidegger, Kierkegaard, et al. And once we see that the existentialist movement existed before and beyond Sartre, we might ask how far back it goes.

The answer to that question is, "way, way back." The oldest book of existentialism that we still regularly read today is Ecclesiastes. In fact, it is the first book I had my students read when I taught existentialism at University of Maryland, College Park.

I suspect most people will be surprised to hear that the Bible contains an existentialist book. But just consider these verses.

> *"Meaningless! Meaningless!" says the Teacher. "Utterly meaningless! Everything is meaningless." (Ecclesiastes 1:2, NIV)*

---

[1] Sartre, "Existentialism Is a Humanism," 349.
[2] I'm paraphrasing Sartre's "Existentialism Is a Humanism," here, though I confess to speaking in a very Thomistic way.

> *The wise have eyes in their heads, while the fool walks in the darkness; but I came to realize that the same fate overtakes them both. Then I said to myself, "The fate of the fool will overtake me also. What then do I gain by being wise?" I said to myself, "This too is meaningless." For the wise, like the fool, will not be long remembered; the days have already come when both have been forgotten. Like the fool, the wise too must die! So I hated life, because the work that is done under the sun was grievous to me. All of it is meaningless, a chasing after the wind.* (Ecclesiastes 2:13–17, NIV)

If that isn't existentialism, I don't know what is (and neither do you). But working through the issues expressed above is what the entire book of Ecclesiastes is about. Ecclesiastes is a masterwork of existentialism.

So, Is Christian Existentialism Possible?

The fact that existentialism in Western culture begins in the Bible ought to give us pause. It shows us, for example, that Sartre does not own existentialism, even if he invented the name we now use for it. Sartre was simply a prominent thinker in the recent past who dealt with a set of concerns and struggles that many had before him, and many have had since. He was a latecomer to existentialism, and his way of working it out was neither the first nor the only way.

The same might be said for the 19th and 20th century thinkers we now call "the Christian existentialists." They each had their own way of working through the issues and concerns of existentialism. But that does not mean their ways were the best or only ways of doing Christian existentialism.

When we ask, therefore, whether Christian existentialism is biblical or unbiblical, we have to distinguish two issues. The first is whether what has been labeled "Christian existentialism" was in fact biblical or unbiblical. The second is whether anything properly labeled "Christian existentialism" *could be* biblical.

Unfortunately, I cannot answer the first question. I simply do not know the Christian existentialists of the 19th and 20th centuries well enough. The one I know best is Kierkegaard, and he seems perfectly fine to me. However, if someone wanted to argue the opposite, I'd be happy to listen.

Even though I have nothing helpful to say about whether any particular 19th or 20th century Christian existentialist was orthodox and biblical, I can say this. The fact that Ecclesiastes is a work of existentialism shows that legitimate, orthodox, biblically-sound Christian existentialism is possible. And I hope that this possibility is one that Christian thinkers continue to take up.

How Should Christians Do Existentialism?
As Christians, we would have to reject Sartre's analysis of the cause of angst, even as we acknowledge the fact of angst. As Christians, we would say that humans struggle with angst not because there is no God, but because God made us free, or because we are cut off from God by sin, or because God is not just another created thing (and thus can seem to us to be no-thing/nothing). Perhaps, furthermore our world seems meaningless because created things only have meaning in relation to their Creator—the source of value and goodness—and we often fail to see that relationship.

Does this mean Christians cannot draw on thinkers whose existentialism is unbiblical? No. Anyone who has spent time and energy working on the same questions and issues you are exploring may have valuable insights to offer. I, for example, found that studying Nietzsche's critiques of Christianity made me a better Christian. I find Camus's commitment to the value of truth inspiring.[1] And I find Sartre and Heidegger's inability to escape morality telling.[2]

I would hope, however, that as Christians we have resources that are not available to our non-Christian friends. We have the doctrines of the Incarnation, of creation, of redemption, and so on, that are relevant to how we examine and deal with existentialist issues. And this means, I would claim, that it is possible for Christian existentialism to be even better than atheist existentialism. Whether the existentialist philosophies and theologies we produce are any good, however, is our responsibility.

---

[1] See his focus on facing the absurd nature of human existence, rather than ignoring it or denying it, in *Myth Of Sisyphus*.
[2] Heidegger, with Camus, clearly values truth, and assumes that authenticity—a kind of faithfulness to the truth—is of ultimate value for humans (see Heidegger, *Being And Time*). Sartre, furthermore, ends up believing in a kind of Kantian deontology (see "Existentialism Is a Humanism," 351).

A Poem to My Anxiety
Buck Salem

Where are you
I want to speak directly to you.
I want to hold you fully in my awareness while I speak to you.
You've been with me my whole life
But I was always afraid of you.
You were never bad
You are only as harmful as we make you.
It's strange, when we treat you as an enemy, you become an enemy.
But when I make you my friend, you cease to be an enemy.
You become a door that I can walk through
A door to freedom
A door that leads to the real world
to a more full life.

In the past, your touch burned my skin
And I drew back from you
The more I pulled away, the more the heat from you burned.
But now, I reach out, and the heat of your touch starts to drop off
It dissipates in front of my very eyes
The scorching heat becomes a gentle warmth.
I realize that you can touch me without hurting me.
In fact, I realize that letting you touch me is the only way to keep
from being hurt.

They tell me I have an anxiety disorder.
They say it's a phobia.
A fear that God is not real.
Truly, I now realize that any potential encounters with God that I
may have in store,
should really happen after I work things out with you, anxiety.
Otherwise, they won't be the encounters that they could or should
be.

So let me get back to the less pondering part of my poem.
Let me imagine you in front of me.
Let me speak to you personally.

I know that you become my friend when I make you my friend.
I'm holding out my hand to you.
I feel your hand in mine.
I'm sorry for treating you poorly.
I'm sorry for running away from you.
I'm not going to run from you anymore.
I want to walk with you.
I want to invite you onto my team
My recovery team.
Thank you for being here.
Thank you my friend
Thank you.

Sorrow and Grief

Sorrow, grief, and lament are pivotal, if oft-neglected, parts of the Christian life. The ways we experience these dark nights shape our faith more powerfully than any sunlit joys. These essays consider the challenges and consternations of sorrow and grief, inviting us to fight for faith in the Risen Son even in our darkest nights.

Essays

You Are Not Okay, *White*

Thoughts, Prayers, and Platitudes, *Quick*

The Longest Lent, *Byrkett*

The Lost Art of Evangelical Weeping, *Cline*

Why God Allows Spiritual Dryness in the Christian Life, *Hall*

Dealing with Pain and Suffering, *McMeans*

The Art of Grieving, *Byrkett*

You Are Not Okay
Barbara White

On April 6, 2012, Thomas Kinkade, who was among the most popular artists in the world at the time, died in his California home from acute intoxication from alcohol and Valium. His death shocked both his fans and the media, which was quick to point out the irony that the Painter of Light™ had lived and died in such darkness.

Kinkade's paintings were, and are, incredibly popular. At the peak of his popularity in 2001, Kinkade generated $130 million. The Thomas Kinkade company estimates that one out of every 20 American homes had a Kinkade print hanging in it. His depictions of bucolic cottages, heavenly golf courses, and cozy looking churches appeared on everything from tea towels to jigsaw puzzles. Prior to the housing crash in 2008 there were plans for a San Francisco Bay area housing development called "The Village, a Thomas Kinkade Community" which offered "cottage style homes" and had the slogan "Calm, not chaos. Peace, not pressure."

This is the ethos of the Thomas Kinkade empire, and it is the reason his ironic death of despair shocked so many. Kinkade offered his viewers a window into a world that few of us could ever hope to live in, but that seemed to call to us like the warm light through mullion windows on a snowy evening. There is a dreamy, sleepy, quality about all of them. They are warm and comforting. Kinkade's paintings are so popular, I think, because they tell you that you are OK. Kinkade's paintings offer us, in the words of Sir Roger Scruton, a "world presented through a veil of self-congratulatory sentiment...[which] tells you that you're a good person, and no further efforts need be made."

The thing is, no one actually believes them. If they did, they would never buy them in the first place. The reason Thomas Kinkade is so popular is that his paintings offer people something that they know they *don't have*. If you actually lived in a Moonlight Cottage ("the tranquil moods of morning light in a setting I dream of stumbling upon") you wouldn't need a painting of one to hang over the mantle in your own, ordinary home. Even those of us who have stable jobs, healthy families, and happy marriages wouldn't describe our quotidian existence as "calm, not chaos. Peace, not pressure."

One only needs to zoom out slightly to see that even the most tranquil home in real life is in the middle of a world that is not OK. The COVID-induced not-OK-ness of 2020 is only the most recent development, following four years of tumultuous politics in the United States, a crisis impacting Uyghurs in China, the 9/11 terrorist attacks and the War on Terror—and, of course, the Fascist and Communist horrors of the 20th century, which claimed many millions of lives. This confronts us every time we turn on the news. Is it any surprise that people want to fill their homes with things that tell them that everything is OK?

The problem, of course, is that putting your hopes into anything that isn't true and doesn't square with your actual life will let you down. Eventually you'll have to leave the world of the painting and go about your day, where you are met with one small tragedy after another. And then you discover that life is still hard, and on top of that you feel like you've been lied to. The tragic early death of Thomas Kinkade from drink and anxiolytics throws the brutality of this betrayal into sharp relief.

Advent, more than any other time of year, reminds us that we are not OK. Advent is, of course, a time of preparing for the Feast of the Incarnation. But its *primary* emphasis is on preparation for the return of Christ as Judge and King. This is why, just as shopping malls across America are attempting to imitate Kinkade's Victorian Christmas Carol, the mood on Sunday mornings turns darker, more urgent, and more intense.

In Advent we hear again the parables of the foolish virgins left in the cold, and about the master who goes away on a journey, with a household anxiously awaiting his return. We are told to keep awake, and are warned of a time when the sun will be darkened and the stars fall from heaven. We walk in the wilderness with the prophets who speak of doom, and yet of salvation. A wild man in camel's hair calls us to repent, with an axe at the root of the tree. We draw ever closer to Christmas and, at the same time, ever closer to the Cross. "Advent," Episcopal preacher and writer Fleming Rutledge reminds us, "begins in the dark."

Scripture is not a self-help book, and it does not tell us that we are OK. In fact, it reminds us over and over again that it is quite the opposite. We are so not OK that God Himself became one of us, took our flesh, bore our sorrows, and died our death precisely *because* we cannot help ourselves. When we prepare the way in the wilderness of Advent we are forced to remember that the baby who is laid in the manger is also the man who is hung on the Cross. Advent refuses to let us skip straight to the happy ending where everything is OK. We are *not* OK, and there is nothing we can do about it. Thanks be to God, we have a Savior who can do what we cannot.

The Gospel doesn't offer dreamy antidotes to the challenges and pain of being human. It offers something deeper, richer, and more real: hope. This hope comes from looking at the sorrow and violence in the world, and trusting that in defeating death, Christ has overcome the world. It means looking at the anger and violence in your own heart, and trusting that Christ loves that wicked and broken heart enough to die for it.

On this dark night in a dark Advent in a dark year, I pray for the repose of the soul of Thomas Kinkade. I pray that the power of the Resurrection might overcome the darkness and despair that consumed him in his mortal life. I pray for those of us who are looking for an escape to a cozy cottage or peaceful garden suffused with pastel light. I ask God for the strength and hope to be willing to walk in a wilderness, where, on the horizon, maybe, we can see that dawn is breaking. God is the true painter of light, because His is the only light that shines forth in the darkness, which the darkness cannot overcome.

Come, Lord Jesus.

Thoughts, Prayers, and Platitudes
Jacob Quick

What good is it, my brothers and sisters, if someone claims to have faith but has no deeds? Can such faith save them? Suppose a brother or a sister is without clothes and daily food. If one of you says to them, "Go in peace; keep warm and well fed," but does nothing about their physical needs, what good is it? In the same way, faith by itself, if it is not accompanied by action, is dead.
James 2:14-17

Not all thoughts and prayers are created equal. A mourning nation struggles with the aftermath of a mass shooting, and struggles to find a path forward that not only does justice to victims, but also prevents the repetition of such senseless violence in the future. It's a story that Americans are all too familiar with. Mass shootings in the US have become so common that we reflexively refer to each occurrence as "*another* mass shooting." Our vernacular exemplifies the prevalence of such tragedies: these mass shootings are not isolated events, but interconnected symptoms of a disease that ails our nation.

The response to this mass shooting has, once again, initiated criticism of sending "thoughts and prayers" to victims and their loved ones. For example, Neil deGrasse Tyson recently tweeted, "Evidence collected over many years, obtained from many locations, indicates that the power of Prayer is insufficient to stop bullets from killing school children."

Tyson's statement, among others in a similar vein, have predictably provoked the ire of many Christians, leading certain sites like The Babylon Bee to sarcastically respond. But is that cynicism toward "thoughts and prayers" offered by prominent Christian leaders and politicians a blatant denigration of Christian practice?

I posit that the backlash against "thoughts and prayers" is not, at its core, a criticism of Christianity or religious practice. It's a condemnation of religious hypocrisy: a critique of those who substitute religious cliches for appropriate action.

Arbitrary Action

The reaction to "thoughts and prayers" is the consequence of a series of inconsistent responses to mass shootings in the US over the years. The San Bernardino mass shooting was invoked as evidence that America needs a Muslim ban (despite overwhelming evidence to the contrary). Likewise, violent crimes committed by immigrants are utilized to promote stricter immigration laws (even though immigrants commit fewer violent crimes, on average, than native-born US citizens). But when a mass shooting is committed by a white US citizen, the same Americans who are so adamant about restrictive laws become arbitrarily reluctant to take legislative action. Instead, they send their "thoughts and prayers."

Recent discussions surrounding the mass shooting in Parkland have highlighted other troubling elements of our national conversation about gun violence. It's common to identify gun violence as stemming from problems of mental health. However, study after study suggests that individuals diagnosed with mental health issues are *less* likely to commit violent crimes (including mass shootings) than those without a diagnosis. In addition, the demonization, stigmatization, and physical abuse of those struggling with mental health is a pervasive problem in America, and further scapegoating the mental health community only perpetuates such disgraceful trends.

The prevalence of mass shootings in the US should cause all of us to carefully assess our assumptions, and work toward finding concrete, evidence-based solutions for the prevention of further atrocities. It's hard to deny Neil deGrasse Tyson's point about "thoughts and prayers": they're not creating the change we need to effectively prevent mass shootings and reduce the alarmingly high rates of gun violence in the US.

Practicing What We Pray

The insufficiency of "thoughts and prayers", however, does not actually reflect the powerlessness of prayer, in and of itself. Prayer is a powerful, transformative, and indispensable aspect of Christian life. It is through prayer that we communicate with God and align every aspect of ourselves with God's mission on earth.

But when we utilize "prayer" as nothing more than paying lip service to tragedy, it's no longer prayer, in the genuine sense. It's a charade. It changes prayer from a transformative spiritual practice to a means of justifying complacency in the face of evil. And God is not pleased when the practice of prayer is manipulated to passively perpetuate an indefensible status quo.

Jesus minced no words when it came to those who prayed for public attention, "And when you pray, do not be like the hypocrites, for they love to pray standing in the synagogues and on the street corners to be seen by others. Truly I tell you, they have received their reward in full" (Matt. 6:5). Jesus' condemnation does not denigrate the power of prayer, but cautions against the instrumentalization of it for personal gain.

The contemporary criticism of "thoughts and prayers" is not some secular attack on Christianity that requires an apologetic defense of religious faith. Such a response betrays a preoccupation with *defending* Christianity rather than actually practicing its teachings. Rather, *the criticism of "thoughts and prayers" correlates with a critique of professing Christians that is repeated throughout Scripture.* It is a call for those of us who follow Christ to actually practice what we preach or, in this context, practice what we pray.

The recent mass shooting should remind us that God has no patience for empty words and platitudes. It should call us to remember the ancient Christian motto, *Lex orandi lex credendi*: "The law of prayer is the law of faith." We must all critically assess our own complicity with evil, repent of it, and embody a relentless love for those who are vulnerable and victimized. *And in so doing, we will begin to genuinely pray as our Lord commanded us.*

As we pray that God's will be done on earth, may we become the very agents through which God makes it so.

The Longest Lent
Johanna Byrkett

Lent began eight months ago today.

Eight months ago I was in a cool, dark sanctuary, listening to my vicar say "You are going to die." I didn't know how accurate that statement would be for this year. We rose, row by row. Ashes were traced across my forehead, I returned to my seat. We rose, row by row, again going forward—this time to receive the bread, the wine. In darkness we stepped into February chill. Ash Wednesday was the only evening Lenten service I got to attend in person this year. Not a single evening of Holy week was spent in that dark church sanctuary with fellow believers. We weren't present together in the darkness of Easter morning that bursts into light and noise and exuberant alleluias.

Oh, yes, I "attended" Holy Week services and Easter morning on-line. But that isn't the same—not even close. I haven't worshipped, truly worshipped, physically together with other believers for *eight* months. It feels like the longest Lent in the history of the church calendar. It feels like Easter was an anticlimax or like it didn't even happen... Like it was swallowed up in the darkness, buried in the ashes of burned hopes, dreams, plans, businesses, cities, and people.

In August I gathered with many others to remember our friend Mike Adams, who took his life in this season of darkness. He is a standout to me, because he is someone I know. . . Yet he is one among many. The number of suicides this year are, in some demographics, outpacing the number of virus deaths. No need to tell me this virus is killing people—I know it is—but the power plays surrounding the virus are killing people in other ways, whether physically through suicide or because of division that makes one citizen stab another for not wearing a mask; or internally, spiritually, emotionally isolating us from one another. . . Keeping us apart at home, or six feet away, cancelling events, or putting masks between our faces, stifling our expressions of vulnerability, kindness, concern, and even of anger or fear. If no one can see our expressions of pain, how can they reach out to us? Are they afraid to hug us? If I can't see the look of loss on someone's face, how will I know "You too? I thought I alone knew that grief. . ." and be able to wrap them in love?

How do we invite others into our pain, into our sorrow, into our deep joys, into a place of hope, if we cannot be close, if we cannot *see* the human expressions of these things across each other's faces? To be isolated while six feet away from someone—to be denied physical affection and warm greetings—is worse than being alone at home. Those six feet are the extreme loneliness of being alone in a crowded room. It is like the searing pain of being close to your beloved, but being just unable to reach them, to touch them.

This season feels like birth pangs gone wrong. It feels like something is terribly wrong with the baby and it isn't moving. . . The thing we've been looking toward, the hope at the end of the morning sickness, the joy at the end of labour, the person to join our family has been snatched away, and we are left to bury our dead in isolated grief—with no hugs, with no real place for grief or anger to go.

It feels like the longest Lent. In the normal Lenten season we are *together* in our lament. We gather together to acknowledge that something isn't right. We encourage one another to take heart that the King *is* coming. We hope for one another, when others can't hope for themselves. But *this* Lenten season is isolation—not the solitude or quiet reflection of Lent—and it is the work of the enemy of our souls. Dividing, separating in every possible way.

Where is the hope? Where is the empty tomb of this season that has killed us in more than body? Where is the Easter coming out of this mourning? Where is the light in this darkness? Where is the King?

Maybe this horrible, longest Lent is in some way our taste of what the disciples felt when Jesus died. We know the end of that story, but they didn't. We know on Good Friday that Easter is coming. They didn't. And maybe this interminable Lent is our truly dark Holy Saturday. It is our season where we can't see what is happening in the spiritual realm. We can't see the Easter about to come.

Maybe we will die before we understand what it was all about, but we must remember that Jesus will never be held down by death. Jesus will never be defeated by the enemy of our souls. Death and satan will one day be undone. The Kingdom will come in its fullness. And that won't be an anticlimactic Easter in the time of covid. It will be the greatest celebration of life and love and sacred community. . . It will be seeing face-to-face and still living.

Easter is coming. . .

The Lost Art of Evangelical Weeping
Timon Cline

There is a mood and practice of forced buoyancy in American evangelical churches. In near Orwellian fashion, this frenzied gaiety tries to sanitize the church of any perceived negativity, sorrow, or grief. I have been in church services where the worship leader mounts the stage, "kicking off" the service with, "How's everybody feeling this morning?" (implying the expectation of a positive reaction), followed by, "Oh, you can do better than that!" when the enthusiasm of the congregation isn't to his liking. *Cue the concert-esque music and lights.* The message is clear: we're here to be happy and celebratory. Negativity is not a component of *our* brand. It's bad for business. And truth be told, business is not really booming.

Russell Moore summed up this attitude of American evangelical churches in a humorous but sobering way:
> "Our most 'successful' pastors and church leaders know how to smile broadly. Some of them are blow-dried and cuff-linked; some of them are grunged up and scruffy. But they are here to get us 'excited' about 'what God is doing in our church.'

Our worship songs are typically celebrative, in both lyrical content and musical expression. In the last generation, a mournful song about crucifixion was pepped up with a jingly-sounding chorus, 'It was there by faith I received my sight, and *now I am happy all the day!*'"[1]

He goes on to suggest that many in the pews assume that others have the kind of happiness that churches keep promising, and wonder why it's passed them by. "By not speaking, where the Bible speaks, to the full range of human emotion—including loneliness, guilt, desolation, anger, fear, desperation—we only leave our people there, wondering why they just can't be 'Christian' enough to smile through it all."[2]

---

[1] Moore, Russell, "Why Facebook (and Your Church) Might Be Making You Sad." *Russell Moore* (blog), January 27, 2011, http://www.russellmoore.com/2011/01/27/why-facebook-and-your-church-might-be-making-you-sad/.
[2] Ibid.

Scripture, however, speaks in direct contradiction of this prevalent evangelical attitude (Matt. 5:4; Jas. 4:9). Indeed, the gospel did not come for the happy and healthy, but for the broken and sick. It also does not promise the eradication of all non-cheerful emotions after salvation, nor does it advocate the inhuman suppression of expression of such. In fact, grief, sorrow, and weeping should not only be welcomed and expected as natural human emotions, but can be beneficial to spiritual growth individually, as well as in the life of the church. These emotions, observed rightly, are "excellent" and "precious to God."[1] This is not to say that the life of Christian faith is not one of celebration and true joy. It is to say that celebration and joy should be correctly motivated.

There are two kinds of "weeping" that should be present in our churches: first, to be examined here, is what I will call "spiritual weeping" (what Thomas Watson calls "evangelical weeping"). Second, to be covered in part two, is what I will call "natural weeping." Contra Watson, I will use "evangelical weeping" as the overarching label for both types delineated above.

Spiritual Weeping
The first kind of weeping is most adequately described and applied by Thomas Watson, an English non-conformist, and Puritan preacher and writer of the late 17th Century. His book *The Godly Man's Picture* is a classic and helpful example of Puritan spirituality. I would wholeheartedly encourage every Christian to read it in its entirety. The section of the book entitled "The Godly Man is an Evangelical Weeper" will be our focus here.

As a preliminary clarification, it should be noted that by "evangelical weeping," Watson does not mean "weeping" as a mechanism for fulfilling Matthew 28:16-20 (i.e., evangelizing), but rather in the sense of it being a requisite practice of a Christian. "Weeping" is often used interchangeably for "grieving" and "mourning" by Watson and therefore should not be confined to mean only the shedding of tears.

As alluded to earlier, in many Christian circles there is an unspoken vendetta against sorrow, grief, and guilt, even when expressed toward

---

[1] Watson, Thomas, *The Godly Man's Picture Drawn in a Scripture Pencil, or, Some Characteristic Marks of a Man who is Going to Heaven* (Edinburgh, UK: Banner of Truth, 2009), 58.

the sin we claim to hate (Rom. 12:9). We have a tendency to eradicate feelings of guilt (especially when guilt is related to one's *personal* behavior, beliefs, or past) in particular. Making someone feel guilty is a cardinal offense of sorts. The Bible speaks differently (as does Watson) about these emotions and their function in the Christian life. *Should we practice and encourage weeping, mourning, and guilt over sin?*

In short, yes. Watson saw "a melting heart" as the *sine qua non* of entering the covenant of grace with God, and evidence of the Spirit's presence in a believer's life. This may be counterintuitive and uncomfortable for the modern evangelical. It's sufferable to have a weepy, come-to-Jesus moment, but then it's time to button it up and take your seat in the happy pew. Yet, unless we believe that sinless perfection is already attained, weeping should be encouraged and expected in all believers. It represents a growing recognition of depravity and an acknowledgement of God's supremacy, grace, and holiness. "The sorrow of the heart runs out at the eye (Ps. 31:9)."[1]

It is by this weeping over sin that we come to rely on Christ and conform to him. An anonymous Puritan prayer exhibits this posture of weeping well:
> "O Fountain of all good, destroy in me every lofty thought,
> Break pride to pieces and scatter it to the winds,
> Annihilate each clinging shred of self-righteousness,
> Implant in me true lowliness of spirit,
> Abase me to self-loathing and self-abhorrence,
> Open in me a fount of penitential tears,
> Break me, then bind me up;
> Thus will my heart be prepared dwelling for my God..."[2]

When was the last time you heard an evangelical worship leader or pastor open a Sunday service with such a prayer?

Why weep?

Watson anticipates objections: *is not pardoned sin the ground for joy? Why does the redeemed Christian continue to weep?* In true

---
[1] Ibid.
[2] *The Valley of Vision*, ed. Arthur Bennett (Edinburgh, UK: Banner of Truth, 2015), 8.

Puritan fashion, he provides a terse preface, "A godly man finds enough reasons for weeping," followed by rich applications.

First, the Christian continues to weep because of "indwelling sin" and "clinging corruption," realizing that the "old self" (Eph. 4:22) remains at war against the soul (1 Pet. 2:11; Gal. 5:17) until death.[1] St. Paul presents this remnant of sin as a law bound to our very existence until our final glorification (Rom. 7:21). John Owen characterized indwelling sin as "a powerful and effectual indwelling principle, inclining and pressing unto actions agreeable and suitable unto its own nature."[2] It is as if indwelling sin is a (now) foreign entity inside the Christian, pulling in the opposite direction for its own sake. Weeping over indwelling sin shows that the Christian recognizes his depraved state and remains in a posture of repentance. "The eye is made both for seeing and weeping. Sin must first be seen before it can be wept for."[3]

In connection to this, a Christian may weep because prevailing sin sometimes overcomes him (i.e., Rom. 7:19; Jer. 44:4-5; Isa. 1:2). This is justifiably troubling to the believer who aspires to holiness. "It troubles him that he shoots so short of the rule and standard which God has set."[4] The genuine Christian weeper will show "habitual desire to live up to the standard which St. Paul sets," but often falls short.[5] Mourning over such should not be discouraged or snuffed out lest we deny truth: that man is sinful, that God has set a standard of perfection, and that holiness is worth the struggle. Also, weeping over prevailing sin propels the believer to war against the sinful habits "embattled against [him]"[6] and arrive at a greater apprehension of the need for the Holy Spirit's work. Our sin should bother us because it is counter to the God we profess to love. And in a sense, the sins of those justified are particularly odious because they act in

---

[1] *The Godly Man's Picture*, 56.
[2] Owen, John, "The Nature, Power, Deceit, and Prevalency of the Remainders of Indwelling Sin in Believers," in *The Works of John Owen*, vol. 6, ed. William H. Goold (Edinburgh, UK: Banner of Truth, 2009), 158.
[3] Watson, Thomas, *The Doctrine of Repentance* (Edinburgh, UK: Banner of Truth, 2011), 12, available at http://www.onthewing.org/user/Watson%20-%20Repentance%20-%20Modern.pdf.
[4] *The Godly Man's Picture*, 57.
[5] Ryle, J.C., *Holiness* (London, UK, James Clarke & Co., 1956), 27.
[6] Saint Augustine, *Confessions*, trans. Henry Chadwick (Oxford University Press, 2008), 140.

contradiction to the truth known by them. As Watson puts it, "The sins of God's people put black spots on the face of religion."[1] As we relinquish the idols of our hearts we should mourn that such things were ever substitutes for God in us.

Therefore, we are to mourn with those who are mourning their sin (Rom. 12:15) because the repentance of sin is a sign of the Holy Spirit's work in our lives and of our incremental sanctification. "Grace dissolves and liquefies the soul, causing a spiritual thaw," says Watson.[2] This process in our fellow congregants should be encouraged and we should endeavor to walk alongside them in it. For it is "in the agony of death [that we] come to life."[3]

Second, Christians may, and should, weep out of awe of God's love and mercy. "Gracious hearts, which are golden hearts, are the soonest melted into tears by the fire of God's love." It is often a lack of apprehension of our own depravity and our unmeritorious reception of the grace of Christ that keeps us from exhibiting Christ-like patience and compassion for others. Mourning over our own sin and reflecting on the mercy of Christ is a sure-fire cure for this tendency that is all too present in many congregations.

Third, Christians should weep for the church. "[B]ut an upright Christian, [...] counts the church's loss his loss, [...] and bleeds in her wounds."[4] Watson suggests that most Christians live like a drunken man sleeping securely in his wine, too conceited and lackadaisical to have concern for the condition of the church.[5] I began this post with a link showing declining commitment to church attendance (and religion in general) in America. Throughout the world we see the church actively persecuted. Despite these issues, the majority of American evangelicals are more likely to be moved to tears by whispers of threats against the Second Amendment than they are by reports of persecution and dwindling congregations. Evangelicals are more likely to be at a ball game than in the church pew and more knowledgeable of their favored political party's platform than the

---

[1] *The Godly Man's Picture*, 58.
[2] Ibid., 55.
[3] *Confessions*, 146.
[4] Watson, Thomas, "The Upright Man's Character," in *The Sermons of Thomas Watson* (Ligonier, PA: Soli Deo Gloria, 1990), 337.
[5] Ibid., 338.

historic creeds and confessions of their Spiritual Mother.[1] This should not be so. "True grace ennobles the heart, dilates the affections, and carries out a man beyond the sphere of his private concernments [sic], making him mind the church's condition as his own."[2] Evangelicals need to recover their emotional identification and connectivity with the church, grieving when she suffers and rejoicing when she flourishes.

To be clear, the purpose of Christian weeping is not to create a culture of despair. Mourning without hope is dishonorable to Christ because it implies that his work is inadequate, that faith is not triumphing. Watson would have concurred in this distinction, I think. Later in the chapter he makes an effort to distinguish between worldly despair and "divine sorrow."

The essential points are: (1) appropriate sorrow is ingenuous, being "more for the spot than the sting." It is concerned with the existence of sin nature, not just the unfavorable repercussions that sin brings. Per Watson, "Hypocrites weep for sin only as it brings affliction." Focusing on the existence of the sin nature, and not just sin's affliction, prohibits an attitude of legalism and unloving judgment towards one another. It is the remainder of sin in *all* of us (both seen and unseen) that sends us to our knees.

(2) Furthermore, appropriate weeping is "influential."[3] It produces spiritual growth and ultimately makes the heart better. Whereas, sorrow over sin that plagues the believer to a fault is not *productive*, if you will. Accordingly, a Christian suffering from prolonged sorrow over sin needs exhortation and encouragement from fellow "weepers," not to continue into ever-deepening sorrow.

Watson warns that some weep in vain over sin because they return to their same wickedness willingly, making the previous weeping superfluous. True sanctification does not consist of "temporary religious feelings" or "outward formalism and external devoutness."[4] "Repenting tears are precious," and not to be wasted or

---

[1] Calvin, John, *Institutes of the Christian Religion*, trans. Henry Beveridge (Peabody, MA: Hendrickson, 2008), 670.
[2] "The Upright Man's Character," 338.
[3] *The Godly Man's Picture*, 59.
[4] *Holiness*, 25.

fabricated.[1] It is those who are not truly wounded over their sin who produce superficial weeping. Their repentance, and subsequently their peace, is only "skin deep."[2] Jonathan Edwards warns against fabricated spirituality masterfully in *Religious Affections*:

> "False affections, however persons may seem to be melted by them while they are new, have a tendency in the end to harden the heart. With the delusion that attends them, they finally tend to stupefy the mind, and shut it up against those affections wherein tenderness of heart consists: and the effect of them at last is that persons become less affected [by] their present and past sins, and less conscientious with respect to future sins, less moved with warnings and cautions of God's word [...] and have far less care of their behavior when they come into the holy presence of God in the time of public or private worship."[3]

Perhaps it is a lack of "evangelical weeping" and an abundance of "temporary religious feelings" that has brought the American evangelical church to the beleaguered state in which it presently finds itself. Christians should not weep for weeping's sake nor for the sake of "external religiousness," but for the sake of mortifying their own sin and growing in greater admiration for Christ and his attributes.[4] American evangelicalism needs to regain the lost art of evangelical weeping over the reality of our sin against Christ, in order that we may recover a steady walk with Christ, true and vibrant worship, and a proper posture before God. To conclude as Watson does, "Let us give Christ the water of our tears and he will give us the wine of his blood."[5]

---

[1] Ibid.
[2] *The Godly Man's Picture*, 57.
[3] Edwards, Jonathan, *The Religious Affections* (Edinburgh, UK: Banner of Truth, 1991), 285. Watson also spoke against "counterfeit repentance" in *The Doctrine of Repentance*, 10.
[4] *The Godly Man's Picture*, 57.
[5] Ibid., 60.

Faith Across Traditions

Why God Allows Spiritual Dryness in the Christian Life
Alyssa Hall

I must confess that I did not begin studying the Scriptures personally on a daily basis until almost two years ago. I grew up having family Bible reading in the mornings and often in the evenings. But, about two years ago, I came to a point when I realized that it was something I really should do faithfully on my own. I readily admit that when I first made the decision to become faithful in reading my Bible daily, I didn't feel especially enthused about it. I wasn't averse to the idea; rather, I had a lethargy, an apathy for it.

But of course, it was always something that was expected of me as a Christian, and I knew that I really should make time for it, so, even though I didn't have a deep, burning desire to read the Bible on a daily basis, like eating your vegetables, I knew it was good for me, so I got together a Bible reading plan and began to delve in. I was extremely dedicated to daily reading of the Word and I let not one day pass in which I did not read four chapters, two from the Old Testament, and two from the New.

The first month or so in which I began to read my Bible faithfully, I fully expected to have a deep inner longing for God and His Word. But I just didn't. I became so frustrated, wondering what I was doing wrong. I was doing my righteous duty as a Christian and I was expecting God, like a vending machine, to make me into an ultra-spiritual person right away. I wasn't getting the emotional closeness from God that I wanted to have, but I kept pressing onward, trusting that if I, in faith, obeyed what I believed He wanted me to do, then surely He would give me a heart for the Scriptures.

I began to pray, asking God to give me a hunger for His Word. I knew I couldn't change my heart to desire it on my own, so I asked Him to conform my desires to His. And, sure enough, as I spent time in the Word of God and as I asked faithfully for His help in changing the desires of my heart, I experienced great spiritual growth, and I actually began to look forward to reading my Bible. I began to take joy in what the Lord was going to say to me in His Word each day. I was so thankful that I could see the Lord working in my heart, conforming my desires to His and helping me to love what He loves. The Lord blessed me with this rich study of the Word for a while, and I grew to love the intimacy with God that I felt while having my daily Bible time. But, as time passed, I noticed something in myself that grieved my heart terribly.

I noticed I would go through seasons in which my time in the Word was full of rich insight and fellowship with the Spirit. But then, I would go through seasons, sometimes days, sometimes weeks, when I simply did not feel on fire. The icy fingers of lethargy and apathy from the early days of my devoted Bible reading would come back to haunt me and I would hear a voice in my head telling me that I don't really desire God, and I knew it was true.

I wondered what I had done to deserve this. After all, was I not doing everything right? I had overcome the adversary of apathy many months ago, hadn't I? And yet, I found myself struggling with the same feelings once again. So I stormed the gates of heaven with tears in my eyes and a heavy heart, begging God for help, knowing that, just as He did before, He must deliver me, for I am powerless to do so myself. And, being the merciful God He is, He did deliver me, at least for a while. But even now, I still wrestle with periods of spiritual dryness from time to time. Why does God let us go through dry spells where we don't desire Him like we ought? I don't believe that God enjoys watching us struggle, but I do know that He works everything together for the ultimate good, even when, in the moment, we can't understand what all is actually going on. So, based on how the Lord has used spiritual dry spells in my life, I want to explore a few of the reasons that I believe God allows them in our walk with Him.

One reason that God allows us to experience seasons of apathy is that He wants us to seek Him diligently. Seeking God ought to be a relentless pursuit and when we get accustomed to receiving everything from Him without us having to ask Him for it we don't appreciate or seek it out nearly as diligently as we ought. Let's observe Matthew 15:22-28 to get a glimpse into the mind of God.
> "And, behold, a woman of Canaan came out of the same coasts, and cried unto him, saying, Have mercy on me, O Lord, thou son of David; my daughter is grievously vexed with a devil. But he answered her not a word. And his disciples came and besought him, saying, Send her away; for she crieth after

us. But he answered and said, I am not sent but unto the lost sheep of the house of Israel. Then came she and worshipped him, saying, Lord, help me. But he answered and said, It is not meet to take the children's bread, and to cast it to dogs. And she said, Truth, Lord: yet the dogs eat of the crumbs which fall from their masters' table. Then Jesus answered and said unto her, O woman, great is thy faith: be it unto thee even as thou wilt. And her daughter was made whole from that very hour."

Here, we see that Jesus wasn't trying to hurt this woman by not answering her pleas right away, nor was He withholding good things from her for no reason. Instead, He wanted to test her faith — He wanted her to ask Him repeatedly. The dogged pursuit of God's help proves to Him our faith, just as it did with this woman, and I believe that He delights not only in hearing our requests, but also in fulfilling them Himself.

Another reason that God allows us to experience dry seasons in our spiritual walk is because it pleases Him to see our persistence despite our lack of passion in the moment. It's easy to follow faithfully when we are feeling excited about it, and when we walk in confidence and security. But it is much more difficult to obey when our hearts don't feel ravished by His Spirit and they are cold and dry. It then becomes a discipline, a sacrifice, to remain faithful. And I believe that such sacrifices warm the heart of God. Our persistence in obedience becomes most glorifying to Him when we follow despite our lack of zeal at the present.

I believe that God allows these times of apathy to fill in specific holes in our individual spiritual maturity. James 1 says, "My brethren, count it all joy when ye fall into divers temptations; Knowing this, that the trying of your faith worketh patience. But let patience have her perfect work, that ye may be perfect and entire, wanting nothing." Here we see that the "trying of your faith" that comes from *asking* God to create perfect desires in us and then *waiting* upon Him to do what we have asked causes us to become "perfect and entire, wanting nothing." In my life particularly, the Lord has used dry seasons to teach me the importance of spending a great deal of time in prayer. I had always been used to praying at mealtimes and before bed for just a few minutes, but the discipline of fervent prayer was not something that I really learned until I began to experience seasons of dryness that forced me to my knees on a moment-by-moment basis for daily sustenance.

Finally, I believe that God gives us times of testing in this way to teach us to depend completely upon Him for everything-even the very *desire* to know Him. As I began my journey of regular Bible study, my mind was convinced that I was doing the right thing, but my heart was not full of passion for what I was doing. I tried to change my own heart, but all of my efforts were worthless. But when I cried out to Jesus for help, confessing my sins and asking for Him to change me, He was faithful! He walked into the field full of dry bones, and said, "O ye dry bones, hear the word of the Lord!" and immediately the dry bones of my heart were clothed with flesh and the breath of life entered into them! (Ezekiel 37:1-14)

If we were powerless to save ourselves from hell, why do we think that any other battles we fight mustn't belong to God as well? As the Apostle Paul said, "**He** which hath begun a good work in you **will perform** it until the day of Jesus Christ." (Philippians 1:6, emphasis added)

In conclusion, then, we understand why God allows us to suffer seasons of apathy and spiritual dryness, but we may yet ask, "Why is this struggle so relentless and ongoing?" My answer is, "Because we are at war!" We have an adversary who is very real and who comes to us in our lowest, driest points and accuses us to no end. He tells us that we are unworthy to call ourselves Christians, that we are just religious hypocrites, and that God is unwilling either to forgive us of this sin or to help us overcome it. But we can see through the façade our enemy puts on, can we not? And whenever we are on our knees, imploring God to help us through our weakness, we are doing hand-to-hand combat with the devil. As John Bunyan said, "Prayer is a shield to the soul, a sacrifice to God, and a scourge for Satan." It feels like a fight because it is one. But it is a fight we are sure to win, for Matthew 7 tells us,

> "Ask, and it shall be given you; seek, and ye shall find; knock, and it shall be opened unto you. For every one that asketh receiveth; and he that seeketh findeth; and to him that knocketh it shall be opened...If ye then, being evil, know how to give good gifts unto your children, how much more shall your Father which is in heaven give good things to them that ask him?"

God delights in answering our prayers, just as a father delights in providing for his children. He will not let us struggle forever, nor will

He tarry in delivering His people. But while we are passing through the valley of dry bones, let us heed Psalm 27:14 and, "Wait on the Lord: be of good courage, and *he shall strengthen thine heart*: wait, I say, on the Lord."

Faith Across Traditions

Dealing With Pain and Suffering
Micah McMeans

It doesn't take a philosophy degree to understand that pain and suffering are two things people are naturally inclined to try and avoid. It is in our nature to run away from suffering, and to simply try and avoid discomfort at all costs. No matter how strong pain makes us, very seldom does anyone truly welcome it. Although time has opened up the windows of my world to the reality of this life, I find myself no longer being able to turn a blind eye to this experience that I have come to understand as suffering. I have found that suffering stands at the heart of our world—for both Christian or unbeliever—and it cannot be avoided, whether we can stomach this truth or not. We try and keep our distance, yet each and every one of us finds ourselves staring in the face of some sort of pain. At times, it can become so grueling that everything inside of us helplessly cries out in anger, demanding some sort of explanation. We yell at God, but receive no response. We search, but there seems to be absolutely no reasonable explanation for why He is letting us experience such tremendous pain. Our brains simply can't seem to comprehend why this life has to be so overbearingly difficult at times. More so, as a Christian, why are we still experiencing such pain when we have God as our father? Why would such a loving father let his beloved experience such agony?

Though the Bible is clear that as a Christian we will endure much tribulation and suffering, sometimes we need more than a Bible verse when wanting an explanation for our trials. Sometimes when in pain the best thing one can do is simply cry out and let the emotions God gave us take their natural course. Though once our heads are clear and we begin to ask why, it is critical that we have logical reasoning to fall back on. Understanding is the one thing that will allow the pain to serve its purpose. It is by far the most important weapon we have against the burden of pain.

The past four years of my life were filled with daily suffering, which in turn were full of daily questions and persistent doubts. Day in and day out, I never found true peace, for my pain was mental. I no longer held Christianity to be true, which in turn led my mind down a very dark, long journey. The uncertainty of life brought forth extreme anxiety, which in turn brought about a deep depression. I saw the brokenness of the world and I saw raw evil for the first time. The pain of everyone around me became too much to bare, and before I knew what was happening I woke up one day and realized that I had become the very thing that I once felt empathy for. I felt helpless, completely and utterly lost. I said I didn't believe in God, but I needed something to blame for my suffering. I had lost my will to live, and I found myself cursing God for not asking my permission to be created. I couldn't think of even one possible reason for why God was allowing me to experience such agony. My pain, the world's pain, it was all too much, and I wanted nothing to do with a God that would create a world such as this.

It was during my fourth year of this suffering that God began to show me why. I don't have time to explain my full story, but an important factor to know is that I (along with most people in this world) relied completely on myself before I became a Christian. I didn't need God. I wanted nothing to do with him and his rules. It would take a perfect storm to bring this young man to his knees, and that is exactly what God let happen. Not only did the continuous pain and suffering bring me to my knees and draw me back to God, but it still continues to brings me closer to him. For I still wander, I still fall away and begin to think I can do life on my own. Only in continuous tribulation do I clearly see how weak I am without God. Only in times of need do I truly rely on him and times of need usually come with pain and suffering. Sometimes to understand pain we must simply be honest with ourselves. God wants all of us, not just our Sunday mornings. Do we really think that we would be willing to do this if he sent nothing but happiness our way?

When my time of suffering was at hand, God at least blessed me with the realization that I should not turn a blind eye to what I was experiencing. Only by God's grace did I not keep myself distracted with entertainment and work. Only by the grace of God was I able to understand that I needed to experience and embrace what I was going through. If I hadn't have done this, I might still be left in an endless cycle of pain and tribulation. The storm God threw my way was going to last however long it took for me to learn what I needed to learn. But we can't learn and grow from the storms in our life if we stay inside and pretend they do not exist. We will only continue to get up from our devices, look outside the window, and curse God for letting the storm last for so long.

We all are guilty of this, we just stick our heads in the sand in different ways. Many of us use entertainment to avoid discomfort and pain. Some of us drown ourselves in alcohol or bury our heads under piles of work. We all have our outlets to escape the reality of this world, we just don't seem to realize the storm is still affecting us no matter how far we stick our head in the sand. Because the truth of the matter is that beyond all the entertainment and distractions of this life lies a world of pain and darkness that is inescapable, and God allows the reality of this life to seep into our daydream to simply wake us up. Sometimes it is to make us realize how much we need him. Other times it is to prepare us for what he has planned for our lives. Either way, God sends tribulation and pain our way for a reason, and the waves of suffering will not let up until we come back down from whatever cloud of escape we have found.

Whether we like it or not, suffering is an essential factor of the Christian faith. To avoid suffering is to avoid fully living for God (1 Peter 2:21). The sooner we learn this the sooner our pain will become sustainable. If we are avoiding pain then we are not letting God change us, and if the pain is not changing us, then we will be left in an endless pit of pain and suffering. *For it is the very pain that we reject and ignore that will give us the insight we need to better comprehend our suffering.* The only way to make our pain bearable is to first understand it, and for this to happen we must quit running. Whether it be dying to ourselves, depression, or dealing with a tragic event, all of these tribulations change us. Think of them as growing pains that we must experience in the process of becoming like Christ. Just like a young child does not understand his parents' discipline until he grows into adulthood, so also we cannot understand the suffering God sends our way until we begin to grow in Christ, and we cannot grow in Christ when running away from the suffering he sends our way.

Only when we are older and mature do we see the reason for our tribulations and suffering. Just like how a young child will always throw a fit while the doctor is trying to give him a shot, for the child simply thinks this man is the white coat is trying to hurt him. The reason we no longer wrestle with shots is because we have grown up. We are no longer children that think the pain of the shot is of no significance, for we are mature enough to understand the pain is for our benefit. Suffering is always more bearable once we understand.

Just like the child that can't understand why the doctor is having to inflict pain upon him, many of us today are stuck at this very same stage in our walk with Christ. But the difference between that child and our walk with Christ is that children grow whether they like it or not. The same cannot be said about our Christian walk. If we keep our head in the sand and don't embrace what God is trying to do, (through suffering) then we will never grow. We will never change and we will be stuck in an endless cycle of pain that we cannot seem to understand. We will stay children of the faith that scream and yell at God whenever he tries giving us a shot for our own good. We must learn to trust our Father, just like a child does in the doctor's office. Our first step is to trust God and take our heads out of the sand, to look upon suffering as a blessing instead of a curse. Only when we wake up and truly experience our pain will we grow and begin to understand our suffering. Only then will the pain make sense, and only then will the healing process begin.

Understood pain is bearable pain, and *we cannot understand pain without fully experiencing it*. I cannot stress this enough. For in the end, it all boils down to our mindset, and we cannot reach the right mindset without first learning to embrace suffering. I used to think this world a living hell, but that was when I was experiencing pain in a world that I thought was for my personal enjoyment and bliss. Now that I have a better understanding of this life, I find myself at a peace I never thought possible. Not because I no longer suffer, but because I understand why I suffer. For if we think of this world as a place for personal enjoyment and happiness, then we might find ourselves in for quite a miserable ride; though, if we think this world as a place for learning, strengthening, and training, then we might not find it to be such a bad place.

The Art of Grieving
Johanna Byrkett

Drip-drop. Drop-drip. Plink! Glorious Spring rain drips off the gutter-less eaves of my cottage this forenoon; every now and then one drop making a sharp ping off something metal below. Steady, strong notes to set the rhythm for the day, those water-drops. I draw icy water for the kettle, waiting for its warm whistle as a Southwest wind kicks up its heels. The song of the rain slows, softens, becomes silent. Whirling this way and that come the downy flakes of snow.

Pungent Earl Grey tickles my senses as I gaze long at the steady, slanting white. I am very much alone, but not in the least lonely. Solitude need not make one *solitary*. Fog, snow, roiling grey skies – they are all friends. The damp, chill, and quiet give one time to pause, to recalibrate the soul toward stillness and Beauty. When we make the time to hush, not writing, nor reading, nor listening to the ever-present music that pervades our senses, we are able to *be*. We are able to grieve or mourn, to ponder and reflect, to pray and listen, to know and be known. Stillness and reflection often seem colossal threats to our current 'culture of noise'. Particularly in the process of grieving, perhaps the greatest conundrum in this age. In times-not-long-past, there was a set period for mourning in which the mourner at the least wore a black band on their arm, if not complete outfits of black. *Now* we hardly even say someone has died, but that they have 'passed away'.

We have funerals and weddings in 'Life Centres' at cemeteries. Our culture seeks to sanitise death from all its ugly brokenness. I am very, very *pro*-life, but even I cannot ignore the effects of the Fall. We cannot pretend that death is routine, neat, and 'part of life'. It is not. It is a violent affront to God the Creator. It is madness and fragmentation at their extreme end. Grieving is a slow process; whether it is the death of a loved one, the loss of a friendship, or the crumbling of a cherished dream. It takes silence and prayer to walk the road of sorrow. Yet, not even the evangelical church seems to accept this. Half-truths are still lies, yet they ring forth from our Postmodern Evangelical churches and the reams of pages in 'Christian' bookstores: *God must always make bad things good. We must always smile and say we are well, that it is good to be alive. Christians are always to be happy, happy, happy* – which translates to fake, fake, fake. God **will** make all things well, but probably not the way we think He should, and often not on this earth. It **is** good to be alive, because we were made for life – but 'good' does not mean 'easy'. The Anglican response to death in the prayer book does not ignore the creeping shadow of death, nor does it wallow in the Fall. It brings one's focus back to God, the Author of life, the Redeemer of death: Thou only art Immortal, Creator and Maker of mankind; and we are mortal, formed of the earth, and unto earth shall we return.

For so Thou did ordain when Thou created me, saying, "Dust thou art, and unto dust shalt thou return." All of us go down to the dust…

Yet even at the grave we make our song: Alleluia, alleluia, alleluia.

Even at the grave we *sing* of the Hope to come. We weep and mourn *in Hope*. This is not easy. We may sing our *alleluias* through teeth clenched, through stinging tears. But we have Hope: Jesus Himself, *the* Resurrection from the dead for all who are 'in Christ'. And when death takes from us one who does not know God, we lament even more. Again, we cannot pretend that death is normal. It is grotesquely abnormal. We still mourn loss.

Learning to lament takes times of silence, of *being*. It can take the form of long walks, writing poetry, playing or writing music, cleaning vigorously, cooking and baking (for oneself or others), painting or drawing, gardening, crying, and many other things. Strikingly, lamentation is often pro-creative. By that I mean that we find an outlet for grief, anger, and sorrow in making, in serving. Look at the first line of the Memorial Prayer – it calls God three things: Immortal, Creator, and Maker. We tend to think of the last two words as being synonyms, but they are Names and have nuances. A 'creator' begets – the thing begotten is from himself, is part of himself, like a child shares the 'humanness' and DNA of its parents. A 'maker' is a companion or a spouse, as well as one who designs or constructs. So, the act of *creation* is intensely personal and part of the creator-begetter. The act of *making* is taking something already in existence and fitting it together; as one takes flour, water, and yeast to *make* bread; or wood, nails, and varnish to *fit* into a wardrobe; or chisels and marble to *form* a sculpture; or a man and a woman together *fashion* a marriage.

In grieving we *image* God by making. We turn to pro-creation to *process* (move forward, continue). We seek solitude and silence in order to better serve, because the act of serving (helping one's neighbour with various tasks, inviting others over for dinner, etc.) brings us outside of ourself so that we do not dead-end in grief. This brings up the other aspect of lamenting. To lament, I said, one needs times of solitude. But one also needs time with others. God says in the beginning that, "It is not good for the Man to be alone". God was right there with the Man, but still says he is 'alone' or without a match (or mate) of his own. We need other persons. We need friends and family who will be still with us, who will listen to us. We need others to serve with our creative acts. We need those close to us to cry with us, and also to make us laugh. The hush of snow is heralding a chance to ponder, time to *be*. This late Spring snow is a gift before I step into the bustle of Summer. The silence of a full day to process and grieve is worth the thanks-giving. Right here and now I learn to be still and know... and to be *known*. Alleluia, alleluia, alleluia!

Contributor Biographies

Aldhizer, George
George lives in North Carolina and works as an accountant. He and his wife Rachel have four kids, and they attend an Anglican church.
- Christmas Is About the Cross (81)
- Toward a Spirituality of Christian Work (145)
- Social Justice Without Resurrection Is Dead (181)
- How Should We Choose the Church We Attend (293)
- The Problem of Predestination (343)

Barrett, Rebecca
Becca is a homeschool mom of three beautiful girls and serves alongside her husband, Colt, in student ministry and missions coordination at First Baptist Church Estancia. She is passionate about teaching the beauty of the Gospel and God's Word to children and teenagers.
- Confessions of a Single Mom (153)

Bryan, Matthew
Matthew is a post-Protestant disciple of Jesus, a disciple maker, a father of three, and the delighted husband of Kristy. He holds a Bachelor of Science summa cum laude from the University of Memphis, has authored four books, including "Forgotten Gospel," and translated a Greek-English interlinear titled the "King Jesus Literal Version." A former church planter, Matthew now serves within the Restoration Movement. He enjoys reading Desiderius Erasmus, researching early Persian Christianity, and encouraging believers to take up Biblical Greek for theological clarity and Church unity.
- Books Removed From the NT (207)
- Maccabees in the New Testament (229)
- The Atonement of Irenaeus (331)

Byrkett, Jody

Johanna has a passion for copyediting and has loved words—their origins, art, and beauty—since before she could write. She studied English and History for a term at Oxford University (New College). Johanna fell in love with Anglican tradition and love for Scripture in her twenties, after being raised in evangelical churches since birth. When she's not drinking tea, reading, or editing, you can find her trekking across the mountains by sunlight or starlight.

- Adventus (73)
- God Is With Us (101)
- Empty Hands (295)
- The Longest Lent (367)
- The Art of Grieving (389)

Cabe, Benjamin

Ben is an ordained priest in the Eastern Orthodox Church and co-founder of *Conciliar Post*. He and his family live in South Bend, IN.

- Why Would a Protestant Convert to Eastern Orthodoxy (17)
- Is Protestantism a Heresy (51)
- Do You Have to Be Anti-Western to Be Eastern Orthodox (65)
- Christmas Is About the Incarnation (87)

Casberg, Chris

Chris is a former U.S. Marine Corps translator. His award-winning writing on faith and culture has appeared in *Christianity Today, The Gospel Coalition, Love Thy Nerd*, and others.

- A Christian Defense of Video Games (149)
- A Sonnet on the Occasion of Super Tuesday (161)
- The Desert Fathers Play *Pokémon Go* (247)
- Things I'd Rather Do on Sunday Morning (267)

Cline, Timon

Timon is editor-in-chief of American Reformer and Director of Scholarly Initiatives at the Hale Institute of New Saint Andrews College. He lives with his wife and son in southwest Florida.

- On Original Sin and Racism (321)
- The Lost Art of Evangelical Weeping (371)

Dickey, Jarrett

Jarrett works as a senior success navigator at a local community college, but many of his greatest life passions are outside his professional work. He and his wife have four children who keep them busy with school activities and sports. Outside of work, Jarrett pastors a small church that meets in a home and coaches youth sports. Over the years, he has learned that coaching, along with pastoral leadership, is an important form of ministry to his neighbors.
- John Wesley and Small Groups (137)
- Augustine on Biblical Interpretation (219)

Ehrett, John

John is a Commonwealth Fellow at the Davenant Institute and a member of the Civitas Group at the Theopolis Institute. His scholarship has appeared in the *Journal of Classical Theology*, *Logia: A Journal of Lutheran Theology*, and many other venues. He holds MAR and STM degrees from the Institute of Lutheran Theology and a J.D. from Yale Law School.
- Why I'm Not Reformed (But Admire Them Anyway) (35)
- The Logic of Closed Communion (61)
- What Re-Enchantment Really Means (131)
- Gnostic Anthropology and Identity Politics (185)
- Visiting D.C.'s Museum of the Bible (215)

Fletcher, Sam

Sam is a priest in the Church of England.
- The Pandemic and the Wrath of God (309)

Grubb, J.D.

J.D. is a published novelist who is passionate about art, outdoor adventure (especially distance running, which he coaches), and world travel. He has lived chapters in the United States and Germany, and intends to explore every corner of the world. He is currently based in San Jose, CA.
- Through the Rain (119)

Hall, Alyssa
Alyssa is an adjunct instructor of music history and voice at Methodist University. She lives in Fayetteville, NC, where she keeps a busy harp and piano studio and serves as harp, piano, and voice faculty at Snyder Music Academy.
- Sola Scriptura's Relevance for the Modern Church (239)
- Why God Allows Spiritual Dryness in the Christian Life (379)

Humphrey, TJ
Rev. TJ is the rector at St Paul's Episcopal Church in Beloit, WI and Trinity Episcopal Church in Janesville, WI.
- Why I Didn't Convert to Orthodoxy (25)

Hyland, Daniel
Daniel is a Roman Catholic father and husband. He is a graduate theology student and earned his B.A. in theology from Catholic Distance University.
- Holy Week (109)
- Mary, Mother of God, Mother of the Church (261)

Johnson, Russell
Russell teaches religious studies at the University of Chicago. He is the author of *Beyond Civility in Social Conflict: Dialogue, Critique, and Religious Ethics*.
- An Open Letter to Christian Bakers in Indiana (173)

Justice, David
David serves as a postdoctoral teaching fellow at Baylor University. He and his wife Mariah have two kids, Abraham and Theo, who keep them on their toes.
- Let Justice Roll Down (127)

Kim, Chad
Chad holds a Ph.D. from Saint Louis University, where he serves as Assistant Professor of Theological Studies & Classical Languages.
- Lex Orandi, Lex Credendi (41)
- What's the Point of the Sermon (285)

Kishi, Aphrodite
Aphrodite is a member of the Eastern Orthodox Church. She lives with her husband in Washington, D.C.
- The Fast Before the Feast (105)

Lambert, Tomerot
Tomerot is a third-year middle school religion teacher at St. Bernard Catholic School in Green Bay, WI. He is also pursuing an online Masters in Catholic Education through the Augustine Institute while being a full-time teacher. His interest lies in moral philosophy, Christian anthropology, Church History, and the theory of education. He is currently engaged to Raven Behringer.
- God Remembers (193)

Landsman, Michael
Rev. Michael serves as the pastor of Zion's Stone UCC in Northampton, PA. He holds an M.Div. from Biblical Theological Seminary (now Missio Seminary) and resides in the Lehigh Valley with his wife Chontey and their children Isaac and Sophia.
- The Insufficiency of Spontaneous Prayer (157)

Maynard, AJ
AJ serves as an ACPE educator (CEC) at Emory Healthcare in Atlanta, GA.
- Remembering Christmas (97)

McMeans, Micah
Micah is currently getting his doctorate in philosophy at St. Patrick's University, Ireland. His research interests revolve around the philosophy of the Church Fathers, Eastern Orthodox Christianity, and philosophy of religion.
- Dealing with Pain and Suffering (385)

Prahlow, Jacob

Jacob serves as lead pastor at Arise Church in Fenton, MO. His wife, Hayley, and their two kids stay busy on their homestead. He is the author of *Encountering God's Story* and co-founder of *Conciliar Post*.

- The Non-Denominational Reformation (45)
- On the Advent of Christ (77)
- What Day Did Jesus Die? (111)
- The Sermon on the Mount and Christian Ethics (123)
- The New Testament in Order (197)
- Acts of Baptism (257)

Quick, Jacob

Jacob is training to be a priest in the Church of England at Westcott House in Cambridge, UK. He is married to Annie, who serves as an Anglican priest.

- Dear White Christians, It's Time for Us to Listen (175)
- Why Is Christian Liturgy So Repetitive (275)
- Thoughts, Prayers, and Platitudes (363)

Rebholtz, Brian

Fr. Brian is the Rector of St. Luke's Episcopal Church in Auburn, CA. He holds an M.A. in Christian Spirituality from the Graduate Theological Union, and a M.Div from the Church Divinity School of the Pacific. His interests include the history of the Bible, liturgy, homiletics, metaphysics and the spiritual aspirations of human beings. He and his wife, Catherine, have five children and are active in Waldorf education.

- In Praise of the English Bible (225)

Salem, Buck

Buck works with international students from around the world through Outreach International and as pastoral intern at Arise Church in Fenton, MO. He holds a B.S. in preaching ministry from Central Christian College of the Bible in Moberly, MO.

- A Poem to My Anxiety (335)

Schellhase, Peter
Peter is a priest serving in the Episcopal Diocese of Albany, where he lives with his wife and three children.
- What John Calvin Taught Me About the Sacraments (271)

Schendel, Joshua
Joshua is professor of theology at Yellowstone Theological Institute in Bozeman, MT. He and his wife, Bethanne, have three kids, Isaiah, Laurel, and Edith.
- Longings (243)

Tillman, Micah
Micah teaches 9th and 10th grade philosophy of science to students who are way smarter than he was at their age. Pennsylvania is both his home and his favorite state.
- Could Liberals and Conservatives Follow the Same Christ? (165)
- Is Christian Existentialism Unbiblical? (349)

Townsend, Luke
Luke is an Associate Professor of Theology and the Director of the Theology Program at Marian University in Fond du Lac, WI. He and his wife, Mary Frances, have one son, Patrick, who just turned two years old.
- It Is Not a Sin to Wear a Facemask (315)

Walker, Wesley
Wesley serves as the Rector of St. Paul's Anglican Church in Crownsville, MD. He and his wife Caroline have two sons, Jude and Rowan. He also co-hosts two podcasts, *The Sacramentalists* and *The Classical Mind*.
- Recovering Koinonia (141)
- CRT and Its Dissidents (187)

White, Barbara

Barbara serves as associate rector for worship and formation at St. Francis in the Fields Episcopal Church in Louisville, KY. She has a B.A. in International Studies with a concentration in the Middle East from Point Loma Nazarene University in San Diego, CA and an M.Div from the Seminary of the Southwest in Austin, TX.
- Tradition Is the Answer to the Questions We've Forgotten (251)
- Three Things That Need to Change About Church (279)
- You Are Not Okay (359)

Winter, Benjamin

Ben is an assistant professor of theology at Divine Word College. Having graduated in 2019 from Saint Louis University with a doctorate in historical theology, he now lives in Dubuque, IA. In his free time, he enjoys reading science fiction, creating electronic music, and travel.
- The Natural Desire to See God (299)
- Dare We Hope for the Salvation of All? (337)

Acknowledgements

While I had the privilege of serving as editor for this volume, this work—and indeed, the entire work of *Conciliar Post* over the past ten years—would not be possible without the tremendous contributions of talent, time, and tears from an incredible group of people.

A huge debt of gratitude is due to each of the executive editors in *Conciliar Post*'s history, including co-founder Rev. Ben Cabe, Dr. Benjamin Wintress (né Winter), and John Ehrett, Esq. Our entire editorial team has spent countless hours creating, drafting, editing, and supporting the mission of *Conciliar Post*, including Andrew Fisher, Micah Carlson, Jody Byrkett, Rev. Wesley Walker, Jarrett Dickey, AJ Maynard, Jeff Reid, and Laura Norris.

Of course, this volume would be far slimmer—and our impact far smaller—without the time and talents of our incredible team of writers, past and present. It has been a tremendous privilege working with and learning from each person who has written for *Conciliar Post* and made our dialogue across traditions possible.

Finally, a big thank you to the team at Arise Press for making this possible and for the opportunity to transform one of those dreams that Ben and I had ten years ago into a reality. A special shout out goes to Ariel Stephens for her editorial prowess.

May the work continue, may the Church continue to strive toward the oneness in faith that our Lord prayed for in the Upper Room, and may *Conciliar Post* continue to encourage and inform faith across traditions.

Rev. Jacob J. Prahlow, Co-Founder and Managing Editor
Pentecost 2024

ConciliarPost.com

Printed by Arise Press in Saint Louis, MO

Faith Across Traditions

Made in the USA
Monee, IL
21 June 2024

76b4c330-8934-4f61-a883-29622cfcdb5bR01